Anne Lindsay's
New Light Cooking

by Anne Lindsay

In co-operation with
Denise Beatty, RD,
and the
Canadian Medical Association

CANADIAN
MEDICAL
ASSOCIATION

Ballantine Books

To my children, Jeff, John and Susie, with love.

Nutrition information provided by Denise Beatty, RD.

Published in Canada by Ballantine Books,
a division of Random House of Canada, Toronto.

Canadian Cataloguing in Publication Data
Lindsay, Anne 1943-
Anne Lindsay's New light cooking
Includes index.
ISBN 0-345-39854-8
1. Low-fat diet—Recipes. I. Title. II. Title: New light cooking.
RM237.7L57 1998   641.5'638   C97-932639-7

Photography: Bradshaw Photography Inc.
Food Styling: Olga Truchan
Prop Styling: Janet Wakenshaw
Book Design: Dianne Eastman
Page Composition: Benny Lee / Richard Hunt

Printed and bound in Canada
10 9 8 7 6 5 4 3 2 1

Front cover: Penne with Sweet Red Peppers, Black Olives and Arugula (page 100)

Contents

Foreword

Good health begins with simple things. Every physician knows proper nutrition is a key to good health. That is why the Canadian Medical Association is so delighted to be associated with Anne Lindsay's *New Light Cooking*. We hope you will consider Anne's latest offering, which benefited from input by medical experts and nutritionists across the country, to be another sign of doctors' commitment to your health.

Helping patients live longer, healthier lives is the ultimate goal of every Canadian physician. This tremendous book is an attempt to answer some of the questions patients routinely ask us concerning nutrition and the food choices they should make. It not only answers your questions but helps you make tasty choices as well.

We are proud to add this book to our growing CMA library. We are sure you will find it a welcome — and delicious — addition to your kitchen.

Bon appetit!

Victor Dirnfeld, MD
President
Canadian Medical Association

President	*Medical Editor*	*Consultants*
Victor Dirnfeld, MD	Catherine Younger-Lewis, MD	Maryann Hopkins, BSP
		Diane Logan, MD
Secretary General	*Advisory Board*	Robert McKendry, MD
Léo-Paul Landry, MD	Susan I. Barr, PhD	W. Grant Thompson, MD
	Gregory P. Curnew, MD	
Director of Professional Development	Shajia Khan, MBBS	*Production Manager*
Stephen Prudhomme	Judith C. Kazimirski, MD	Deborah A. Rupert
	Cynthia Mannion, RN, MSc(A)	
Editor-in-chief	Suzanne Robinson, MSW	*Director, Marketing and Business*
John Hoey, MD		*Development*
		Ken Elsey

Canadian Medical Association
1867 Alta Vista Drive, Ottawa, Ontario K1G 3Y6
888-855-2555; fax 613-731-9102   www.cma.ca

Acknowledgments

With each cookbook I write, I'm asked, "What's different about this one?" Well, with this book, a great deal is new, including an association with the Canadian Medical Association and a new look that includes beautiful color on every page. But at the top of the list I would put a very special feeling of excitement and enthusiasm that has been present from the beginning when the Canadian Medical Association first spoke to me about combining our concerns for healthy eating into a new cookbook. The excitement accelerated when my terrific agent, Denise Schon, got involved, and it has picked up speed as each new person brought his or her own contribution to the project.

Writing a book like this involves dedication and enormous attention to detail. Many people have devoted huge amounts of time, enthusiasm and expertise to it, and I'm extremely grateful to all of them. They have all been a pleasure to work with.

I'd like to thank the Canadian Medical Association, especially the Advisory Board (listed in full on page iv), Steve Prudhomme, Dr. Catherine Younger-Lewis, Ken Elsey, Deborah Rupert, Nadine Mathieu and Christine Pollock, for their tremendous commitment to this book and its success; Denise Beatty, RD, for undertaking the difficult task of researching and writing the nutrition information found throughout the book; Shannon Graham, Daphna Rabinovitch, Heather Epp and Susan Pacaud, my wonderful recipe testers, for their creativity and patience especially when retesting and retesting; Doug Pepper at Random House, who loves food, cooking and publishing cookbooks, for generating so much excitement and for putting together a wonderful editorial and design team; Dianne Eastman, the art director, for making the book look so beautiful; Jennifer Glossop and Bev Renahan for their editorial expertise; Barbara Schon, indexer; everyone at Random House, including David Kent, Duncan Shields and his Ballantine sales team, Pat Cairns, Susan Roxborough, Jennifer Shepherd, Alan Terakawa, and Vicki Black; Barbara Selley, RD, for the nutrient analysis of the recipes; Katherine Younker for the Canadian Diabetes Association Food Choice Values; Nancy Williams for running my office; Michael Levine, my lawyer; Angus Reid for the national poll asking what nutrition questions you have asked your doctor; photographers Doug Bradshaw and Josef Teschl, food stylist Olga Truchan and props co-ordinator Janet Wakenshaw, for the beautiful photographs.

And, as always, a huge thanks to my expert taster and wonderful husband, Bob, for his support, guidance, enthusiasm and love.

Introduction

Everyday, new research confirms that what we eat affects our health. Less fat lowers our chances of heart disease: more milk improves our chance of avoiding osteoporosis. The list goes on and on.

For years now I've been committed to finding ways to make healthy foods tasty, satisfying and easy to prepare. I was delighted, therefore, when the Canadian Medical Association, the most respected medical organization in the country, asked me to work with them to create a new cookbook that would provide more great recipes and up-to-date nutrition information that didn't require a doctorate to understand. Together we hoped to produce a book that would have a sound basis in scientific research but would also dispel the idea that healthy foods have to be bland and boring.

This book is the result of that collaboration. It includes a wealth of information and research on nutrition issues that registered dietitian Denise Beatty assembled and presented in manageable pieces that you will find throughout the book. Her choices are based partly on a survey the CMA and the 43,000 doctors it represents conducted, asking doctors what nutrition issues most concerned their patients.

What most concerns you? The CMA found that weight loss and blood cholesterol are two of the most pressing issues. Dietary supplements and nutrition for children were also of concern. In this book you'll find not only the most recent findings in these areas, but also delicious dishes that will help meet your goals or needs, whether they are losing weight or watching your salt intake.

Another poll, run by Angus Reid, asked Canadians what nutrition-related concerns they had raised with their doctor in the past year. Again cholesterol was a prime concern. Other popular topics were fats, dieting and weight loss, vitamins and minerals, fiber and diabetes. You'll find information on these topics throughout the book as well.

The prevention of disease is not our only goal here. Eating not only fuels the body; it provides pleasure and companionship — and the delight of new experiences. Everyone asks me how I keep coming up with new recipes. The answer, simply, is that it is what I love to do. I love creating new healthy dishes to feed my family and friends. I sometimes just take an old favorite like chocolate cake and find ways to make it healthier by reducing the amount of fat; I substitute oil and buttermilk for butter and increase the flavor by adding extra cocoa. That's how I came up with the recipe for Easy Chocolate Cake with Chocolate Buttermilk Icing on page 264. Sometimes I take flavor combinations I love — like lemon, coriander and coconut milk — and I try them out in new ways. The recipe for Thai Chicken Curry in Coconut Milk on page 164 is the result of such an exploration. And to meet the growing interest in vegetarian eating, I often experiment with meatless versions of curries, stews, pasta and burgers.

After all the mixing and cooking — and eating — recipes that are well received are tested again and again and eventually find their way into my books. First, however, they are checked for their nutrient content. You'll find this information accompanying each recipe. And in this book for the first time they are also assessed for their contribution to the Canada's Food Guide recommendations. Accompanying each recipe are symbols that tell you how many Canada's Food Guide servings the recipe contributes to your daily total. (See pages 2 and 293 for more information.)

As in my other books, the recipes here are quick and easy to prepare and use ingredients you can find in supermarkets everywhere. I hope that you will enjoy them as much as my family and I have, and that you will find in the nutrition information accompanying these recipes a resource that will lead you to good health and great eating.

Anne Lindsay

Healthy Eating: What's It All About?

Throughout this book we refer to healthy eating and a healthy eating pattern. This pattern is the starting point from which all nutrition-related advice is given. Whatever your specific goal — to have a healthy pregnancy, to raise healthy children, to live to an old age, to reduce your chance of developing colon cancer or to lower your blood pressure — you need to start from the basic healthy eating pattern, adjusting it to suit your particular needs.

A healthy eating pattern means building meals and snacks around foods that are low in fat but high in complex carbohydrates (starches), fiber, vitamins, minerals and natural plant chemicals known to benefit health.

A Healthy Eating Pattern: The Basics

Healthy eating means:

- eating more vegetables and fruit;
- eating more starchy foods like legumes (dried beans, peas and lentils), cereal, bread, pasta and rice;
- choosing whole grain foods such as whole wheat bread and brown rice as much as possible;
- eating smaller portions of meat and poultry, and eating fish more often;
- choosing low-fat milk products as much as possible;
- cutting back on foods high in fat, including butter, margarine, fast foods, snack foods, cookies and pastries, rich sauces and dressings;
- consuming alcohol, caffeine-containing beverages and highly salted foods in moderation.

In addition to the foods eaten, healthy eating means developing a healthy relationship with food. Eating should be enjoyable, not fraught with fear and guilt. Healthy eating also means eating in moderation, steering clear of fads and unfounded food claims, and knowing when and how to include favorite foods and treats without overdoing it or feeling guilty or remorseful.

Canada's Food Guide Simplifies Healthy Eating

Canada's Food Guide to Healthy Eating

Food Group	Range of Servings Needed Each Day
Grain Products	5 to 12
Vegetables & Fruit	5 to 10
Milk Products	2 to 4 (for adults)
Meat & Alternatives	2 to 3

Key to Canada's Food Guide Serving

= 1 serving of Grain Products

= 1 serving of Vegetables & Fruit

= 1 serving of Milk Products

= 1 serving of Meat & Alternatives

Canada's Food Guide to Healthy Eating (see following pages) simplifies healthy eating principles by organizing foods into four food groups and recommending the number and size of servings you need each day from each group.

The upper range of servings recommended for both Grain Products and Vegetables & Fruit often takes people by surprise. Don't panic at the thought of eating 12 servings of grain or 10 of fruits and vegetables each day. These higher ranges aren't meant for everyone. The number of servings right for you depends on various factors — your age, sex, body size, activity level and caloric needs. Women and children likely need less than teenage boys or people working in physically demanding jobs.

It is also difficult to tell what a recipe contributes to your overall nutrition needs as outlined in Canada's Food Guide to Healthy Eating. To help you, each recipe in this book is accompanied by a row of symbols that indicate the food groups and number of Canada's Food Guide servings provided by a serving of that recipe. If, for example, a recipe is accompanied by these symbols: **2** 1 , it means that one serving of that recipe will contribute 2 Grain Products and 1 Meat & Alternative servings to your daily total.

Nutrition in the News

These are exciting times in the ever-expanding field of nutrition. The sheer volume of information we receive daily can drive even the most health-conscious people crazy. However, as promising as each new discovery is, it is important to maintain a dose of healthy skepticism when applying these new findings to your own life. Scientific studies are works in progress, not absolute truths. Findings are tentative until the evidence becomes so overwhelming that they are widely accepted. A good strategy is to wait and not make changes based on the results of a single research study.

This book includes information and advice based on many of the more recent nutrition-related discoveries, but above all we stress the power and pleasure of healthy eating as the foundation of good health. Food itself is the only thing we know for sure will provide the natural mix of nutrients and other components known to promote good health, safely and without undue risk.

Health Canada / Santé Canada

CANADA'S Food Guide
TO HEALTHY EATING

Enjoy a variety
of foods from each
group every day.

Choose lower-
fat foods
more often.

Grain Products
Choose whole grain
and enriched
products more often.

Vegetables & Fruit
Choose dark green
and orange vegeta-
bles and orange fruit
more often.

Milk Products
Choose lower-fat
milk products more
often.

Meat & Alternatives
Choose leaner meats,
poultry and fish, as well
as dried peas, beans and
lentils more often.

Canada

3

CANADA'S

Food Guide

TO HEALTHY EATING
FOR PEOPLE FOUR YEARS AND OVER

Different People Need Different Amounts of Food

The amount of food you need every day from the 4 food groups and other foods depends on your age, body size, activity level, whether you are male or female and if you are pregnant or breast-feeding. That's why the Food Guide gives a lower and higher number of servings for each food group. For example, young children can choose the lower number of servings, while male teenagers can go to the higher number. Most other people can choose servings somewhere in between.

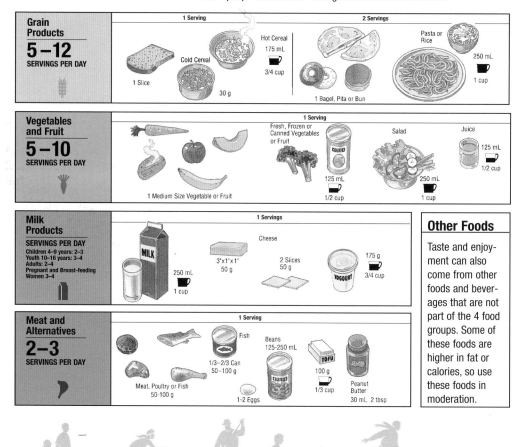

Grain Products
5–12
SERVINGS PER DAY

1 Serving
1 Slice
Cold Cereal 30 g
Hot Cereal 175 mL 3/4 cup

2 Servings
1 Bagel, Pita or Bun
Pasta or Rice 250 mL 1 cup

Vegetables and Fruit
5–10
SERVINGS PER DAY

1 Serving
1 Medium Size Vegetable or Fruit
Fresh, Frozen or Canned Vegetables or Fruit 125 mL 1/2 cup
Salad 250 mL 1 cup
Juice 125 mL 1/2 cup

Milk Products
SERVINGS PER DAY
Children 4–9 years: 2–3
Youth 10–16 years: 3–4
Adults: 2–4
Pregnant and Breast-feeding Women 3–4

1 Servings
MILK 250 mL 1 cup
Cheese 3"x1"x1" 50 g
2 Slices 50 g
YOGOURT 175 g 3/4 cup

Meat and Alternatives
2–3
SERVINGS PER DAY

1 Serving
Meat, Poultry or Fish 50-100 g
Fish 1/3–2/3 Can 50–100 g
1-2 Eggs
Beans 125-250 mL 1/3 cup
TOFU 100 g
Peanut Butter 30 mL 2 tbsp

Other Foods

Taste and enjoyment can also come from other foods and beverages that are not part of the 4 food groups. Some of these foods are higher in fat or calories, so use these foods in moderation.

Enjoy eating well, being active and feeling good about yourself. That's VITALIT

Changing for the Better

At some time or another we all face aspects of our lives we would like to change, such as quitting smoking or adopting healthier eating and cooking habits. These changes are frequently difficult to make, but knowing how other people make positive alterations in their lives can help us succeed.

According to the research of three clinical psychologists,* successful change unfolds through predictable stages, each of which involves different approaches, techniques and coping skills. Each stage is crucial for success. For instance, people who plunge unprepared into the fourth stage, Action, set themselves up for failure since they have not adequately readied themselves.

THE STAGES OF CHANGE

Stage 1 Precontemplation: At this stage you are not even thinking about change. A significant event — a fortieth birthday or a high school reunion or a health crisis — typically moves you to the next stage.

Stage 2 Contemplation: You acknowledge a problem exists but put off doing anything about it. If you are overweight, you might talk about your weight, read about weight loss or buy diet books but never quite get around to losing weight.

Stage 3 Preparation: You enter this stage when you begin to make a solid commitment to change. The focus switches from the problem to the solutions. Using the weight loss example, you might look for a weight loss program, talk to your doctor about a diet or purchase a cookbook like this one in anticipation of learning to cook in healthier ways.

Stage 4 Action: You purposefully modify your life and substitute healthy habits for poor ones. You join a weight loss program, read food labels, buy lower calorie foods, eat less, use recipes from a cookbook like this and become more physically active.

Stage 5 Maintenance: You enter the maintenance stage when you have accomplished the change you set out to make, when, for example, you have lost all the weight you set out to lose. The challenge then becomes to continue to manage your eating and activity patterns so you don't regain the weight.

Stage 6 Relapse: Relapse occurs if you abandon the new habit. It's quite common to cycle forward and backward through the stages. For instance, you may be doing well in the Action stage when a crisis in another area of your life shifts you back to the Contemplation stage. The key to recovering from the Relapse stage is to review the unsuccessful change attempt, learn from it and try again.

* Prochaska JO, Norcross JC, DiClemente CC. *Changing for Good: A Revolutionary Six-stage Program for Overcoming Bad Habits and Moving Your Life Positively Forward.* New York: Avon Books, 1994.

Appetizers

Grilled Quesadillas

Shrimp Quesadillas

Mini Phyllo Tart Shells

Mango Salsa in Mini Phyllo Tarts

Spicy Hummus

Caramelized Onion and Basil Dip

Creamy Crab Dip

Black Bean Dip with Veggie Topping

Creamy Coriander Mint Dip

Smoked Trout Spread

Herbed Yogurt-Cheese

Mushroom Bruschetta

Marinated Mussels

Crab Cakes

Spiced Shrimp

Hoisin Smoked-Turkey Spirals

Sesame Wasabi Spirals

Roasted Red Pepper and Arugula Spirals

Smoked Salmon and Cream Cheese Spirals

Teriyaki Chicken Bites

Citrus Mint Iced Tea

Nutrition Notes

Losing Weight: "Losing Weight in Good Health"

Heart Disease: "Take Healthy Eating to Heart"

Cancer: "Cancer and Healthy Eating"

Alcohol: "Wine, Whisky and Your Health"

Grilled Quesadillas

These make a terrific snack, lunch or light supper. You can substitute Cheddar cheese for the mozzarella. Serve with salsa.

1	small avocado	1
1	tomato, diced	1
1/2 cup	corn kernels	125 mL
1/4 cup	chopped canned green chilies or green onion	50 mL
1/4 tsp	salt	1 mL
Pinch	pepper	Pinch
8	flour tortillas (8 inch/20 cm)	8
1 cup	grated skim or part-skim mozzarella cheese	250 mL
1/3 cup	chopped fresh coriander (cilantro) or parsley	75 mL

1 Peel and pit avocado; place half in bowl and mash until smooth. Chop remaining half; stir into bowl along with tomato, corn, green chilies, salt and pepper.

2 Spread mixture evenly over half of each tortilla. Sprinkle cheese and coriander over mixture. Fold uncovered half over filling; gently press edges together.

3 In nonstick skillet or on grill over medium heat, cook quesadillas for 1-1/2 minutes until bottom is lightly browned. Turn and cook for 1-1/2 minutes or until filling is heated through and cheese is melted. *Makes 8 servings.*

Make ahead: Through step 2; cover and refrigerate for up to 4 hours.

Per serving:

calories	217
protein	8 g
total fat	8 g
saturated fat	2 g
cholesterol	8 mg
carbohydrate	28 g
dietary fiber	2 g
sodium	424 mg

R.D.I. Vit A 6%, E 4%, C 13%, Folate 10%, Ca 11%(124 mg), Iron 13%, Zinc 10%.

Canada's Food Guide Serving:

1½ ½ ¼

Shrimp Quesadillas

I love the fresh dill flavor here; however, chopped fresh basil or coriander also taste wonderful. If available, add a few spoonfuls of chopped mild green chilies. Serve these for lunch, as a first course or an hors d'oeuvre.

1 cup	grated skim (7% b.f.) or part-skim (15% b.f.) mozzarella cheese	250 mL
8	flour tortillas (8 inch/20 cm)	8
1/2 cup	diced tomato	125 mL
1/2 cup	salad shrimp (2 oz/60 g)	125 mL
1/2 cup	crumbled feta or firm goat cheese (chèvre)	125 mL
1/3 cup	chopped fresh dill	75 mL
1/4 cup	chopped red or green onion	50 mL
1/4 tsp	hot pepper sauce	1 mL

Serving Tip

Use a pizza cutter or long chef's knife to cut quesadillas into wedges.

1 Sprinkle half of the mozzarella evenly over half of each tortilla.

2 In small bowl, stir together tomato, shrimp, feta cheese, dill, onion and hot pepper sauce; spoon evenly over mozzarella. Top with remaining mozzarella. Fold uncovered half over filling; gently press edges together.

3 In large non-stick skillet over medium-high heat, cook quesadillas, two at a time, for 3 to 5 minutes or until bottom is lightly browned. Turn and cook until cheese is melted and bottom is lightly browned. Cut each into 3 wedges. *Makes 24 pieces.*

Make ahead: Through step 2, cover and refrigerate for up to 4 hours.

Per piece:	
calories	**70**
protein	**4 g**
total fat	**2 g**
saturated fat	**1 g**
cholesterol	**9 mg**
carbohydrate	**8 g**
dietary fiber	**1 g**
sodium	**126 mg**

R.D.I. Vit A 2%, E 1%, C 2%, Folate 2%, Ca 5%(55 mg), Iron 4%, Zinc 4%.

Canada's Food Guide Serving:

½ 🌾 ¼ 🐟

Mini Phyllo Tart Shells

These phyllo pastry shells are very easy to make, keep for weeks and are wonderful
hors d'oeuvres when filled. Basically, the shells are made of 4 thicknesses
of phyllo stacked with a light brushing of melted butter between them and cut
into 2-inch (5 cm) squares. Fill with Seafood Salad (page 231),
Mango Salsa (opposite page), or Smoked Salmon (opposite page).

3	**phyllo pastry sheets**	3
4 tsp	**butter, melted**	20 mL

1 Lay one sheet of phyllo on work surface, keeping remainder covered to prevent drying out. Brush with butter; fold in half to measure 12 x 8 inches (30 x 20 cm). Brush top with butter; cut into 2-inch (5 cm) squares.

2 Stack squares on angle to make four thicknesses for each shell; press into tiny 1-1/2 inch (4 cm) tart cups.

3 Bake in 375°F (190°C) oven for 3 to 5 minutes or until golden brown. Let cool. *Makes 36 shells.*

Make ahead: Store in cookie tin or cardboard box in dry place for up to 1 month.

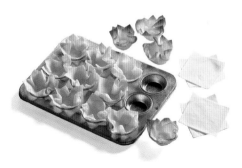

Per tart shell:
calories	**10**
protein	**0 g**
total fat	**1 g**
saturated fat	**trace**
cholesterol	**1 mg**
carbohydrate	**1 g**
sodium	**14 mg**

R.D.I. Iron 1%.

Mango Salsa in Mini Phyllo Tarts

This winning combination of paper-light buttery pastry shells with a juicy, fragrant filling is one of my favorite hors d'oeuvres.

1	mango, peeled and finely diced	1
1/2 cup	finely diced red onion	125 mL
1/2 cup	finely chopped sweet green pepper	125 mL
2 tbsp	fresh lemon or lime juice	25 mL
2 tbsp	finely chopped fresh coriander (cilantro) and/or mint	25 mL
1/4 tsp	each ground cumin and pepper	1 mL
30	Mini Phyllo Tart Shells (opposite page)	30

1 In small bowl, combine mango, onion, green pepper, lemon juice, coriander, cumin and pepper.

2 Spoon into tart shells. Serve immediately.

   Makes 1-1/2 cups (375 mL) salsa and 30 pieces.

   Make ahead: Through step 1, cover and refrigerate for up to 1 day.

Smoked Salmon with Lime-Ginger Mayonnaise in Mini Phyllo Tarts

Fill each tart shell with 1/2 tsp (2 mL) Lime Ginger Mayonnaise (page 205).
Top with 1 tsp (5 mL) smoked salmon bits; garnish with leaf of fresh coriander.

Per piece:

calories	17
protein	trace
total fat	1 g
saturated fat	trace
cholesterol	1 mg
carbohydrate	3 g
dietary fiber	trace
sodium	16 mg

R.D.I. Vit A 3%, E 1%, C 7%,
Folate 1%, Ca 0%(2 mg), Iron 1%,

Spicy Hummus

Serve this hummus as a dip for fresh vegetables or whole wheat pitas or as a spread in sandwiches, bagels or pitas. Because hummus is so easy to make at the last minute, I always keep a can of chick-peas in the cupboard.

1	can (19 oz/540 mL) chick-peas, drained and rinsed	1
3 tbsp	each fresh lemon juice and water	50 mL
2	cloves garlic, minced	2
1 tbsp	sesame oil or 2 tbsp (25 mL) tahini or peanut butter	15 mL
1-1/2 tsp	ground cumin	7 mL
1/2 tsp	hot pepper sauce or cayenne pepper	2 mL
3 tbsp	chopped fresh parsley or coriander (cilantro)	50 mL
2 tbsp	chopped bottled jalapeño pepper (optional)	25 mL

1 In food processor, purée chick-peas, lemon juice, water, garlic, sesame oil, cumin and hot pepper sauce. (If too thick, add more water, 1 tbsp/15 mL at a time, until hummus is a soft spreadable consistency.) Transfer to serving bowl. Sprinkle with parsley, and jalapeño pepper (if using). *Makes about 2 cups (500 mL).*

Make ahead: Cover and refrigerate for up to 1 week.

Lemon-Dill Hummus: Increase lemon juice to 1/4 cup (50 mL). Omit sesame oil, cumin, parsley and jalapeño pepper. Add 2 tbsp (25 mL) olive oil and 1/4 cup (50 mL) packed chopped fresh dill and purée with chick-peas.

Sun-Dried Tomato Hummus: Pour 1/2 cup (125 mL) boiling water over 1/2 cup (125 mL) dry-packed sun-dried tomatoes; let stand for 10 to 15 minutes or until softened. Drain, saving liquid. Prepare Spicy Hummus, substituting 1/4 cup (50 mL) soaking liquid for the water. Add half of the tomatoes to processor with chick-peas. Add extra soaking liquid if processed mixture is too thick. Coarsely chop remaining tomatoes and stir into hummus.

White Bean Hummus: Substitute 1 can (19 oz/540 mL) white kidney beans, drained and rinsed, for the chick-peas. Omit jalapeño pepper.

Caramelized Onion and Basil Dip

Slowly cooked onions add a richness that complements fresh basil wonderfully.
This versatile dip can also be used as a sauce or a spread, in sandwiches or on bagels.

2 tsp	olive or vegetable oil	10 mL
2	large onions, sliced (4 cups/1 L)	2
1 tbsp	balsamic vinegar	15 mL
1-1/2 tsp	granulated sugar	7 mL
1 cup	light (5%) sour cream	250 mL
1/2 cup	2% plain yogurt	125 mL
1/4 cup	chopped fresh basil*	50 mL
1/4 tsp	each salt and pepper	1 mL

1 In nonstick skillet, heat oil over medium-high heat. Stir in onions and cook, stirring, for 5 minutes. Stir in vinegar and 1 tsp (5 mL) of the sugar. Reduce heat to low; cook, covered but stirring occasionally, for 20 to 30 minutes or until well caramelized and deep golden. Let cool completely.

2 Coarsely chop cooked onions; place in bowl. Stir in sour cream, yogurt, basil, salt, pepper and remaining sugar. Add more salt to taste. Cover and refrigerate for 30 minutes before serving. *Makes about 2-1/2 cups (625 mL).*

Make ahead: Cover and refrigerate for up to 2 days.

Note about Salt

The amount of sodium in the salt you add to taste is not included in the mg of sodium in the recipe's nutrition information. If you add 1/2 tsp (2 mL) of salt, you will add 1300 mg of sodium to the total recipe. To determine the amount per serving, divide the total sodium added by the number of servings.

*Substitution Tip

Instead of fresh basil, you can use 1/4 cup (50 mL) chopped fresh parsley plus 1 tsp (5 mL) dried basil.

Homemade Tortilla Chips

You can make you own crisp, flavorful, lower-fat tortilla chips. Cut soft flour tortillas into wedges; spread in single layer on baking sheet and bake in 375°F (190°C) oven for 3 to 5 minutes or until crisp.

For seasoned chips, before baking, brush very lightly with beaten egg white and sprinkle with dried or chopped fresh oregano or rosemary or with a combination of herbs, or with sesame seeds, poppy seeds or freshly grated Parmesan cheese.

Per 2 tbsp (25 mL):

calories	35
protein	2 g
total fat	1 g
cholesterol	2 mg
carbohydrate	5 g
sodium	44 mg

R.D.I. Vit A 1%, E 1%, C 2%, Folate 2%, Ca 4%(41 mg), Iron 1%, Zinc 1%.

Canada's Food Guide Serving:
1/4

13

Creamy Crab Dip

*I find that frozen crabmeat has more flavor and a better texture than canned.
Imitation crab is also fine. Of course, fresh Canadian crab is a hands-down
winner to be used as a special treat. In summer, use chopped fresh chives instead of the
parsley. This makes a tasty dip for vegetables, sliced French bread or
low-fat chips such as baked tortilla chips (or Homemade Tortilla Chips on page 13).*

1-1/2 cups	frozen crabmeat, thawed and thoroughly drained (7 oz/200 g)	375 mL
1 cup	light (5%) sour cream	250 mL
1/2 cup	2% plain yogurt	125 mL
1/2 cup	finely chopped celery	125 mL
2 tbsp	chopped fresh parsley and/or fresh dill	25 mL
1 tbsp	prepared horseradish	15 mL
1/2 tsp	Dijon mustard	2 mL
1/4 tsp	each salt, pepper and hot pepper sauce	1 mL

I   In small bowl, combine crab, sour cream, yogurt, celery, parsley, horseradish, mustard, salt, pepper and hot pepper sauce; mix well. Cover and refrigerate for 1 hour. *Makes 2-1/2 cups (625 mL).*

Make ahead: Cover and refrigerate for up to 2 days.

Per 2 tbsp (25 mL):

calories	24
protein	2 g
total fat	1 g
saturated fat	trace
cholesterol	5 mg
carbohydrate	2 g
dietary fiber	0 g
sodium	103 mg

R.D.I. Vit A 1%, C 2%, Folate 1%,
Ca 4%(40 mg), Iron 2%, Zinc 1%.

Black Bean Dip with Veggie Topping

This dip is a favorite with all my children. When Susie makes it, she cooks the onions and spices in the microwave (see sidebar). My sons sometimes omit the cooking and just mix everything in a food processor. Serve with baked tortilla chips or vegetables.

1 tsp	vegetable oil	5 mL
1/4 cup	chopped onion	50 mL
1	large clove garlic, minced	1
1	sweet green pepper, chopped	1
1/2 tsp	each ground coriander, ground cumin and chili powder	2 mL
1/4 tsp	cayenne pepper or crushed red pepper flakes	1 mL
1	can (19 oz/540 mL) black beans, drained and rinsed	1
2 tbsp	fresh lime or lemon juice	25 mL
3 tbsp	chopped packed fresh coriander (cilantro)	50 mL
1	small tomato, chopped	1

1 In large nonstick skillet, heat oil over medium heat; cook onion, garlic and half of the green pepper until onion is tender, about 5 minutes, stirring occasionally. Add ground coriander, cumin, chili powder and cayenne; cook, stirring, for 30 seconds. Remove from heat.

2 In food processor, process beans and lime juice. Add onion mixture and half of the fresh coriander; process until smooth. If too thick, add up to 1/4 cup (50 mL) water, 1 tbsp (15 mL) at a time, processing until smooth. Cover and refrigerate for at least 1 hour or for up to 3 days.

3 Spoon into serving dish. Sprinkle with remaining green pepper, coriander and tomato. *Makes 2 cups (500 mL).*

Make ahead: Through step 2, refrigerate for up to 3 days.

Pinto Bean Dip

Substitute 1 can (19 oz/540 mL) pinto beans, drained and rinsed, for the black beans. If using pinto beans, it may not be necessary to add water.

Microwave Method

In microwaveable dish, combine oil, onion, garlic, half of the green pepper, ground coriander, cumin, chili powder and cayenne. Cover with plastic wrap, slightly vented; microwave on High for 2 minutes. Continue recipe at step 2 of Black Bean Dip.

Per 2 tbsp (25 mL):

calories	39
protein	2 g
total fat	trace
cholesterol	0 mg
carbohydrate	7 g
dietary fiber	2 g
sodium	57 mg

R.D.I. Vit A 1%, E 1%, C 12%, Folate 17%, Ca 1% (10 mg), Iron 4%, Zinc 3%.

Canada's Food Guide Serving:
¼

Losing Weight in Good Health

When the Canadian Medical Association asked its members what nutrition questions they were asked most frequently, how to lose weight topped the list by a long shot. And it's no wonder. Canadians are getting fatter despite what seems to be a full-time preoccupation with weight and weight loss. Almost one-third of adults are overweight, and in the past decade the prevalence of obesity has increased 8% in boys and 10% in girls. (See page 250 for advice for overweight children.)

These figures are not good news. Aside from the toll on our emotional well-being, being overweight increases our risk of high blood pressure, high blood cholesterol and triglycerides, diabetes, gallbladder disease, arthritis and joint problems, certain cancers, sleep disorders and menstrual and fertility problems.

The good news is that losing weight — even 10 to 20 pounds (5 to 10 kg) — can be beneficial in reducing blood pressure, blood lipids and improving glucose tolerance.

Are You Ready to Lose Weight Once and For All?

According to the Stages of Change model (see page 5), people sometimes try to change many times before they finally succeed. And success is dependent on the strength of their commitment to and preparation for change.

To assess your readiness to lose weight, ask yourself these questions.

- Are you really determined to lose weight?
- Do you have a sense, deep down inside, that you can do it?
- Do you want to lose weight for yourself and no one else?
- Have you taken responsibility for being overweight, without making excuses and blaming other factors and people?
- Are you being realistic about your size and shape and what is possible for you to achieve?
- Do you accept that the lifestyle changes you need to make are permanent, not just until you lose the weight you want to lose?

Your chances of achieving and maintaining weight loss will be better if you answered yes to all these questions.

Are You Destined to be Fat?
Being overweight is a complex problem with many causes. Although some people are more prone to being overweight because of genetic traits and hormonal influences, being prone to fatness is no different from being prone to heart disease or diabetes. You can defy or alter your genetic destiny by altering lifestyle habits.

What's the Best Way to Lose Weight?

Anyone who has tried to lose weight knows it's not a simple process. What's even harder is maintaining a healthy weight once the weight is lost. Success depends on learning to eat and to respond to food in healthy ways.

What seems to work best in the long run is a commitment to healthy eating and regular physical activity. This method involves hard work, and the progress is slow, but it does increase your chances of losing and maintaining the weight loss permanently.

Many diet plans such as the high-protein/low-carbohydrate diet may offer quicker weight loss, but some are downright dangerous. What's more, few people can stick with these unbalanced programs for long. While you can lose weight, often very quickly, the loss is rarely maintained. We recommend that you resist quick-fix approaches to weight loss and tackle the problem by eating more healthfully and becoming more active.

Keep Active

Becoming more active is a critical part of weight loss, weight maintenance and healthy living in general.

Choose a physical activity that you enjoy and can keep with. If you are currently inactive, don't set yourself up for failure by taking on too much, too soon. Start slowly and work up to more activity.

Walking is one of the easiest, most enjoyable and affordable activities, especially if you are overweight and unfit. All you need are good walking shoes and comfortable clothes.

As you become more physically active, aim for 20 to 30 minutes of daily physical activity. In addition, think about other ways to include more activity into your routine. For instance, ride your bike to the local variety store; park your car in a back lot at the shopping center; take the stairs whenever possible.

Counting Calories: How Many?

No single calorie and fat level is right for everyone; your calorie needs vary depending on your metabolism, your level of activity and your medical conditions. When you start a weight-loss plan, consume about 1500 calories and 40 to 45 grams of fat daily.

If after the first two weeks you are losing more than 2 pounds (1 kg) weekly or feeling hungry all the time, increase your calorie intake to the point that you are not hungry and are losing just 1 or 2 pounds (500g to 1 kg) a week. If after the first two weeks you are not losing at least 1 pound (500g) a week, drop back to 1400 calories and increase physical activity.

Never restrict yourself to diets of 1000 to 1200 calories a day. This calorie level is too low and will leave you hungry and thinking about food all the time. People who overeat and binge do so in response to severe food restriction.

HEALTHY EATING TIPS: Losing Weight

- Follow the basic principles of healthy eating (see page 1).
- Reduce both your calorie and your fat intake.
- Use calorie- and fat-reduced products such as light mayonnaise, low-fat yogurt and light cheese.
- Avoid high-fat snack foods such as chips, snacking crackers and cookies.
- Include your favorite foods and treats once in a while to avoid feelings of deprivation and to learn to fit these foods into a healthy eating pattern.
- Learn to eat in response to hunger but stop eating once you are satisfied.
- Don't subject yourself to hunger. Eat a banana; have a light hot chocolate; or drink a glass of tomato juice to carry you over to the next meal.
- Eat at least three times a day, more often if you are hungry. Spread calories out so that 300 to 500 calories are consumed at regular intervals throughout the day.
- Watch portion sizes. Big bagels, oversized muffins and Caesar salads often contribute two to three times the calories and/or fat you think they do.
- Keep track of what you eat. Weighing and measuring food at first is a good reality check since research shows that people tend to underestimate what they are eating.

HEALTHY EATING TIPS: Maintaining a Healthier Weight

People who have lost weight and kept it off view weight control as a lifelong effort. They use the same strategies to maintain weight as they used to lose weight — healthy eating and an active lifestyle. For these people, weight loss was not an end in itself but a means to an end that included better health, more confidence, improved self-esteem and ability to do other things in life.

Try these strategies to help you maintain weight loss:

- Weigh yourself at least once a week to keep tabs on your weight.
- Deal with small weight gains immediately. It's normal for weight to fluctuate, but set a top weight limit for yourself. Once your weight hits this point, be ready with a plan to reduce this weight immediately. For example, you might exercise more, have no desserts for two weeks, or cut back on portions.
- Keep in touch with friends, family members or programs that helped you lose weight.
- Learn to deal with life's problems without turning to food. While there's nothing wrong with taking a break with a cup of tea and a few cookies, if you find yourself repeatedly overeating in response to stress and anxiety, you may want to seek some professional counseling.
- Don't let your hard-earned efforts to be healthier be thwarted by minor setbacks such as an eating binge or overindulgence during holidays or celebrations. Forget it and get back on track as soon as you can.

Hot Chili Peppers

- Mild: green, poblano
- Medium: jalapeño, banana
- Hot: serrano
- Very hot: Scotch bonnet
- Hottest: Habañero

To Use Peppers

If your hands are sensitive, wear rubber gloves (inexpensive ones are available at drugstores). Don't touch your eyes or your lips when chopping peppers. If you don't wear gloves, thoroughly wash your hands in soapy water after handling peppers. For a milder taste, remove a pepper's seeds and ribs.

Pepper Fact

Chipotle is a dried, smoked jalapeño pepper.

Creamy Coriander Mint Dip

*Coriander and mint give this dip or sauce a lively taste.
It's also great as a sandwich spread, in pitas or as a sauce with Crab Cakes (page 28)
or with grilled chicken or fish or Chick-Pea Burgers (page 121).*

1 cup	light (5%) sour cream	250 mL
1/2 cup	2% plain yogurt	125 mL
1	fresh jalapeño pepper, seeded, deribbed and minced (about 1 tbsp/15 mL) or 1/4 tsp (1 mL) hot pepper sauce	1
1/4 cup	chopped fresh coriander (cilantro)	50 mL
2 tbsp	each chopped fresh mint and chives	25 mL
1/2 tsp	salt	2 mL
Pinch	pepper	Pinch

1 In bowl, combine sour cream, yogurt, jalapeño pepper, coriander, mint, chives, salt and pepper; mix well. If using hot pepper sauce, add more to taste.
Makes 1-2/3 cups (400 mL).

Make ahead: Cover and refrigerate for up to 2 days.

Smoked Trout Spread

This easy-to-make spread is one of my long-time favorites. Spread it on crackers or slices of French bread. Or use it in canapés by cutting thin slices of pumpernickel bread into 2-inch (5 cm) pieces, topping with a small spoonful of trout spread and garnishing with sprig of dill. It's also tasty stuffed into cherry tomatoes or spooned onto cucumber rounds. Smoked trout is available at specialty food stores and many supermarkets.

8 oz	skinless smoked trout fillet	250 g
1/2 cup	extra-thick (Greek-style) or drained plain yogurt	125 mL
3 tbsp	light mayonnaise	50 mL
3 tbsp	chopped fresh dill	50 mL
2 tbsp	fresh lemon juice	25 mL
1 tbsp	minced onion or green onion	15 mL
2 tsp	prepared horseradish	10 mL
1/4 tsp	pepper	1 mL

I In food processor, combine trout, yogurt, mayonnaise, dill, lemon juice, onion, horseradish and pepper; process until smooth. Cover and refrigerate for at least 1 hour. *Makes 1-2/3 cups (400 mL).*

Make Ahead: Cover and refrigerate for up to 3 days. (Actually better after 1 day.)

Smoked Trout Sour Cream Spread: This spread is also very delicious made with 1/2 cup (125 mL) light (5%) sour cream instead of the yogurt and 3 tbsp (50 mL) plain yogurt instead of the light mayonnaise.

To Drain Yogurt

Place plain (no gelatin) yogurt in a cheesecloth-lined sieve set over bowl or in yogurt drainer. Refrigerate for about 4 hours or until reduced by half. Discard liquid or use in soups. Liquid contains B vitamins and minerals and is low in fat.

Per 2 tbsp (25 mL):

calories	45
protein	4 g
total fat	2 g
saturated fat	trace
cholesterol	11 mg
carbohydrate	1 g
sodium	40 mg

R.D.I. Vit A 1%, C 2%, Folate 2%, Ca 3%(37 mg), Iron 2%, Zinc 3%.

Canada's Food Guide Serving:

¼ 〉

Herbed Yogurt-Cheese

I keep this versatile yogurt-cheese in the refrigerator and use it as a topping for baked potatoes, as a spread in pita sandwiches or to mix with a little light mayonnaise when making tuna or chicken sandwiches. Don't overdo the garlic because it becomes much stronger in flavor after a few days.

Herbed Light Cream Cheese

Substitute 1 cup (250 mL), or 8 oz (250 g), light, tub or 17% cream cheese for the drained yogurt, or mix the light cream cheese with 1/2 tsp (2 mL) each herbes de Provence and grated lemon rind.

2 cups	2% plain yogurt (Balkan-style or no gelatin) or 1 cup (250 mL) extra-thick yogurt	500 mL
2 tbsp	chopped green onions or chives	25 mL
2 tbsp	finely chopped fresh parsley	25 mL
1 tbsp	finely chopped fresh dill and/or basil	15 mL
Half to 1	clove garlic, minced	Half to 1
1/4 to 1/2 tsp	each salt and pepper	1 to 2 mL

1 Place plain yogurt in cheesecloth-lined sieve set over bowl or in yogurt drainer; refrigerate for 3 hours or overnight or until reduced to 1 cup (250 mL).

2 In bowl, combine drained yogurt, onions, parsley, dill, garlic, salt and pepper, mixing well. Cover and refrigerate for at least 4 hours. *Makes 1 cup (250 mL).*

Make ahead: Cover and refrigerate for up to 3 days.

Per 2 tbsp (25 mL):
calories	29
protein	3 g
total fat	1 g
saturated fat	trace
cholesterol	2 mg
carbohydrate	3 g
sodium	99 mg

R.D.I. Vit A 1%, C 3%, Folate 4%, Ca 9%(97 mg), Iron 1%, Zinc 5%.

Canada's Food Guide Serving:
¼

Mushroom Bruschetta

*Pile any kind or combination of mushrooms — shiitake, portobello, oyster —
on this tasty bruschetta. Serve as a starter at brunch, as a snack or cut
into smaller pieces for hors d'oeuvres.*

1	piece (6-inch/15 cm) baguette or Italian loaf	1
1	clove garlic, halved	1
1 tbsp	butter	15 mL
6 cups	sliced mushrooms (1 lb/500 g)	1.5 L
1/4 cup	chopped green onions	50 mL
1/4 cup	chopped fresh basil or 2 tsp (10 mL) dried	50 mL
1/4 cup	coarsely chopped fresh parsley	50 mL
1/2 cup	freshly grated Parmesan cheese	125 mL

1 Slice bread crosswise into 1/2-inch (1 cm) thick diagonal slices. Place on baking sheet; broil, turning once, for 2 minutes or until golden. Rub tops with cut side of garlic; discard garlic.

2 In large nonstick skillet, melt butter over medium-high heat. Add mushrooms; cook, shaking pan and stirring often, for about 8 minutes or until mushrooms are browned and liquid is evaporated. Stir in onions, basil and parsley; cook for 1 minute.

3 Spoon mixture over garlic side of bread; sprinkle with cheese.

4 Broil for about 3 minutes or until cheese melts. Serve hot or warm. *Makes 12 pieces.*

Make ahead: Through step 2, cover and refrigerate for up to 1 day. Through step 3 up to 1 hour ahead.

Tomato Basil Bruschetta

In bowl, toss together 2 large tomatoes, diced, 1/4 cup (50 mL) chopped fresh basil (lightly packed), 1 clove garlic, finely chopped, and salt and pepper to taste; let stand for 15 minutes. Prepare bread with garlic as directed. Brush lightly with olive oil and top with tomato mixture.

Per piece:

calories	**57**
protein	**3 g**
total fat	**3 g**
saturated fat	1 g
cholesterol	6 mg
carbohydrate	**6 g**
dietary fiber	**1 g**
sodium	**136 mg**

R.D.I. Vit A 2%, E 1%, C 3%, Folate 4%, Ca 6% (69 mg), Iron 6%, Zinc 5%.

Canada's Food Guide Serving:
¼ 🌾 ½ 🥕

Marinated Mussels

Tantalizing tastes make these a winning hors d'oeuvre. They are also perfect for a first course at a dinner party or as part of an antipasto platter.

2 lb	mussels (45 to 50)	1 kg
Half	each small yellow and red sweet pepper, diced	Half
1/4 cup	chopped fresh coriander (cilantro)	50 mL
1/4 cup	minced green onions	50 mL
2 tbsp	fresh lime or lemon juice	25 mL
2 tbsp	each soy sauce and roasted sesame oil	25 mL
1 tbsp	minced gingerroot	15 mL
1/2 tsp	hot chili paste or hot pepper sauce	2 mL

1 Wash mussels and remove any hairy beards; discard any mussels that have broken or open shells or don't close when tapped.

2 Place in large heavy saucepan; add 1/2 cup (125 mL) water. Cover and cook over medium-high heat until mussels open, about 5 minutes; drain and let cool. Discard any mussels that do not open.

3 Meanwhile, in large bowl, stir together sweet peppers, coriander, onions, lime juice, soy sauce, sesame oil, ginger and hot chili paste.

4 Remove mussels from shells, reserving shells. Add mussels to bowl; cover and marinate for at least 30 minutes.

5 Arrange half the mussel shells on large platter; fill each with mussel and some marinade. *Makes about 45 pieces or 6 first-course servings.*

Make ahead: Through step 4, cover and refrigerate for up to 6 hours.

Per piece:
calories   **12**
protein   **1 g**
total fat   **1 g**
        cholesterol   **2 mg**
carbohydrate   **1 g**
sodium   **38 mg**
R.D.I. Vit A 1%, C 7%, Folate 1%,
Ca 0%(2 mg), Iron 2%, Zinc 1%.

Take Healthy Eating to Heart

In the past two decades we have learned a lot about what causes heart disease and how to reduce the risk of developing it. Healthy eating clearly plays an important role in preventing heart disease and stroke and promoting heart health overall. It is also one of the cornerstones for treating aspects of heart disease such as elevated blood cholesterol.

Other Ways to Protect your Heart

In addition to the main dietary strategies for heart health, which focus on weight loss, cutting dietary fat, increasing complex carbohydrates (starches) and fiber, other food and nutrition-related therapies may be useful for some people at a high risk for heart disease. However, since some vitamin supplements are potentially harmful and may interfere with the absorption and metabolism of other nutrients and medications, these types of therapies should be undertaken only with the knowledge of your doctor and used as a part of a total risk reduction program.

- *Antioxidant vitamins:* Antioxidant vitamins C, E and beta carotene hold promise as therapies, although their benefits have not been proved and they are not widely recommended by doctors. The best advice is to increase your intake of these vitamins through foods (see page 214). If you decide to take supplements, do not exceed these daily guidelines: **Vitamin C: 250 to 500 mg**
  Vitamin E: 100 to 800 IU
  Beta carotene: 6 to 15 mg

  There is also some question about the safety of beta carotene supplements for smokers. A Finnish study published in 1994 unexpectedly found an increased risk of lung cancer in smokers who took supplements of beta carotene, a finding that continues to be the subject of ongoing debate and study.

- *Niacin:* A supplement of 1.5 to 3 grams of niacin or nicotinic acid, a B vitamin, lowers LDL (bad) cholesterol and triglycerides and raises HDL (good) cholesterol. However, since niacin can have some unpleasant side-effects (flushing of the skin among them) and is potentially harmful, it should be taken only under a doctor's supervision.

- *Omega-3 fat:* Eicosapentaenoic acid (EPA) and docosahexaenoic acid (DHA) are omega-3 fats that reduce the stickiness of blood, lower triglyceride levels and may lower blood pressure. Supplements are not widely recommended because long-term effects remain uncertain, but eating more fish to obtain omega-3 fats is advocated.

Risk Factors for Cardiovascular Disease

- smoking
- high blood pressure
  (see page 208)
- a high-fat diet
  (see page 64)
- high LDL (low-density lipoprotein) cholesterol
  (see page 166)
- low HDL (high-density lipoprotein) cholesterol
  (see page 166)
- elevated triglycerides
  (see page 166)
- diabetes (see page 268)
- being overweight
  (see page 16)
- not being physically active

- *Folic acid and other B vitamins:* There is mounting evidence that folic acid and, to a lesser extent, vitamins B6 and B12 may protect against heart disease by keeping levels of homocysteine down. High levels of homocysteine, a by-product of amino acid metabolism, have been linked to artery-clogging atherosclerosis and heart attacks. To ensure a healthy intake of folic acid, eat more dark green vegetables, citrus fruits, whole grains, bran cereal, legumes (dried beans, peas and lentils), and foods fortified with folic acid such as enriched pasta, rice and corn meal products. Check the nutrition analysis that accompanies each recipe to see how much folic acid the dish contains.
- *Garlic:* Eating 1 to 2 raw cloves of garlic daily or taking a 600 mg garlic supplement may be helpful. Allicin, the active ingredient in garlic, can reduce blood cholesterol up to 9%.

Cancer and Healthy Eating

The development of some forms of cancer is influenced by dietary factors such as fat, fiber, antioxidant vitamins and alcohol. As with preventing heart disease, healthy eating is the key to lowering your risk of these nutrition-related cancers.

HEALTHY EATING TIPS: Lowering the Risk of Cancer

- Reduce your fat intake. High-fat diets are linked to several cancers including colorectal, breast, ovarian, prostate and kidney.
- Eat more fiber. Diets high in insoluble fiber like that found in wheat bran, whole grain breads and cereals, vegetables and fruit have been linked to a lower risk of colorectal cancer and more recently with a lower risk of breast cancer. (See page 226.)
- Eat lots of vegetables and fruits. These foods contain a variety of antioxidant vitamins, minerals and plant chemicals (phytochemicals), which are linked with lower cancer rates. (See page 146.)
- Lose weight. Excess weight, particularly in women, seems to increase the risk for certain cancers such as breast and uterine. (See page 16.)
- Limit your alcohol intake. Excessive drinking has been linked to mouth and throat cancer, especially when combined with cigarette smoke. Alcohol consumption is also linked to breast cancer. (See page 34.)

Crab Cakes

Crab Balls

Perfect for cocktail parties. Shape crab mixture into forty-eight 1-inch (2.5 cm) balls. Bake as directed for 10 to 12 minutes or until golden. Serve with Creamy Coriander Mint Dip (page 20) or substitute fresh or dried tarragon to taste for the coriander in the dip. *Makes 48.*

Ginger, Coriander Crab Cakes

Substitute chopped fresh coriander (cilantro) for the dill. Add 1 tsp (5 mL) grated gingerroot and 1 to 2 tsp (5 to 10 mL) minced fresh jalapeño pepper.

Serve these as an elegant first course with Creamy Coriander Mint Dip (page 20) as a sauce. Or serve with salsa mixed with a little light mayonnaise and garnished with stems of chives or sprigs of watercress. For lunch serve with a Spinach Salad, (page 38) or Carrot Slaw with Radicchio (page 39) and Spanish-Style Asparagus (page 136).

1/4 cup	finely chopped green onions	50 mL
1/4 cup	light mayonnaise	50 mL
2 tbsp	each chopped fresh parsley, dill and celery	25 mL
1	egg, lightly beaten	1
1 tsp	finely grated lemon rind	5 mL
1 tsp	each Dijon mustard and hot pepper sauce	5 mL
1/4 tsp	each salt and pepper	1 mL
1 cup	fine dry bread crumbs	250 mL
1 lb	crabmeat (fresh, thawed or imitation*)	500 g
1 tbsp	vegetable oil	15 mL

1 In bowl, stir together onions, mayonnaise, parsley, dill, celery, egg, lemon rind, mustard, hot pepper sauce, salt and pepper. Stir in 1/4 cup (50 mL) of the bread crumbs and crab; mix lightly until combined. Shape into 6 patties.

2 Place remaining crumbs on plate; coat each patty on both sides with crumbs, using spatula to help turn patties as they will be soft.

3 Pour oil onto rimmed baking sheet. Place in 400°F (200°C) oven for 2 to 3 minutes or until very hot. Gently transfer crab cakes to hot baking sheet. Bake for 15 minutes or until golden on both sides, turning after 7 minutes. *Makes 6 servings.*

Make ahead: Through step 2, cover and refrigerate for up to 4 hours.

Per serving:

calories	191
protein	21 g
total fat	7 g
saturated fat	1 g
cholesterol	89 mg
carbohydrate	10 g
dietary fiber	1 g
sodium	816 mg

R.D.I. Vit A 6%, D 3%, E 3%, C 12%, Folate 19%, Ca 6% (64 mg), Iron 23%, Zinc 33%.

Canada's Food Guide Serving:
½ 🌾   1½ 🍖

* If using imitation crab meat, use 400g and chop before adding. Mixture will be crumbly but will hold together after baking.

Spiced Shrimp

*Pass these hot, spicy shrimp in a bowl along with toothpicks for an hors d'oeuvre
your guests will love.*

1 tsp	each paprika, ground cumin and packed brown sugar	5 mL
1/2 tsp	each salt, dry mustard and dried oregano	2 mL
1/4 tsp	chili powder	1 mL
Pinch	cayenne pepper	Pinch
1 lb	raw or cooked peeled extra-large or large shrimp	500 g
1 tbsp	vegetable oil	15 mL
	Lime wedges (optional)	

1 In small bowl, combine paprika, cumin, sugar, salt, mustard, oregano, chili powder
and cayenne. Sprinkle over shrimp and toss to coat evenly. Refrigerate for up to
3 hours.

2 In large nonstick skillet, heat oil over medium-high heat; stir-fry shrimp until pink
and no longer opaque, 3 to 4 minutes for raw, 2 to 3 minutes for cooked. Serve hot
with wedges of lime (if using). *Makes about 40 pieces.*

ANTIPASTO PLATTER

For a fabulous appetizer or a light lunch, arrange a selection of roasted or marinated
vegetables, salads, cheeses, fish and meats on a large platter and serve with crusty
bread, focaccia or bruschetta. Give guests small plates and let them serve themselves.

Choose a colorful selection from: Marinated Mussels (page 24), Spicy Hummus
(page 12), Spiced Shrimp (this page), sardines, marinated artichokes, grilled or roasted
sweet peppers, zucchini or eggplant drizzled with olive oil and Italian herbs (page 156),
cherry tomatoes, cooked sliced beets drizzled with balsamic vinegar, black and green
olives, thinly sliced prosciutto, wedges of Asiago or Parmigiano-Reggiano or rounds of
Bocconcini cheese, wedges of fresh melon and fresh figs, chick-peas or white kidney
beans drizzled with vinaigrette. Garnish with fresh basil leaves, arugula or watercress.

Per 3 shrimp:

calories	**48**
protein	**7 g**
total fat	**2 g**
cholesterol	**52 mg**
carbohydrate	**1 g**
sodium	**137 mg**

R.D.I. Vit A 3%, E 2%, C 2%,
Folate 1%, Ca 1%(11 mg), Iron 6%, Zinc
4%.

Canada's Food Guide Serving:

½

29

Hoisin Smoked-Turkey Spirals

These are truly fast and easy to make but
your guests will think you spent hours in the kitchen.

Tortilla Roll-Ups

Any of the spirals on these pages can be cut into larger pieces and served as a sandwich platter. Add cooked, cooled asparagus spears to the Hoisin Smoked-Turkey Spirals, and thinly sliced smoked ham or turkey to the Sesame Wasabi Spirals.

4	10-inch (25 cm) flour tortillas	4
1/2 cup	hoisin sauce	125 mL
1/3 cup	finely chopped green onions	75 mL
2 cups	thinly sliced or shredded smoked turkey (8 oz/250 g)	500 mL
4	large leaves leaf lettuce or enough spinach to cover tortillas	4

1 Spread each tortilla with hoisin sauce; sprinkle with green onions. Arrange turkey in single layer, not overlapping, over tortilla, leaving 1-inch (2.5 cm) border around edge. Cover turkey with lettuce leaf. Roll up tightly, jelly-roll fashion.

2 Wrap tightly in plastic wrap. Refrigerate for at least 1 hour or for up to 6 hours.

3 Cut each on the diagonal into 12 slices; discard or eat ends. *Makes 40 pieces.*

Make ahead for all spirals: Through step 2, refrigerate for up to 6 hours.

Per piece:

calories	35
protein	2 g
total fat	1 g
cholesterol	4 mg
carbohydrate	0 g
dietary fiber	trace
sodium	83 mg

R.D.I. Folate 1%, Ca 0% (5 mg), Iron 3%, Zinc 1%.

Canada's Food Guide Serving:
¼

Sesame Wasabi Spirals

A hit of wasabi, the hot flavor in sushi, makes this my favorite roll-up bite.

4	10-inch (25 cm) flour tortillas	4
1/3 cup	light mayonnaise or Herbed Yogurt Cheese (page 22)	75 mL
4 tsp	wasabi powder	20 mL
4	strips (8- x 1/2-inch/20 x 1 cm) peeled seeded cucumber	4
1/4 cup	toasted sesame seeds	50 mL
1/4 cup	coriander (cilantro) leaves or 4 leaves of leaf lettuce	50 mL

1 Spread each tortilla with mayonnaise, leaving 1-inch (2.5 cm) border around edge. Mix wasabi powder with 1 tbsp (15 mL) water; spread in thin line across tortilla, about one-quarter of the way down. Beside wasabi, arrange row of cucumber. Sprinkle mayonnaise with sesame seeds and top with coriander. Starting at wasabi side, roll up tightly and press to seal edge.

2 Follow steps 2 and 3 as in previous recipe. *Makes 40 pieces.*

To Toast Sesame Seeds

Place sesame seeds in small skillet over medium heat and cook 5 minutes or until golden, stirring occasionally.

Shopping Tip

Small tins of wasabi powder, or Japanese horseradish, are available at Asian grocery stores.

Per piece (with light mayonnaise):

calories	31
protein	1 g
total fat	2 g
cholesterol	0 mg
carbohydrate	4 g
dietary fiber	trace
sodium	41 mg

R.D.I. Folate 1%, Ca 0% (4 mg), Iron 2%, Zinc 2%.

Canada's Food Guide Serving:
¼

Roasted Red Pepper and Arugula Spirals

Cooking Tip

To roast your own red peppers, broil, grill or roast them in a 400 F (200 C) oven, turning often, until blistered. Then peel off the skin.

You can roast your own peppers or use the ones from a jar, available at most supermarkets. Instead of Herbed Light Cream Cheese (page 22), you can use light, tub or 17% plain cream cheese mixed with 1/4 cup (50 mL) chopped fresh basil or coriander. Or mix soft chèvre cheese with half its volume of light sour cream (to make it spreadable) and basil or coriander.

4	10-inch (25 cm) flour tortillas	4
1/2 cup	Herbed Light Cream Cheese (page 22) or soft chèvre	125 mL
4	roasted red peppers, well drained	4
Half	bunch arugula or enough watercress or lettuce to cover	Half

1 Spread each tortilla with cream cheese. Cut red peppers into 1-inch (2.5 cm) wide strips; arrange, in single layer, in row over cream cheese. Cover with arugula, leaving 1-inch (2.5 cm) border around edge.

2 Follow steps 2 and 3 as in previous recipe. *Makes 40 pieces.*

Per piece:
calories	29
protein	1 g
total fat	1 g
cholesterol	3 mg
carbohydrate	4 g
dietary fiber	trace
sodium	41 mg

R.D.I. Vit A 5%, C 33%, Folate 1%, Ca 1%(8 mg), Iron 2%, Zinc 1%.

Canada's Food Guide Serving:
¼ ¼

Smoked Salmon and Cream Cheese Spirals

These spirals are a lighter version of the original, long-time favorite of caterers.

4	10-inch (25 cm) flour tortillas	4
1 cup	Herbed Yogurt Cheese (page 22) or 2/3 cup (150 mL) Herbed Light Cream Cheese (page 22)	250 mL
10 oz	thinly sliced smoked salmon	300 g
1 cup	lightly packed watercress or coriander (cilantro) leaves	250 mL

1 Spread each tortilla with yogurt cheese. Arrange salmon in single layer over cheese, leaving 1-inch (2.5 cm) border around edge; sprinkle with watercress.

2 Follow step 2 as in previous recipe. *Makes 40 pieces.*

Per piece with Herbed Yogurt Cheese:
calories	33
protein	2 g
total fat	1 g
cholesterol	2 mg
carbohydrate	4 g
dietary fiber	trace
sodium	103 mg

R.D.I. Vit A 1%, E 1%, C 2%, Folate 1%, Ca 2%(24 mg), Iron 2%, Zinc 2%.

Canada's Food Guide Serving:
¼

Teriyaki Chicken Bites

*I absolutely love fresh coriander, but this appetizer is also delicious
with fresh basil or even with no herb at all. The marinade
can also be used to marinate chicken pieces for baking or grilling.
It will be enough for up to 2 lb (1 kg) chicken.*

1 lb	boneless skinless chicken breasts	500 g
1	large sweet green or red pepper	1
1/4 cup	soy sauce	50 mL
2 tbsp	liquid honey	25 mL
1 tbsp	rice vinegar	15 mL
1 tbsp	minced gingerroot	15 mL
1	clove garlic, minced	1
1/4 tsp	hot pepper sauce or chili paste	1 mL
24	fresh coriander (cilantro) leaves	24

1 Cut chicken into 1/2-inch (1 cm) thick 1-inch (2.5 cm) pieces; place in bowl. Cut green pepper into 1-inch (2.5 cm) pieces; set aside.

2 In small bowl, combine soy sauce, honey, vinegar, ginger, garlic and hot pepper sauce. Pour over chicken; stir to coat. Cover and refrigerate for at least 1 hour or for up to 24 hours.

3 Soak wooden skewers or toothpicks in cold water for 20 minutes. Thread 2 pieces of chicken onto skewer along with 1 piece of green pepper and 1 coriander leaf between chicken.

4 Place on baking sheet. Bake in 350°F (180°C) oven for 10 to 12 minutes, or broil for 5 minutes, or until chicken is no longer pink inside. Serve hot. *Makes 24 pieces.*

Make ahead: Through step 2 for up to 1 day. Through step 3 for up to 3 hours.

Teriyaki Chicken Bites with Basil

Substitute fresh basil leaves, cut in pieces, for fresh coriander leaves.

Cooking Tip

To double the recipe, use the same amount of marinade, but double the amount of chicken, sweet pepper and coriander.

Per piece:

calories	**26**
protein	**4 g**
total fat	**trace**
cholesterol	**11 mg**
carbohydrate	**1 g**
sodium	**96 mg**

R.D.I. Vit C 7%, Folate 1%, Ca 0% (2 mg), Iron 1%, Zinc 2%.

Canada's Food Guide Serving:
¼ 🍗

Wine, Whisky and Your Health

In recent years the so-called French paradox has received lots of media coverage. The paradox is that the French, with their diet of cream sauces, rich pastries and cheese, have the lowest rate of heart disease of any country, save Japan. Many researchers attributed this unlikely situation to a high consumption of wine. And, in fact, it's now well accepted that small amounts of all forms of alcohol, not just red wine, do reduce the risks of death from heart disease, probably by increasing levels of the good HDL cholesterol and reducing the risk of blood clotting.

But don't uncork the bottle just yet! Alcohol consumption has its down sides. The French may not be as likely to die of heart disease but cirrhosis of the liver and cancer of the digestive system are more common. Most health experts agree that the negatives associated with alcohol consumption far outweigh its benefits.

What's a Drink?

One drink equals:

- a 5 oz (142 mL) glass of wine (12% alcohol)
- a 12 oz (341 mL) bottle of beer (5% alcohol)
- a 1.5 oz (45 mL) shot of liquor (40% alcohol)
- a 3 oz (90 mL) glass of sherry or port (18% alcohol)

To Drink or Not to Drink?

Are you one of the people who might benefit from moderate alcohol consumption? It depends. Older people with a low HDL-cholesterol level, normal triglycerides, normal blood pressure, who are slim and have no bleeding disorders might benefit from 1 to 2 drinks a day. But those of all ages who are prone to alcohol abuse, who have high blood pressure, high triglyceride levels or pancreatitis, or who are overweight or planning a pregnancy are best off avoiding alcohol altogether. Even moderate intakes may be too much for some women since alcohol is known to increase the risk of breast cancer.

HEALTHY TIPS: Drinking

- If you choose to drink alcohol, limit yourself to 1 drink a day if you are a woman and 2 drinks a day if you are a man. Don't "save" your daily drinks so that you can drink more on the weekends. Studies show that beyond 2 drinks a day the heart protective effects of alcohol are lost and the harmful effects of alcohol are more likely.
- Try these non-alcoholic cocktails:
  - Fruit spritzers made with fruit juice, soda water and a twist of lime or lemon
  - Virgin Bloody Mary or Virgin Bloody Caesar spiced with hot pepper sauce and Worcestershire sauce and garnished with lemon or lime
  - Frozen daiquiri mix without the alcohol
  - Soda water with a dash of angostura bitters and a slice of lemon or lime

Citrus Mint Iced Tea

Consider this cool refresher when entertaining or relaxing on the porch.
I served this tea at a summer baby shower.

2/3 cup	water	150 mL
1/3 cup	granulated sugar	75 mL
1/4 cup	finely chopped fresh mint leaves	50 mL
2 cups	freshly brewed tea	500 mL
2/3 cup	grapefruit juice (optional)	150 mL
2/3 cup	fresh orange juice	150 mL
1/4 cup	fresh lemon juice	50 mL
	Sprigs of mint	

1 In saucepan, bring water and sugar to boil; boil for 1 minute. Add mint leaves; let stand for 30 minutes.

2 Strain into large bowl, using back of spoon to press mint leaves. Add tea, grapefruit juice (if using), orange juice and lemon juice; mix well.

3 Serve over ice. Garnish with mint. *Makes 4 cups (1 L), about 6 servings.*

Make ahead: Through step 2 for up to 1 day

Fruit Smoothies

In blender or food processor, blend fruit juice, yogurt and pieces of fresh fruit. Use any fresh fruit (melons, berries, peaches, pineapple, banana). For a thicker drink, use chunks of frozen fruit.

Fruit Spritzers

For a refreshing drink, mix soda water with fruit juice or fruit nectar. Cranberry juice, soda water and ginger ale are a particularly pleasing combination.

Per serving:

calories	59
protein	trace
total fat	0 g
cholesterol	0 mg
carbohydrate	15 g
dietary fiber	trace
sodium	4 mg

R.D.I. Vit A 2%, C 33%, Folate 6%, Ca 1%(7 mg), Iron 1%, Zinc 1%.

Salads

Spinach Salad with Walnut Vinaigrette

Carrot Slaw with Radicchio

Garlic Green Beans with Flavored Oil

Fresh Beet and Onion Salad

Watercress, Orange and Chick-Pea Salad

Indonesian Coleslaw

Thai Vegetarian Salad

Black Bean and Corn Salad

Marinated Shrimp and Mango Salad

Arugula Salad with Grilled Chèvre

Curried Lentil, Wild Rice and Orzo Salad

Chicken Penne Salad with Thai Dressing

Tomato and Corn Pasta Salad

Pesto Pasta Salad with Chicken and Sun-Dried Tomatoes

Couscous, Orange and Carrot Salad

Yogurt Parsley Dressing

Herb and Ginger Vinaigrette

Nutrition Notes

Folic Acid: "Folic Acid for a Healthy Pregnancy"

Feeding Young Children: "Young Children and Hassle-Free Mealtimes"

Spinach Salad with Walnut Vinaigrette

Kitchen Tip

Keep walnut oil in the refrigerator.

* Substitution Tip

Any kind or combination of greens and lettuces can be used; the darker the color, the more vitamins and fiber. Add extra ingredients such as chopped fresh basil, dill, coriander or chives; grated carrots; apple or mango slices; orange segments; alfalfa, radish, or bean sprouts; dried cranberries; chick-peas or shrimp.

This simple leafy salad goes well on most menus. In place of the walnut oil, you can use extra-virgin olive oil or a mixture of 2 tsp (10 mL) sesame oil and 2 tbsp (25 mL) canola oil. If you toss the salad thoroughly (easiest in a large bowl), you'll be surprised at how little dressing you actually need.

Half	pkg (10 oz/284 g) fresh spinach, trimmed*	Half
1	small head Boston lettuce*	1
1	clove garlic, chopped	1
1/4 tsp	each salt (approx.) and Dijon mustard	1 mL
1 tbsp	balsamic or red wine vinegar	15 mL
3 tbsp	walnut oil	50 mL
	Pepper	

1 Wash, dry and tear spinach and lettuce to make about 10 cups (2.5 L).

2 In salad bowl, using pestle or fork, crush garlic with salt to form paste; whisk in mustard and vinegar, then oil.

3 Add prepared greens; toss thoroughly to coat. Season with pepper and more salt to taste. *Makes 8 servings.*

Make ahead: Through step 1, wrap in paper towels, then place in plastic bag and refrigerate for up to 1 day. Through step 2 for up to 2 hours.

OILS AND THEIR USES

- Don't be fooled by bottles of olive oil that are labeled "light." The term refers to the oil's color and flavor, not to the amount of fat or calories.
- When the taste of the oil is front and center, as in salad dressings, choose cold-pressed extra-virgin olive oil for its superior flavor. The color — yellow or green— depends on the variety of olives used. Pure olive oil, which is further processed, is lighter in color and less flavorful.
- When flavor from oil is not important or not wanted (stir-fries, muffins), canola oil is a good choice.

Per serving:

calories	53
protein	1 g
total fat	5 g
cholesterol	0 mg
carbohydrate	2 g
dietary fiber	1 g
sodium	88 mg

R.D.I. Vit A 13%, E 5%, C 10%, Folate 20%, Ca 2% (22 mg), Iron 4%, Zinc 1%.

Canada's Food Guide Serving: ½

Carrot Slaw with Radicchio

This easy-to-make salad is not only a crunchy side dish with meat or chicken, it can also be packed into pita halves along with meat slices or chick-peas.

2 cups	coarsely grated carrots	500 mL
1 cup	thinly sliced radicchio or red cabbage	250 mL
1/4 cup	chopped green onions	50 mL
2 tbsp	sunflower seeds, toasted	25 mL
Balsamic Vinaigrette:		
2 tbsp	balsamic vinegar or wine vinegar	25 mL
1 tbsp	olive oil	15 mL
1 tsp	each Dijon mustard and granulated sugar	5 mL
1/4 tsp	each salt and pepper	1 mL

1 Balsamic Vinaigrette: In bowl, whisk together vinegar, 2 tbsp (25 mL) water, oil, mustard, sugar, salt and pepper. Add carrots, radicchio and onions; toss to coat.

2 Sprinkle sunflower seeds over top. *Makes 4 servings.*

Make ahead: Through step 1, cover and refrigerate for up to 6 hours.

VINEGAR SUBSTITUTIONS

Vinegars vary greatly in harshness and sweetness. Still, it's easy to make substitutions for fancy ones:

- For fruit-flavored vinegars, substitute balsamic or red wine vinegar, adding a pinch of granulated sugar as needed to achieve desired sweetness.
- If a recipe calls for rice wine vinegar, substitute a slightly reduced amount of cider vinegar with a pinch of granulated sugar.
- Fresh lemon juice is also a good substitute for vinegar. Indeed, it is preferable to pure white vinegar, especially in dressings.

Cooking Tip

Toast sunflower seeds in skillet over medium heat for 3 to 6 minutes or until fragrant.

Nutrition Tip

Sunflower seeds are high in vitamin E.

Per serving:

calories	97
protein	2 g
total fat	6 g
saturated fat	1 mg
cholesterol	0 mg
carbohydrate	10 g
dietary fiber	2 g
sodium	182 mg

R.D.I. Vit A 155%, E 32%, C 12%, Folate 13%, Ca 3% (29 mg), Iron 6%, Zinc 5%.

Canada's Food Guide Serving:

1

Garlic Green Beans with Flavored Oil

When I visited Wendy Bowle-Evans, at her home in the tiny village of Regusse in the Provence area of France, she made this with flavorful walnut oil and the skinny green beans you find everywhere in France. In the center of the platter, she heaped marinated wild mushrooms, which her husband, Jean-Jacques Virgros, had picked.

To Serve Hot

Drain cooked beans but do not cool. Add hot beans in step 3, garnish and serve immediately.

1-1/2 lb	green beans	750 g
1	clove garlic, chopped	1
1 tsp	salt	5 mL
1 tbsp	balsamic or red wine vinegar	15 mL
1 tbsp	walnut or sesame oil	15 mL
Garnish:		
1	tomato, cut in wedges, or 1/4 cup (50 mL) thinly sliced red cabbage	1

1 Remove stem ends from green beans. In large pot of boiling water, cook beans for 4 to 5 minutes or until tender; drain and cool under cold water. Drain well.

2 On serving platter and using pestle or back of fork, crush garlic with salt to form paste: stir in vinegar then oil.

3 Add green beans; stir to coat in garlic mixture. Let stand for 15 minutes.

4 Garnish with tomato or red cabbage. *Makes 8 servings.*

Make ahead: Through step 1, wrap in paper towels then place in plastic bag and refrigerate for up to 1 day. Through step 2 for up to 2 hours.

Per serving:

calories	46
protein	2 g
total fat	2 g
saturated fat	trace
cholesterol	0 mg
carbohydrate	7 g
dietary fiber	2 g
sodium	290 mg

R.D.I. Vit A 6%, E 2%, C 17%, Folate 12%, Ca 3% (35 mg), Iron 7%, Zinc 3%.

Canada's Food Guide Serving:
1½

Fresh Beet and Onion Salad

This simple yet tasty Spanish salad goes well with almost any meat, fish or poultry.
Be sure to use extra-virgin olive oil and coarsely ground black pepper.

4	medium beets (1 lb/500 g)	4
2 tbsp	red wine vinegar	25 mL
1 tbsp	extra-virgin olive oil	15 mL
1/4 tsp	each granulated sugar, salt and coarsely ground pepper	1 mL
	Lettuce leaves or watercress (optional)	
1 cup	thinly sliced Spanish onion	250 mL

1 Trim beets, leaving 1 inch (2.5 cm) of stems. In pot of boiling water, cook beets, covered, until tender when tested with fork, about 40 minutes. Drain and let cool; slip off skins. Cut into 1/4-inch (5 mm) thick slices.

2 Combine vinegar, oil, sugar, salt and pepper.

3 Line shallow serving dish with lettuce (if using). Arrange half of the beets on dish; top with half of the onion. Drizzle with half of the dressing. Repeat layers. Let stand for 30 minutes. *Makes 4 servings.*

Make ahead: Through step 2, cover and refrigerate for up to 6 hours. Through step 3, set aside for 30 minutes.

Serving Tip

Slice, dice or coarsely grate cold cooked beets then drizzle with balsamic vinegar or toss with Herb and Ginger Vinaigrette (page 57)

Cooking Tip

See page 140 for more information on beets.

Nutrition Tip

Beets are high in folate, potassium and fiber. Beet greens are very high in beta carotene (vitamin A) and potassium and are a source of vitamin C and folate.

Per serving:

calories	85
protein	2 g
total fat	4 g
cholesterol	0 mg
carbohydrate	13 g
dietary fiber	2 g
sodium	211 mg

R.D.I. Vit E 7%, C 10%, Folate 35%, Ca 2% (23 mg), Iron 6%, Zinc 4%.

Canada's Food Guide Serving:
1½

Watercress, Orange and Chick-Pea Salad

*The fresh mint, juicy orange and crisp onion make a pleasing contrast
to the smooth chick-peas and delicate watercress or arugula.*

1	orange	1
1 cup	chick-peas, drained and rinsed	250 mL
1/4 cup	chopped red onion	50 mL
2 tbsp	chopped fresh mint	25 mL
1/4 cup	fresh orange juice	50 mL
1 tsp	red wine vinegar	5 mL
1 tsp	sesame oil	5 mL
1/2 tsp	grated gingerroot	2 mL
1	bunch watercress or arugula	1

1 Slice rind and white membrane from orange. Holding orange over bowl to catch juices, cut between sections and membranes, adding sections to bowl. Add chick-peas, red onion and mint.

2 Whisk together orange juice, vinegar, oil and ginger; pour over chick-pea mixture and toss to mix.

3 Remove any tough stems from watercress; arrange on small serving platter or individual plates. Spoon chick-pea mixture over top. *Makes 4 servings.*

Make ahead: Through step 3, cover and refrigerate for up to 6 hours.

Per serving:

calories	105
protein	5 g
total fat	2 g
saturated fat	trace
cholesterol	0 mg
carbohydrate	18 g
dietary fiber	3 g
sodium	117 mg

R.D.I. Vit A 14%, E 4%, C 63%,
Folate 20%, Ca 6% (61 mg), Iron 5%,
Zinc 5%.

Canada's Food Guide Serving:

Indonesian Coleslaw

*This colorful, crunchy salad from Daphna Rabinovitch,
associate director of the food department at* Canadian Living *magazine,
is refreshing any time of year. However, it is especially tasty in August and
September when new cabbages are in the markets.*

4 cups	finely shredded cabbage	1 L
1	small sweet red pepper, cut in thin short strips	1
2	medium carrots, grated	2
4	green onions, chopped	4
1 cup	bean sprouts	250 mL
1/4 cup	chopped fresh coriander (cilantro)	50 mL
1/4 cup	chopped peanuts	50 mL
Dressing:		
3 tbsp	each rice vinegar and hoisin sauce	50 mL
2 tsp	each sesame oil and minced gingerroot	10 mL
1 tsp	each soy sauce and granulated sugar	5 mL
1	clove garlic, minced	1

1 In large bowl, toss together cabbage, red pepper, carrots, onions and bean sprouts.

2 Dressing: In separate bowl, whisk together vinegar, hoisin sauce, sesame oil, ginger, soy sauce, sugar and garlic.

3 Pour dressing over coleslaw. Add coriander and peanuts; toss to mix well.
Makes 8 servings.

Make ahead: Through step 2, cover and refrigerate for up to 1 day.

Greek Salad

During tomato season, I make a Greek salad at least once a week. In a shallow dish, I toss together 3 large tomatoes, cubed, 2 medium cucumbers, peeled and cubed, and 4 to 6 oz (125 to 190 g) feta cheese, crumbled. I sprinkle with oregano, salt and pepper, add a squeeze of fresh lemon juice and a drizzle of extra-virgin olive oil, then top with a few Greek olives.

Per serving:

calories	80
protein	3 g
total fat	4 g
saturated fat	1 g
cholesterol	0 mg
carbohydrate	11 g
dietary fiber	2 g
sodium	155 mg

R.D.I. Vit A 63%, E 5%, C 57%,
Folate 18%, Ca 3% (37 mg), Iron 6%,
Zinc 6%.

Canada's Food Guide Serving:
1¼ 🥕

Thai Vegetarian Salad

Nutrition Tips

Tofu is a good source of protein and can be high in calcium if it is set with a calcium compound, which will be indicated in the list of ingredients. Check calcium values on labels.

Carrots are extremely high in the antioxidant beta carotene, which the body converts to vitamin A.

Fish Sauce

A staple in Thai cooking, fish sauce adds a salty, fish flavor. Although the smell of it raw is very unappealing, it mellows during cooking. It keeps for ages in your cupboard. It is high in sodium.

The combination of fresh mint and coriander gives this salad a delightful zing. You could also add diced cucumber, radishes or cabbage.

1 cup	cubed firm tofu (5 oz/140 g)	250 mL
1/4 cup	finely sliced red onion	50 mL
Half	sweet green pepper, cut in short strips	Half
2	carrots, coarsely grated	2
1/4 cup	each chopped fresh mint and fresh coriander (cilantro)	50 mL
2 tbsp	chopped peanuts	25 mL
Dressing:		
1/4 cup	fresh lemon or lime juice	50 mL
1 tbsp	granulated sugar	15 mL
1 tbsp	fish sauce or soy sauce	15 mL
Pinch	red pepper flakes	Pinch

1 In bowl, combine tofu, red onion, green pepper and carrots.

2 Dressing: Mix together lime juice, sugar, fish sauce and red pepper flakes; pour over salad and toss well.

3 Stir in mint and coriander. Sprinkle peanuts over top. *Makes 4 servings.*

Make ahead: Through step 2, cover and refrigerate for up to 2 hours.

Per serving:

calories	121
protein	8 g
total fat	6 g
saturated fat	1 mg
cholesterol	0 mg
carbohydrate	13 g
dietary fiber	2 g
sodium	215 mg

R.D.I. Vit A 117%, E 6%, C 38%, Folate 14%, Ca 9% (99 mg), Iron 31%, Zinc 11%.

Canada's Food Guide Serving:

1 🥕 ½ 🥖

Black Bean and Corn Salad

*Black beans, yellow corn, sweet red pepper and green coriander make
this a colorful salad, a favorite of my son, Jeff. For a more substantial dish,
add diced feta cheese. If coriander isn't available, use fresh parsley or basil.*

1	can (19 oz/540 mL) black or kidney beans, drained and rinsed	1
1	sweet red pepper, chopped	1
2 cups	cooked corn kernels	500 mL
1/2 cup	chopped celery	125 mL
1/4 cup	chopped green onions	50 mL
2 tbsp	chopped fresh coriander (cilantro)	25 mL
Dressing:		
3 tbsp	rice or cider vinegar	50 mL
1-1/2 tsp	Dijon mustard	7 mL
1/4 tsp	each granulated sugar, salt and pepper	1 mL
1 tbsp	each water and vegetable oil	15 mL

1 In bowl, combine beans, red pepper, corn, celery, onions and coriander.

2 Dressing: In small bowl, whisk together vinegar, mustard, sugar, salt and pepper;
whisk in water and oil. Pour over salad and stir to mix. *Makes 8 servings.*

Make ahead: Cover and refrigerate for up to 1 day.

Lentil and Corn Salad: Substitute 1 can (19 oz/540 mL) drained and rinsed
lentils for the beans. Regular-size lentils are better in this salad than the tiny ones.

Nutrition Tip

Black and romano beans are
very high in fiber and folate, or
folacin, an important B vitamin,
and contain some calcium.

Per serving:

calories	117
protein	6 g
total fat	2 g
saturated fat	trace
cholesterol	0 mg
carbohydrate	21 g
dietary fiber	4 g
sodium	204 mg

R.D.I. Vit A 10%, E 5%, C 52%,
Folate 40%, Ca 2% (22 mg), Iron 9%,
Zinc 8%.

Canada's Food Guide Serving:
¾ ½

Marinated Shrimp and Mango Salad

For years, I have been part of a women's gourmet dinner group. This is one of our favorite starter salad recipes, but it would also make a spectacular luncheon dish.

Lower-Fat Cooking

This recipe uses chutney instead of some of the oil; it adds flavor and helps to emulsify and thicken salad dressings.

Cooking Tip

Use whole sprigs of watercress and coriander but remove bottom of large, tough stems. You could also use half arugula and half watercress.

2 lb	large peeled raw shrimp (or thawed and completely dried)	1 kg
1 tsp	vegetable oil	5 mL
2	bunches watercress (8 cups/2 L lightly packed)	2
1 cup	packed fresh coriander sprigs	250 mL
2	sweet red peppers, cut in thin strips	2
2	large ripe mangoes, peeled and cut in thin strips	2
Shrimp Marinade:		
2 tsp	each ground cumin, ground coriander and paprika	10 mL
2/3 cup	2% plain yogurt	150 mL
2 tbsp	minced gingerroot	25 mL
1 tbsp	minced garlic	15 mL
2	fresh jalapeño peppers, seeded and chopped, or 1 tbsp (15 mL) chopped bottled peppers	2
	Grated rind of 1 lime	
Dressing:		
1/2 cup	mango chutney	125 mL
1/3 cup	fresh lime juice	75 mL
3 tbsp	vegetable oil	50 mL
Dash	hot pepper sauce	Dash

1 Shrimp Marinade: In small nonstick skillet, dry-roast cumin, coriander and paprika over medium heat, stirring occasionally, for about 2 minutes or until darkened slightly and fragrant. Let cool.

2 In large bowl, stir together yogurt, ginger, garlic, jalapeño peppers, lime rind, roasted spices, and salt and pepper to taste. Add shrimp; mix to coat. Cover and refrigerate for 1 hour or for up to 24 hours.

Per main-course serving:

calories	379
protein	35 g
total fat	11 g
saturated fat	1 g
cholesterol	231 mg
carbohydrate	37 g
dietary fiber	5 g
sodium	312 mg

R.D.I. Vit A 100%, E 34%, C 242%, Folate 15%, Ca 16% (178 mg), Iron 32%, Zinc 22%.

Canada's Food Guide Serving:

2¼ 🍴 2 🍞

3 Dressing: In food processor, purée chutney. Add lime juice, oil and hot pepper sauce; process to mix. Set aside.

4 In large nonstick skillet, heat oil over medium-high heat; cook shrimp and marinade, turning once, for 3 to 4 minutes or until pink and opaque.

5 In large bowl, toss together watercress, coriander, red peppers, mangoes, shrimp and dressing. Arrange on individual salad plates. *Makes 12 appetizer servings, or 6 main-course servings.*

Make ahead: Through step 3, cover and refrigerate for up to 1 day.

Folic Acid for a Healthy Pregnancy

If you are planning a pregnancy, consider taking a supplement of folic acid now and during the first few months of pregnancy to reduce the incidence of neural tube defects (NTDs). NTDs result in serious birth defects such as spina bifida and brain malformations.

To reduce the risk of having a NTD-affected pregnancy, women are usually advised to take a supplement of 0.4 mg folic acid in addition to choosing a diet rich in folic acid.

Food Sources for Folic Acid

A well-chosen diet is estimated to provide about 0.2 mg of folic acid. To increase your intake, include these sources of folic acid in your diet:

**Excellent Sources of Folic Acid
(0.05 mg or more folic acid per serving)**

- 3 oz (90 g) cooked liver*
- 2/3 cup (150 mL) cooked spinach, broccoli, asparagus, green peas, brussels sprouts, beets
- 3 oz (60 g) dark green lettuce
- 1 cup (250 mL) orange or pineapple juice
- 1/4 cup (50 ml) sunflower seeds
- 3/4 cup (175 mL) chick-peas, lentils, dried beans

* Use sparingly if pregnant because of high vitamin A content: excess vitamin A is associated with birth defects.

**Good Sources of Folic Acid
(0.03 mg or more folic acid per serving)**

- 3/4 cup (175 mL) cooked lima beans
- 2/3 cup (150 mL) corn kernels or bean sprouts
- Half cantaloupe, 1 orange
- 2 eggs
- 2 tbsp (25 mL) wheat germ
- 3/4 cup (175 mL) enriched All-Bran cereal

Foods Fortified with Folic Acid (as of 1998)

- white flour – bread, crackers, baked goods
- pasta, instant rice, and cornmeal products labeled "enriched"

Arugula Salad with Grilled Chèvre

Arugula and chèvre are two of my favorite foods. To have them together is heaven.
This salad makes a fabulous first-course for a dinner party.

8 oz	chèvre cheese round (15% b.f.), chilled	250 g
1	egg, beaten	1
1 cup	homemade whole-grain bread crumbs	250 mL
3 cups	arugula, large stems removed, torn	750 mL
8 cups	red leaf lettuce or Boston lettuce, torn	2 L
1 tbsp	olive oil	15 mL
Dressing:		
1/4 cup	1% or 2% plain yogurt	50 mL
1 tbsp	white wine vinegar	15 mL
1 tbsp	olive oil	15 mL
1 tsp	minced fresh tarragon or 1/4 tsp (1 mL) dried	5 mL
1/2 tsp	each Dijon mustard, salt and pepper	2 mL

1 Dressing: In bowl, whisk together yogurt, vinegar, oil, tarragon, mustard, salt and pepper.

2 Slice cheese into 8 rounds; dip in egg then in bread crumbs to coat all sides.

3 Toss arugula and lettuce with dressing; divide among 8 salad plates.

4 In nonstick skillet, heat oil over medium heat. Cook cheese, turning once, for 3 to 5 minutes or until crisp and golden outside and slightly melted inside. Place each round on salad. *Makes 8 servings.*

Make ahead: Through step 2, cover and refrigerate for up to 2 hours.

Per serving:

calories	114
protein	5 g
total fat	8 g
saturated fat	4 g
cholesterol	32 mg
carbohydrate	6 g
dietary fiber	1 g
sodium	297 mg

R.D.I. Vit A 11%, D 1%, E 6%, C 7%, Folate 15%, Ca 9% (96 mg), Iron 4%, Zinc 4%.

Canada's Food Guide Serving:
1 🥕 ½ 🍞

48

Curried Lentil, Wild Rice and Orzo Salad

Canadian Living magazine's food director, Elizabeth Baird, served this at her niece's wedding. It's also a good choice for buffets and picnics and makes a delicious vegetarian meal. I've adapted it slightly by replacing some of the oil with water.

1/2 cup	wild rice	125 mL
2/3 cup	green or brown lentils	150 mL
1/2 cup	orzo pasta	125 mL
1/2 cup	currants	125 mL
1/4 cup	chopped red onion	50 mL
1/3 cup	slivered almonds, toasted	75 mL
Dressing:		
1/4 cup	white wine vinegar	50 mL
2 tbsp	water	25 mL
1 tsp	ground cumin	5 mL
1 tsp	Dijon mustard	5 mL
1/2 tsp	each granulated sugar, salt and ground coriander	2 mL
1/4 tsp	each turmeric, paprika, ground nutmeg and ground cardamom	1 mL
Pinch	each cinnamon, cloves and cayenne pepper	Pinch
1/4 cup	vegetable oil	50 mL

1 In separate pots of boiling water, cook wild rice for 35 to 40 minutes, lentils for 25 to 30 minutes and orzo for 5 minutes or until each is tender but not mushy. Drain well and transfer to large bowl. Add currants and onion; set aside.

2 Dressing: In small bowl, whisk together vinegar, water, cumin, mustard, sugar, salt, coriander, turmeric, paprika, nutmeg, cardamom, cinnamon, cloves and cayenne; whisk in oil. Pour over rice mixture and toss gently. Let cool completely; cover and refrigerate for at least 4 hours.

3 Serve sprinkled with almonds. *Makes 8 servings.*

Make ahead: Cover and refrigerate for up to 2 days.

Chicken Penne Salad with Thai Dressing

I've served this salad to guests for lunch and at a summer supper.
It's also a great way to use up leftover cooked chicken or turkey.
Serve with a green salad and whole wheat French bread.

8 oz	penne (2-1/2 cups/625 mL) or short pasta	250 g
3 cups	cubed cooked chicken or turkey	750 mL
2 cups	packed coarsely chopped trimmed spinach	500 mL
1 cup	julienned carrot	250 mL
1 cup	coarsely shredded red cabbage	250 mL
1/4 cup	chopped fresh coriander (cilantro) or parsley	50 mL
Thai Dressing:		
1/4 cup	unsalted peanuts	50 mL
3 tbsp	coarsely chopped gingerroot	50 mL
1/4 cup	each fresh lemon juice and water	50 mL
2 tbsp	sodium-reduced soy sauce	25 mL
1 tbsp	granulated sugar	15 mL
1 tbsp	roasted sesame oil (not light)	15 mL
1/4 tsp	each salt, pepper and hot pepper sauce	1 mL

1 In large pot of boiling water, cook penne for 8 to 10 minutes or until tender but firm; drain and rinse under cold water. Drain again and place in salad bowl.

2 Add chicken, spinach, carrot, red cabbage and coriander; toss to combine.

3 Thai Dressing: In food processor or blender, finely chop peanuts and ginger. Add lemon juice, water, soy sauce, sugar, sesame oil, salt, pepper and hot pepper sauce; process to mix well.

4 Pour over pasta mixture; toss to mix. *Makes 6 servings.*

Make ahead: Through step 3 (dressing), cover and refrigerate for up to 3 days. Through step 2 for up to 4 hours. Through step 4 for up to 1 hour.

Per serving:

calories	**362**
protein	**28 g**
total fat	**11 g**
saturated fat	**2 g**
cholesterol	**62 mg**
carbohydrate	**37 g**
dietary fiber	**3 g**
sodium	**382 mg**

R.D.I. Vit A 71%, E 14%, C 32%, Folate 29%, Ca 5% (57 mg), Iron 17%, Zinc 29%.

Canada's Food Guide Serving:

1¼ 🌾 ¾ 🥕 1 🍗

Young Children and Hassle-Free Mealtimes

Since battles with children over food are almost impossible to win, don't try. Instead, listen to the experts' advice on how to help your children develop healthy eating habits and attitudes about food and eating.

HEALTHY EATING TIPS: Feeding Kids

- Offer kids simple, good-tasting meals and make a point of eating with them.
- Provide a wide variety of nutritious foods. Then let your child decide what and how much to eat. Don't pressure a child into eating.
- If children refuse to eat, keep your cool! Don't get into a routine of pleading, begging, coaxing or threatening children to get them to eat. Your job is over once the food is served.
- Serve small portions, leaving the option open to ask for more. Then back off.
- When meals are pushed aside, remove the food and excuse the child from the table. Don't prepare a favorite item to replace the refused food.
- When children consistently refuse to eat, check how much eating and drinking is going on between planned snacks and meals. Make sure snacks are about 2 hours before the next meal. Drinking a lot of juice can dull a young child's appetite, too. Limit juice to snack times and offer water at other times.
- Offer new foods, but respect a child's decision not to try them. Don't give up, however. Just because a child refuses new food once doesn't mean he or she won't try it the third or fourth time you offer it. To make new foods more appealing, try these ideas:
  - Introduce a new food along with old favorites to a child who is hungry.
  - Let children help in the preparation. For example, let them add the tomato, lettuce and cheese to a filled taco.
  - Make the new food look appealing. Serve bite-sized or finger-sized portions; use a sense of color to combine foods; sprinkle a few chocolate chips on top of a fruit dessert; float some croutons in soup.
- Don't turn dinnertime into a long lecture about shortcomings and chores. Make it a relaxing and enjoyable time of the day.

Tomato and Corn Pasta Salad

Beans, tomatoes and corn add lots of fiber to this fresh-tasting pasta dish,
which is perfect for a buffet, brunch, barbecue, light supper or even a packed lunch.

1 lb	penne pasta (about 5 cups/1.25 L)	500 g
2 lb	tomatoes, seeded and cut in chunks (about 5)	1 kg
2 tbsp	each olive oil and fresh lemon juice	25 mL
2	cloves garlic, minced	2
1 tsp	salt	5 mL
1/4 tsp	pepper	1 mL
1 cup	corn kernels	250 mL
1 cup	crumbled feta cheese	250 mL
1 cup	coarsely chopped fresh parsley	250 mL
1	can (19 oz/540 mL) kidney or black beans, drained and rinsed	1
1/2 cup	finely chopped fresh coriander (cilantro)	125 mL

1 In large pot of boiling water, cook penne for 8 to 10 minutes or until tender but firm; drain. Rinse under cold water; drain well.

2 Meanwhile, in large bowl, combine tomatoes, oil, lemon juice, 1/4 cup (50 mL) water, garlic, salt and pepper; let stand for 5 minutes.

3 Add pasta, corn, cheese, parsley, beans and coriander; toss to combine. *Makes 8 servings.*

Make ahead: Cover and refrigerate for up to 4 hours.

Nutrition Tip

Feta cheese is lower in fat than many cheeses. You can often find it at 15% b.f. which is the same as part-skim mozzarella.

Fiber-Booster

With more than 6 grams of fiber per serving, legumes (dried beans, peas and lentils) can help boost your daily intake. Lentil soup, minestrone, split pea soup, baked beans, bean salad, hummus (chick-pea spread) are all tasty choices.

Per serving:

calories	382
protein	15 g
total fat	9 g
saturated fat	3 g
cholesterol	14 mg
carbohydrate	63 g
dietary fiber	8 g
sodium	632 mg

R.D.I. Vit A 13%, E 10%, C 55%, Folate 33%, Ca 11%(117 mg), Iron 18%, Zinc 20%.

Canada's Food Guide Serving:

2 🌾 1¼ 🥕 ¼ 🥫 ½ 🍗

Pesto Pasta Salad with Chicken and Sun-Dried Tomatoes

This is a lightened-up version of the most popular salad at Hannah's Kitchen,
a Toronto restaurant.

Cooking Tip

Commercial pesto sauces will vary in flavor and content of oil; add the store bought variety to the recipe to taste.

16	dry-packed sun-dried tomatoes	16
1 lb	boneless skinless chicken breasts	500 g
1 tsp	olive oil	5 mL
1 lb	penne or radiatore pasta	500 g
	Pesto Sauce (page 85) or 1 cup (250 mL) commercial pesto sauce	
2 tbsp	toasted pine nuts (optional)	25 ml

1 Pour boiling water over tomatoes to cover; let stand until softened, 3 to 5 minutes. Drain and chop coarsely.

2 Cut chicken into 1/4-inch (5 mm) thick strips about 2 inches (5 cm) long. In nonstick skillet, heat oil over medium-high heat; stir-fry chicken for about 5 minutes or until no longer pink in center.

3 In large pot of boiling water, cook penne for 8 to 10 minutes or until tender but firm; drain, reserving 1/4 cup (50 mL) cooking water. Rinse under cold water; drain again.

4 In large bowl, toss together penne, tomatoes, chicken and pesto sauce, adding reserved cooking water if necessary to moisten. Add salt and pepper to taste. Sprinkle with pine nuts (if using). *Makes 6 servings (about 2 cups/500 mL each).*

Make ahead: Cover and refrigerate for up to 1 day.

Luncheon Menu

Fruit Spritzers (page 35)

Pesto Pasta Salad with Chicken and Sun-Dried Tomatoes (this page)

Spinach Salad with Walnut Vinaigrette (page 38)

Fig and Cottage Cheese Quick Bread (page 245)

Citrus Frozen Yogurt with Mango (page 270)

Double-Chocolate Cookies (page 251)

Per serving:

calories	465
protein	30 g
total fat	9 g
saturated fat	2 g
cholesterol	48 mg
carbohydrate	63 g
dietary fiber	4 g
sodium	436 mg

R.D.I. Vit A 1%, E 9%, C 3%, Folate 13%, Ca 10% (107 mg), Iron 12%, Zinc 22%.

Canada's Food Guide Serving:

3 ½ 1

Couscous, Orange and Carrot Salad

*Serve this particularly pleasing combination of flavors and textures with a platter of
sliced tomatoes and grilled vegetables or meats for a summer meal.*

1-3/4 cups	water or chicken stock	425 mL
1-1/4 cups	couscous	300 mL
2	oranges, sectioned and chopped (see page 42)	2
1 cup	coarsely shredded carrots	250 mL
1/2 cup	raisins or currants	125 mL
1/4 cup	chopped fresh coriander (cilantro) or parsley or mint	50 mL
Ginger Vinaigrette:		
2 tbsp	each balsamic vinegar and fresh lemon juice	25 mL
2 tbsp	each olive or vegetable oil and water	25 mL
1 tbsp	each granulated sugar and minced gingerroot	15 mL
1/4 tsp	each salt, pepper and ground cumin	1 mL

1 In saucepan, bring water to boil; add couscous and stir quickly to mix. Cover and
remove from heat; let stand for 10 minutes to absorb liquid. Using fork, fluff
couscous; let cool.

2 In salad bowl, combine oranges, carrots, raisins, coriander and couscous.

3 Ginger Vinaigrette: In small bowl, whisk together vinegar, lemon juice, oil, water,
sugar, ginger, salt, pepper and cumin.

4 Pour vinaigrette over salad and toss to mix. *Makes 6 servings.*

Make ahead: Through step 3, cover and refrigerate for up to 1 day.

Cooking Tip

To cool couscous quickly,
fluff with a fork, then spread it
out on a large baking sheet,
breaking up any lumps.

Per serving:

calories	270
protein	6 g
total fat	5 g
saturated fat	1 g
cholesterol	0 mg
carbohydrate	52 g
dietary fiber	3 g
sodium	113 mg

R.D.I. Vit A 53%, E 9%, C 47%,
Folate 16%, Ca 4% (43 mg), Iron 7%,
Zinc 5%.

Canada's Food Guide Serving:
1¼ 🌾 1¼ 🥕

55

Yogurt Parsley Dressing

This delicious, creamy, all-purpose dressing goes well in almost any salad, such as seafood, potato, cooked vegetable or just plain leafy greens. The parsley is essential — it adds a fresh flavor — but I like to add other fresh herbs as well.

1 cup	1% or 2% plain yogurt	250 mL
1/2 cup	light mayonnaise	125 mL
1/2 cup	chopped fresh parsley	125 mL
2 tbsp	fresh lemon juice	25 mL
1	small clove garlic, minced	1
1 tsp	each Dijon mustard and salt	5 mL
1/4 tsp	pepper	1 mL

� In small bowl, stir together yogurt, mayonnaise, parsley, lemon juice, garlic, mustard, salt and pepper. Cover and refrigerate. *Makes 1-2/3 cups (400 mL).*

Make-ahead: Cover and refrigerate for up to 1 week.

Buttermilk Dill Dressing: Substitute buttermilk for yogurt; add 1/3 cup (75 mL) (or more to taste) chopped fresh dill or 1 tsp (5 mL) dried dillweed.

Basil Yogurt Dressing: Add 1/3 cup (75 mL) chopped fresh basil.

Tarragon Yogurt Dressing: Add 1/4 cup (50 mL) chopped fresh tarragon or 2 tsp (10 mL) dried.

Creamy Caesar Yogurt Dressing: Add another clove garlic, minced, and 1/4 cup (50 mL) freshly grated Parmesan cheese.

Per 1 tbsp (15 mL):

calories	20
protein	1 g
total fat	1 g
cholesterol	0 mg
carbohydrate	1 g
sodium	125 mg

R.D.I. Vit A 1%, C 3%, Folate 1%, Ca 2% (18 mg), Iron 1%, Zinc 1%.

Herb and Ginger Vinaigrette

You'll love this combination of herbs, ginger and garlic tossed with a mixture of fresh greens or drizzled over a plate of thickly sliced tomatoes. If fresh coriander (cilantro) and basil aren't available, substitute 1/4 cup (50 mL) chopped fresh parsley and a pinch each of crushed dried basil and coriander leaves.

2 tbsp	balsamic or rice vinegar	25 mL
1 tbsp	each soy sauce, fresh lemon juice and olive oil	15 mL
2 tsp	granulated sugar	10 mL
1 tsp	minced gingerroot	5 mL
1	clove garlic, minced	1
2 tbsp	each chopped fresh basil and coriander (cilantro)	25 mL

I In small bowl, whisk together vinegar, soy sauce, lemon juice, oil, sugar, ginger and garlic. Stir in basil and coriander. Season with salt and pepper to taste.
Makes about 1/2 cup (125 mL), enough for green salad to serve 8.

Tomato, Arugula and Red Onion Salad: In salad bowl or on platter, toss 4 medium tomatoes, cut in wedges, 1 bunch arugula and a few paper-thin slices of red onion separated into rings with enough of this vinaigrette to moisten.
Makes 4 servings.

Substituting Dried Herbs For Fresh

As a rough guideline, substitute one-third the amount of dried herb for the amount of fresh herb. For example, in a recipe calling for 1 tbsp (15 mL) fresh rosemary, use 1 tsp (5 mL) dried. For the mild herbs, such as parsley, dill and basil, because I use large amounts of the fresh, I use less than one-third of the dried, usually about 1 tsp (5 mL). Dried coriander seeds should not be substituted for the fresh. In some cases you can use a bit of the dried leaves.

Add fresh herbs toward or at the end of the cooking time or just before serving. Dried herbs are usually added near the beginning of the cooking time.

Per 1 tbsp (15 mL):

calories	26
protein	0 g
total fat	2 g
saturated fat	trace
cholesterol	0 mg
carbohydrate	3 g
sodium	130 mg

R.D.I. Vit E 2%, C 2%, Ca 0% (3 mg), Iron 1%.

Soups

Tortellini Vegetable Soup

Portuguese Chick-Pea and Spinach Soup

Soup au Pistou

Winter Vegetable Soup

Sweet Potato and Ginger Soup

Lightly Curried Carrot and Ginger Soup

Asian Carrot and Mushroom Noodle Soup

Spicy Thai Chicken Noodle Soup

Chinese Shrimp and Scallop Soup

Thai Coconut, Ginger and Chicken Soup (Gai Tom Ka)

Porcini Mushroom Bisque

Lentil, Barley and Sweet Potato Soup

Mulligatawny Soup

Quick Black Bean, Corn and Tomato Soup

Onion and Potato Soup

Gazpacho

Nutrition Notes

Fat: "Lower Fat for Healthy Eating"

Nutrition for Seniors: "Eating Well As We Get Older"

Tortellini Vegetable Soup

*I keep a package of frozen tortellini in my freezer and a can of chicken broth
in the cupboard so I can make a very fast meal by adding whatever vegetables I have on
hand. Sometimes I substitute bean sprouts, celery, spinach, pesto sauce, fresh herbs,
dill, basil, garlic, shrimp, ham, lemon juice or soy sauce.*

*Substitution Tip

I prefer the flavor of canned stock or broth to that of stock made from a cube or powder. However, instead of water and canned broth, you can use 5 cups (1.25 L) homemade chicken stock, which, of course, is best of all if you happen to have it. You may need to add more stock depending on how much is absorbed by the tortellini in cooking.

3	cloves garlic, minced	3
1 tsp	dried Italian herb seasoning	5 mL
1	pkg (8 oz/250 g) cheese tortellini	1
1	can (10 oz/284 mL) chicken broth (undiluted)*	1
1 cup	frozen mixed vegetables or corn and/or peas	250 mL
3	green onions, chopped (1/2 cup/125 mL)	3
1 cup	sliced mushrooms	250 mL
2 tbsp	chopped fresh parsley	25 mL
1/4 cup	freshly grated Parmesan cheese	50 mL

1 In large saucepan, bring 4 cups (1 L) water, garlic and Italian seasoning to boil over high heat. Add tortellini, stirring to prevent sticking; return to boil. Reduce heat and simmer, covered, for 5 minutes.

2 Add undiluted broth, frozen vegetables, green onions and mushrooms; simmer for about 5 minutes or until tortellini is tender and vegetables are hot. Stir in parsley and pepper to taste.

3 Ladle into bowls; sprinkle with Parmesan cheese.
Makes 4 servings, about 1-1/2 cups (375 mL) each.

Make ahead: Through step 2, cover and refrigerate for up to 1 day.

Per serving:

calories	**247**
protein	**15 g**
total fat	**6 g**
saturated fat	**3 g**
cholesterol	**43 mg**
carbohydrate	**33 g**
dietary fiber	**4 g**
sodium	**793 mg**

R.D.I. Vit A 23%, E 3%, C 10%, Folate 14%, Ca 18% (197 mg), Iron 15%, Zinc 17%.

Canada's Food Guide Serving:
1½ ¾ ¼

Portuguese Chick-Pea and Spinach Soup

Portuguese cooks make marvelous soups — thick, hearty and flavorful.
This popular one uses canned chick-peas (garbanzo beans).

1 tbsp	olive or vegetable oil	15 mL
4	cloves garlic, chopped	4
2	onions, chopped	2
1	potato, peeled and cut in chunks	1
4 cups	chicken or vegetable stock	1 L
2 tbsp	each minced fresh parsley and coriander (cilantro)	25 mL
1 tsp	crumbled dried marjoram	5 mL
1	can (19 oz/540 mL) chick-peas, drained and rinsed*	1
Half	pkg (10 oz/284 g) fresh spinach, trimmed and chopped	Half

1 In large heavy saucepan, heat oil over medium-low heat; cook garlic and onions, stirring occasionally, until softened, about 5 minutes.

2 Add potato; stir for 1 minute. Add stock, parsley, coriander and marjoram; cover and simmer until potatoes are very tender, about 15 minutes.

3 Add chick peas. In food processor or using hand blender in saucepan, purée just until chick-peas are coarse; return to pan. Add spinach; simmer for 5 minutes. *Makes 6 servings, 1-1/4 cups (300 mL) each.*

Make ahead: Cover and refrigerate for up to 2 days.

* Substitution Tip

If desired, use 1 cup (250 mL) dried chick-peas to yield 2 cups (500 mL) cooked. Soak overnight. Drain and boil in fresh water for 10 minutes, then simmer for 1 to 2 hours or until tender. Drain.

Reduced-Sodium Cooking

To reduce sodium, substitute cooked, dried or frozen beans for the canned, and use home-made stock with no added salt.

Per serving:

calories	170
protein	9 g
total fat	4 g
saturated fat	1 g
cholesterol	0 mg
carbohydrate	24 g
dietary fiber	3 g
sodium	672 mg

R.D.I. Vit A 18%, E 6%, C 15%, Folate 33%, Ca 6% (65 mg), Iron 15%, Zinc 11%.

Canada's Food Guide Serving:

Soup au Pistou

Pistou is a Provençale version of pesto. In France, this soup is typically made
in late summer, when gardens are full of basil and vegetables.
It usually contains fresh beans such as white haricots, lima or flageolet.

1 tbsp	olive oil	15 mL
2	onions or leeks, chopped	2
1/2 tsp	each dried thyme and pepper	2 mL
2	each carrots and stalks celery, chopped	2
3 cups	each vegetable or chicken stock and water	750 mL
2 cups	chopped fresh tomatoes (or one 19 oz/540 mL can)	500 mL
1/2 cup	small pasta (such as macaroni or shells)	125 mL
1	can (19 oz/540 mL) cannellini or navy (pea) beans, drained and rinsed	1
1 cup	shredded fresh basil leaves*	250 mL
6	large cloves garlic, minced	6
1/2 cup	freshly grated Parmesan or Gruyère cheese	125 mL

1 In large saucepan, heat oil over medium heat; cook onions, stirring often, for
5 minutes. Add thyme, pepper, carrots and celery; reduce heat, cover and simmer,
stirring occasionally, for 5 minutes.

2 Stir in stock, water, tomatoes, pasta and beans; simmer, uncovered, for 15 minutes or
until pasta is tender.

3 Stir in fresh basil, garlic, and salt to taste; simmer for 3 minutes. Ladle into bowls;
sprinkle with cheese. *Makes 6 servings, about 1-1/2 cups (375 mL) each.*

Make ahead: Cover and refrigerate for up to 3 days.

Winter Lunch Menu

Crudité with Creamy Crab Dip (page 14)
Soup au Pistou (this page)
Fig and Cottage Cheese Quick Bread (page 245) or Focaccia (page 246)
Apple Berry Crisp (page 271)

Cooking Tip

Don't use canned white
kidney beans because they are
too soft and will turn to mush.

*Substitution Tip

If fresh basil is not available
and you have pesto, add 1/4
cup (50 mL) or to taste just
before serving. Or add 1 tsp
(5 mL) dried basil and half
the garlic in step 1. In step 3,
add remaining garlic, 1 cup
(250 mL) coarsely chopped
fresh parsley, 1 tbsp (15 mL)
fresh lemon juice and 1 tsp
(5 mL) granulated sugar.

Per serving:
calories	242
protein	15 g
total fat	6 g
saturated fat	2 g
cholesterol	7 mg
carbohydrate	33 g
dietary fiber	7 g
sodium	868 mg

R.D.I. Vit A 69%, E 8%, C 22%,
Folate 29%, Ca 18% (195 mg), Iron 17%,
Zinc 15%.

Canada's Food Guide Serving:
¼ 🌾 2 🥕 ¾ 🍖

Winter Vegetable Soup

*Improvise with this soup. Using this recipe as a guide, add whatever
vegetables you have on hand — spinach, broccoli, cauliflower —
or throw in some cooked rice, lentils or beans.*

2 tsp	vegetable oil	10 mL
1/2 cup	chopped onion	125 mL
2 cups	diced potatoes	500 mL
1/2 cup	each chopped carrots and celery	125 mL
2 cups	vegetable or chicken stock	500 mL
1 cup	shredded cabbage	250 mL
1 tsp	dried basil or 2 tbsp (25mL) chopped fresh	5 mL
1	bay leaf	1
1	can (19 oz/540 mL) tomatoes	1
1/2 cup	frozen peas or sliced snow peas	125 mL
1/4 cup	chopped fresh parsley	50 mL
1/3 cup	freshly grated Parmesan cheese	75 mL

1 In saucepan, heat oil over medium heat; cook onion for 2 minutes. Add potatoes, carrots and celery; cook, stirring, for 3 minutes or until onions are softened.

2 Add stock, cabbage, basil and bay leaf; bring to boil. Reduce heat, cover and simmer for 15 to 20 minutes or until vegetables are tender.

3 Stir in tomatoes, peas and parsley; cook until peas are tender. Add salt and pepper to taste. Discard bay leaf.

4 Ladle into bowls; sprinkle with Parmesan cheese.
Makes 4 servings, about 1-1/2 cups (375 mL) each.

Make ahead: Through step 3, cover and refrigerate for up to 1 day.

Reduced-Sodium Cooking
To cut sodium in half, use homemade stock with no added salt.

Fiber-booster
For extra fiber, add green peas to soups, stir-fries and rice. Put chick-peas in your salads. Throw an extra can of red kidney beans into the chili.

Per serving:

calories	186
protein	8 g
total fat	6 g
saturated fat	2 g
cholesterol	7 mg
carbohydrate	28 g
dietary fiber	4 g
sodium	740 mg

R.D.I. Vit A 47%, E 12%, C 47%, Folate 17%, Ca 17% (190 mg), Iron 14%, Zinc 11%.

Canada's Food Guide Serving:
3

How Much Fat Is Too Much?

What does 30% of a day's calories from fat mean? For healthy adults it means about:

- 90 grams or less of fat for most men
- 65 grams or less of fat for most women

On average, most men need to cut back by about 20 grams of fat and women by 15 grams of fat a day.

Product 1

NUTRITION INFORMATION
PER 298 G SERVING

Energy	272 cal/1140 kJ
Protein	19 g
Fat Total	4.1g
Carbohydrate	40 g

Product 2

NUTRITION INFORMATION
PER 298 G SERVING

Energy	353 cal/1470 kJ
Protein	27 g
Fat Total	12 g
Carbohydrate	34 g

In comparing these two brands of Lasagna with Meat Sauce, Product 1 is clearly the better choice.

Lower Fat for Healthy Eating

The typical Canadian diet is too high in fat. On average, Canadians get 36% of the day's calories from fat, whereas today's recommendation is that only 30% or less of the day's calories come from fat. And for those with a high blood cholesterol or triglyceride level, fat intake should be even lower. (See page 166.)

HEALTHY EATING TIPS: Lower Fat

While some people clearly need to overhaul their diet in order to reduce fat, most people need simply to make small changes like these:

- Allow extra time for shopping, planning meals and trying new recipes. Soon you'll be able to shop for lower-fat foods and prepare lower-fat meals as quickly as you shop and prepare foods now.
- Pay close attention to food preparation; that's where a lot of fat gets added. The recipes and tips in this book will show you how to prepare delicious recipes using lower-fat ingredients and cooking methods. For example, to lower the fat when baking quick breads and muffins, try substituting applesauce or low-fat yogurt for a portion of the fat.
- When packaged food is labeled with nutrition information, use the information on fat per serving to compare products and make lower-fat food choices. (See sidebar.)
- Limit or reduce portions of foods that contain a lot of saturated and trans fat (partially hydrogenated fat). (See the Appendix for these and other terms.) To do this, buy the leanest cuts of meat. Eat smaller portions of meat. Choose lower-fat milk products most of the time. Avoid foods containing partially hydrogenated oil or fried in shortening, for example, cookies, crackers, pastries, fast foods and snack foods.
- Aim to eat lower-fat foods most of the time but don't fret about occasional higher-fat foods or meals. Enjoy the brief break from routine but get back on track as soon as possible.

All Fats Are Not Equal

Reducing the fat in your diet doesn't mean eating no fat. Not only would a no-fat diet be virtually impossible, it would be unhealthy since some fatty acids are essential for life. However, not all fats are equal. In general, you are advised to choose foods containing mostly monounsaturated and polyunsaturated fats (vegetable oils, soft margarines, whole grains, fish, nuts and seeds) over foods high in saturated or trans fat (butter, meat, full-fat milk products, baked goods made with shortening or hydrogenated or partially hydrogenated vegetable oils). See the Appendix for a detailed description of the main types of fat in food and the potential impact of these fats on health.

Children and Low-Fat Diets

Healthy eating habits should start early in life but children's needs are different from adults', particularly when it comes to fat. A committee of the Canadian Paediatric Society and Health Canada concluded that children should not be put on low-fat diets intended for adults. Children often need the calories and nutrients provided by higher-fat foods to grow and develop.

Childhood can be seen as the step-down period between infancy, when 50% of calories should come from fat, and adulthood, when 30% or less of a day's calories should come from fat. During their growth years, children can learn to eat and enjoy lower-fat foods and meals but higher-fat foods such as cheese, peanut butter, nuts, seeds and ice cream may also be included in a child's diet. As children approach the end of physical growth — around age 14 to 15 for girls, 17 to 18 for boys — higher-fat foods can give way to more lower-fat choices.

What's the Fuss about Cholesterol?

Cholesterol is a fat-related compound that is both manufactured in your body and obtained through food. Contrary to popular belief, the cholesterol in food such as eggs is not a major factor in raising blood cholesterol. The body compensates for a dietary intake of cholesterol by reducing the cholesterol's absorption and the body's own production of cholesterol. For this reason people with a healthy blood cholesterol level need not worry unnecessarily about cholesterol-containing foods if they are eaten in moderation. The most important action is to cut down on fat. When you do this, your cholesterol intake falls too, since cholesterol naturally occurs in many of the same foods as saturated fat.

Sweet Potato and Ginger Soup

Ginger, lime juice and coconut milk complement the mellow flavor of sweet potatoes. If the soup is too thick, stir in extra chicken stock.

6 cups	cubed peeled sweet potatoes (about 3 large)	1.5 L
3-1/2 cups	chicken stock	875 mL
1 tbsp	minced gingerroot	15 mL
1/2 cup	unsweetened coconut milk	125 mL
3 tbsp	fresh lime juice	50 mL
1/2 tsp	salt	2 mL
1/4 tsp	pepper	1 mL
1/4 cup	sliced almonds, toasted	50 mL
1/4 cup	chopped fresh coriander (cilantro)	50 mL

1 In saucepan, combine potatoes, stock and ginger; bring to boil. Reduce heat, cover and simmer for about 10 minutes or until potatoes are tender.

2 Transfer to food processor; purée until smooth.

3 Return to saucepan; whisk in coconut milk, lime juice, salt and pepper. Cook over low heat just until heated through.

4 Ladle into bowls; sprinkle with almonds and coriander.
Makes 8 servings, about 3/4 cup (175 mL) each.

Make ahead: Through step 3, cover and refrigerate for up to 1 day.

Lightly Curried Carrot and Ginger Soup

Carrots thicken this soup and give it a rich flavor.
You can substitute yogurt and coconut milk for some of
the milk. For extra calcium, replace some of the stock with milk.

2 tsp	vegetable oil	10 mL
2	cloves garlic, minced	2
1	onion, chopped	1
2 tbsp	minced gingerroot	25 mL
1 tsp	ground coriander	5 mL
1/2 tsp	ground cumin	2 mL
1/4 tsp	each curry powder, salt and pepper	1 mL
4 cups	thickly sliced peeled carrots (about 1-1/2 lb/750 g)	1 L
3 cups	vegetable or chicken stock	750 mL
2 cups	2% milk (or one-third each milk, 2% plain yogurt and coconut milk)	500 mL
1/4 cup	chopped fresh coriander (cilantro) or parsley	50 mL

1 In large saucepan, heat oil over medium heat; cook garlic, onion, ginger, coriander, cumin, curry powder, salt and pepper; stirring occasionally, for about 5 minutes or until onion is softened.

2 Stir in carrots. Pour in stock; bring to boil. Reduce heat and simmer, covered, for 30 minutes or until carrots are very soft.

3 In batches, purée mixture in blender or food processor. Return to saucepan; whisk in milk (then yogurt and coconut milk if using); reheat just until hot. Stir in salt and pepper to taste.

4 Ladle into bowls, sprinkle with coriander. *Makes 6 servings, about 1 cup (250 mL) each.*

Make ahead: Through step 3, cover and refrigerate for up to 3 days or freeze for up to 1 month.

Cooking Tip

Vegetable cream soups are much smoother if puréed in a blender rather than a food processor.

Per serving:

calories	108
protein	4 g
total fat	4 g
saturated fat	1 g
cholesterol	6 mg
carbohydrate	15 g
dietary fiber	2 g
sodium	504 mg

R.D.I. Vit A 188%, D 17%, E 7%, C 7%, Folate 7%, Ca 12% (133 mg), Iron 5%, Zinc 7%.

Canada's Food Guide Serving:

🥕 ¼ 🥛

Asian Carrot and Mushroom Noodle Soup

Light and fresh tasting yet with the heartiness of pasta and chicken, this soup can be a main course or appetizer. For variety, use other kinds of noodles and substitute spinach or chopped bok choy for the snow peas.

*Substitution Tip

Substitute rice stick noodles or rice vermicelli for the egg noodles; add them with the coriander and simmer for 2 minutes or until noodles are tender.

1 tsp	vegetable oil	5 mL
2	cloves garlic, minced	2
1 tbsp	minced gingerroot	15 mL
3	green onions, chopped	3
1/8 tsp	red pepper flakes	0.5 mL
1 cup	thickly sliced mushrooms	250 mL
3/4 cup	thinly sliced carrots	175 mL
2 cups	each chicken stock and water	500 mL
1 tbsp	fresh lime or lemon juice	15 mL
2 tsp	each fish sauce, sodium-reduced soy sauce and sesame oil	10 mL
2 oz	fine egg noodles (approx. 3/4 cup/175 mL)*	60 g
6 oz	boneless skinless chicken breast (about 1), cut in thin strips	175 g
3/4 cup	trimmed halved snow peas	175 mL
3 tbsp	chopped fresh coriander (cilantro)	50 mL

Per serving:

calories	135
protein	13 g
total fat	4 g
saturated fat	1 g
cholesterol	31 mg
carbohydrate	13 g
dietary fiber	2 g
sodium	596 mg

R.D.I. Vit A 43%, E 3%, C 13%, Folate 9%, Ca 3% (31 mg), Iron 9%, Zinc 11%.

Canada's Food Guide Serving:
¼ 🌾 ¾ 🥕 ¼ 🍗

1 In saucepan, heat oil over medium heat; cook garlic, ginger, onions and red pepper flakes, stirring, for 2 minutes.

2 Add mushrooms and carrots; cook, stirring, for about 5 minutes or until moisture is evaporated.

3 Add stock, water, lime juice, fish sauce, soy sauce and sesame oil; bring to boil. Reduce heat and simmer, uncovered, for 10 minutes.

4 Stir in noodles and chicken; bring to boil. Reduce heat and simmer for 5 minutes. Add snow peas; cook for 2 minutes. Stir in coriander.
Makes 5 servings, about 1 cup (250 mL) each.

Make ahead: Cover and refrigerate for up to 1 day.

Spicy Thai Chicken Noodle Soup

Liven up an old favorite by adding Thai seasonings. I think you'll like the freshness of lime juice and rind. Use rice stick vermicelli noodles, available at many supermarkets.

To measure, first break into about 3-inch (8 cm) pieces. If you prefer an even spicier soup, add more hot chili paste to taste before serving.

1 tsp	vegetable oil	5 mL
3	cloves garlic, minced	3
1 tbsp	ground cumin	15 mL
1/2 tsp	turmeric	2 mL
8 oz	boneless skinless chicken breasts, thinly sliced	250 g
5 cups	chicken stock	1.25 L
2 tsp	each minced gingerroot and granulated sugar	10 mL
1 tsp	hot chili paste	5 mL
1/2 tsp	grated lime rind	2 mL
2 tbsp	fresh lime juice	25 mL
2 cups	broken rice stick vermicelli (3-1/2 oz/100 g)	500 mL
1 cup	each bean sprouts and coarsely chopped romaine lettuce	250 mL
2 tbsp	chopped fresh coriander (cilantro)	25 mL

1 In saucepan, heat oil over medium heat; cook garlic, cumin and turmeric, stirring constantly, for 1 minute.

2 Add chicken, chicken stock, ginger, sugar, chili paste, lime rind and juice; bring to boil. Reduce heat and simmer for 5 minutes.

3 Add rice stick vermicelli; simmer for 3 minutes. Add bean sprouts and lettuce; cook for 1 minute. Ladle into bowls; sprinkle with coriander.

Makes 6 servings, about 1-1/4 cups (300 mL) each.

Make ahead: Through step 2, cover and refrigerate for up to 1 day.

Per serving:

calories	163
protein	15 g
total fat	3 g
saturated fat	1 g
cholesterol	22 mg
carbohydrate	18 g
dietary fiber	1 g
sodium	677 mg

R.D.I. Vit A 4%, E 3%, C 10%, Folate 12%, Ca 3% (36 mg), Iron 13%, Zinc 10%.

Canada's Food Guide Serving:
¼ 🌾 ½ 🥕 ½ 🍗

Chinese Shrimp and Scallop Soup

This meal-in-a-pot is really a soup with unlimited possibilities. Smaller servings make a wonderful first course as well. Use raw shrimp if possible — because they are more flavorful.

1 oz	dried Chinese or shiitake mushrooms (about 1 cup/250 mL)	30 g
4 oz	rice stick vermicelli or fine egg noodles, broken (about 1-3/4 cups/425 mL)	125 g
1 tbsp	sesame oil	15 mL
3	green onions (including tops), chopped	3
2	large cloves garlic, minced	2
1 tbsp	grated gingerroot	15 mL
3-1/2 cups	each chicken stock and water	875 mL
1/4 cup	rice wine vinegar	50 mL
1 tbsp	soy sauce	15 mL
1 tsp	granulated sugar	5 mL
1/4 tsp	hot pepper sauce or hot chili paste	1 mL
4 cups	coarsely chopped bok choy (leaves and stalks)	1 L
8 oz	large shrimp, peeled and deveined	250 g
8 oz	sea scallops, halved horizontally	250 g

Cooking Tips

For a heartier soup, add 1/2 cup (125 mL) thickly sliced bamboo shoots or celery along with the stock.

For a spicier soup, add more hot pepper sauce to taste. Garnish with chopped fresh coriander (cilantro).

1 In small bowl, cover mushrooms with hot water; let stand for 20 minutes. Drain. Discard tough stems; thinly slice caps. Set aside. Meanwhile, if using rice stick vermicelli, cover with hot water; let soak for 20 minutes. Drain and set aside.

2 In large saucepan, heat 1 tsp (5 mL) of the oil over medium heat; cook onions, garlic and ginger, stirring, for 2 minutes. Stir in mushrooms. Pour in stock, water, vinegar, soy sauce, remaining 2 tsp (10 mL) oil, sugar and hot pepper sauce; bring to boil. Reduce heat to low and simmer, uncovered, for 15 minutes.

3 Stir in egg noodles if using; cook, uncovered, for 4 to 5 minutes. Stir in bok choy, shrimp and scallops; simmer for 2 minutes or until shrimp turn pink and bok choy wilts. Stir in rice stick noodles if using.

Makes 8 servings, about 1 cup (250 mL) each.

Make ahead: Through step 2, cover and refrigerate for up to 1 day.

Per serving:

calories	152
protein	13 g
total fat	3 g
saturated fat	1 g
cholesterol	42 mg
carbohydrate	17 g
dietary fiber	1 g
sodium	566 mg

R.D.I. Vit A 11%, E 2%, C 18%, Folate 13%, Ca 6% (64 mg), Iron 10%, Zinc 12%.

Canada's Food Guide Serving:
¼ 🌾 ½ 🥕 ½ 🍗

Thai Coconut, Ginger and Chicken Soup
(Gai Tom Ka)

Everyone loves this unique and flavorful soup. Next to Pad Thai, it's the most popular menu item in Thai restaurants. For this Canadian version, I've used grated lime rind for kaffir lime leaves, grated lemon rind for lemongrass and fresh gingerroot for galangal. However, I don't recommend using soy sauce instead of fish sauce. This version is quite hot. For a milder soup, use less red pepper flakes.

1-2/3 cups	light unsweetened coconut milk (1 can/398 mL)	400 mL
1 cup	chicken stock	250 mL
	Grated rind from 1 medium lime	
	Grated rind from half medium lemon	
2 tbsp	grated gingerroot	25 mL
1/4 tsp	red pepper flakes	1 mL
4 oz	boneless skinless chicken breasts, thinly sliced and cut in 1-inch (2.5 cm) lengths	125 g
1 cup	straw mushrooms or 4 mushrooms, sliced (optional)	250 mL
Quarter	sweet red pepper, cut in thin strips	Quarter
2 tbsp	fish sauce	25 mL
2 tbsp	chopped fresh coriander (cilantro)	25 mL

1 In saucepan over medium heat, cook coconut milk, stock, lime and lemon rinds, ginger and red pepper flakes until hot but not boiling.

2 Add chicken, mushrooms (if using) and red pepper; cook, stirring often, until chicken is no longer pink inside, about 5 minutes. Stir in fish sauce and coriander. *Makes 4 servings, about 3/4 cup (175 mL) each.*

Per serving:

calories	119
protein	9 g
total fat	6 g
saturated fat	5 g
cholesterol	17 mg
carbohydrate	8 g
sodium	627 mg

R.D.I. Vit A 8%, E 1%, C 42%, Folate 4%, Ca 1% (12 mg), Iron 3%, Zinc 4%.

Canada's Food Guide Serving:
¼ 🥕 ¼ 🍗

Porcini Mushroom Bisque

I absolutely love the rich, woodsy flavor of porcini mushrooms and sometimes double the amount in this recipe. This very elegant dinner party starter can be a clear soup or a cream soup, puréed in a food processor or left chunky.

3/4 cup	dried porcini mushrooms (0.3 oz or 10 g pkg)	175 mL
1/2 cup	boiling water	125 mL
1 tsp	olive oil	5 mL
1	small onion, finely chopped	1
Pinch	dried thyme	Pinch
1 lb	fresh mushrooms, coarsely chopped (about 5 cups/1.25 L)	500 g
2 tbsp	all-purpose flour	25 mL
2 cups	vegetable or chicken stock	500 mL
2 cups	2% milk	500 mL
1/4 cup	chopped fresh parsley or green onions (including tops)	50 mL

1 Rinse dried porcini mushrooms under cold water to remove grit. Place in small bowl and pour in boiling water; let stand for 30 minutes. Drain, reserving liquid; chop mushrooms and set aside.

2 In heavy or nonstick saucepan, heat oil over medium heat; cook onion and thyme for 3 minutes. Add fresh and porcini mushrooms; cook, stirring often, for 5 minutes. Sprinkle with flour and stir until mixed; cook, stirring, for 1 minute. Add stock and reserved porcini mushroom liquid; bring to boil. Reduce heat, cover and simmer for 20 minutes.

3 In food processor or blender, purée half of the mixture. Return to saucepan and stir until blended. Stir in milk; heat over medium heat, stirring, until hot.

4 Add salt and pepper to taste. Ladle into bowls; sprinkle with parsley.
Makes 6 servings, about 3/4 cup (175 mL) each.

Make ahead: Through step 3, cover and refrigerate for up to 2 days.

Mushroom Soup

Follow recipe for Porcini Mushroom Bisque but omit the porcini mushrooms and soaking liquid. Add bay leaf along with stock; discard before puréeing.

Lactose Intolerant?

Follow recipe for Porcini Mushroom Bisque but replace milk with more stock.

Per serving:

calories	85
protein	5 g
total fat	3 g
saturated fat	1 g
cholesterol	6 mg
carbohydrate	11 g
dietary fiber	2 g
sodium	258 mg

R.D.I. Vit A 5%, D 17%, E 2%, C 10%, Folate 9%, Ca 10% (110 mg), Iron 9%, Zinc 11%.

Canada's Food Guide Serving:
1 🌿 ¼ 🥛

Eating Well As We Get Older

As we age it gets harder to meet our nutrition needs, and healthy eating becomes even more important. In addition to the gradual declines in gastrointestinal function, muscle mass and immunity, most of us face some additional stress and disability such as arthritis, high blood pressure, elevated cholesterol levels or diabetes. What's more, medications more commonly used later in life, such as diuretics, laxatives, heart and cancer drugs, may promote nutrient losses or affect our appetites.

HEALTHY EATING TIPS: Older People

- Follow the same basic principles of healthy eating (page 1). Keep your diet low in fat and increase your intake of complex carbohydrates and fiber by eating more vegetables, fruit, whole grains and legumes (dried beans, peas and lentils).
- Make every food choice count nutritionally. As your metabolism slows down, your need for calories drops but your need for nutrients doesn't. You may need even more of some nutrients since the gastrointestinal tract doesn't absorb nutrients as well as it once did.
- Vegetables, fruits, legumes (dried beans, peas and lentils) and whole grains take on an even greater significance — not just for the complex carbohydrate and fiber but as the main source of antioxidant vitamins and minerals. Antioxidant nutrients fight against heart disease and cancer and keep the immune system in top form.
- Pay close attention to your intake of calcium and vitamin D, particularly if you don't get outdoors. (See pages 94 and 97.)
- Make sure you drink lots of fluids. Declining kidney function and a poor thirst response can put you at risk of dehydration. Dehydration is linked to mental confusion.
- Lastly, consider a multivitamin supplement if your food intake is low or restricted for any reason. A multivitamin doesn't make up for a faulty diet but it can help you meet your needs for certain nutrients like calcium and vitamin D.

Lentil, Barley and Sweet Potato Soup

*I freeze some of this thick, comforting, yet light winter soup for those times
when there is no time to cook. The fresh dill and parsley make this soup special.
It is better to omit them than to use dried. If the soup seems too thick
after cooking the potato, add more stock.*

1/2 cup	dried green lentils	125 mL
2 tsp	vegetable oil	10 mL
2	cloves garlic, minced	2
2	carrots, coarsely chopped (about 1 cup/250 mL)	2
2	stalks celery, chopped	2
1	medium onion, chopped	1
1-1/2 tsp	dried thyme	7 mL
1/3 cup	pearl or pot barley	75 mL
6 cups	chicken or vegetable stock	1.5 L
2	bay leaves	2
1	sweet potato (12 oz/375 g), peeled and diced (2 cups/500 mL)	1
1/4 cup	each chopped fresh dill and parsley	50 mL

1 Rinse lentils, discarding any blemished or shrivelled ones; set aside.

2 In large saucepan, heat oil over medium heat; cook garlic, carrots, celery, onion and
thyme, stirring often, for about 5 minutes or until softened.

3 Stir in lentils and barley; pour in stock. Add bay leaves; bring to boil. Reduce heat
and simmer, covered, for 50 minutes.

4 Stir in sweet potato; cover and simmer for 20 minutes or until barley and potato are
tender. Discard bay leaves.

5 Stir in dill and parsley. Season with salt and pepper to taste.
Makes 8 servings, about 1 cup (250 mL) each.

Make ahead: Through step 4, cover and refrigerate for up to 2 days or freeze for up
to 1 month. After 4 hours, soup thickens (because barley absorbs the liquid); add
2 cups (500 mL) more stock and reheat.

Lentil, Barley, Sweet Potato and Fennel Soup

Substitute 3 cups (750 mL)
chopped fresh fennel for the
carrots and celery. It's delicious!

Lentils

Lentils are an excellent source
of fiber, the B-vitamin folate and
vegetable protein. Unlike most
dried beans, they do not require
any soaking, making them not
only more convenient, but also an
ideal addition to soups and stews.

To use canned lentils, add
1 can (19 oz/540 mL), drained,
during last 10 minutes of cooking.

Per serving:	
calories	161
protein	9 g
total fat	3 g
saturated fat	0 g
cholesterol	0 mg
carbohydrate	26 g
dietary fiber	4 g
sodium	611 mg

R.D.I. Vit A 103%, E 8%, C 18%,
Folate 38%, Ca 4% (43 mg), Iron 18%,
Zinc 12%.

Canada's Food Guide Serving:
¼ 🌾 1 🥕 ¼ 🍗

Mulligatawny Soup

*British ingredients teamed with Indian spicing
make this a popular soup in India. Serve this simplified Canadian
version when you have leftover chicken or turkey.*

2 tsp	vegetable oil	10 mL
4	cloves garlic, minced	4
4 tsp	minced gingerroot or 2 tsp (10 mL) ground ginger	20 mL
1 to 2 tsp	curry powder or curry paste	5 to 10 mL
1/2 tsp	cinnamon	2 mL
1	potato, peeled and chopped	1
1	apple, peeled and chopped	1
3 cups	turkey or chicken stock	750 mL
2 cups	fresh or frozen chopped mixed vegetables	500 mL
2 cups	diced cooked chicken or turkey	500 mL
1/2 tsp	salt	2 mL
2 tbsp	chopped fresh coriander (cilantro) or parsley	25 mL

1 In large nonstick saucepan, heat oil over medium heat; cook garlic, ginger, curry powder and cinnamon, stirring, for 1 minute.

2 Add potato, apple, stock and mixed vegetables; cover and simmer for 20 minutes or until vegetables are tender.

3 In food processor or blender, purée vegetable mixture until smooth; return to saucepan. Add chicken and salt; heat through.

4 Ladle into bowls; sprinkle with coriander. *Makes 6 servings, about 1 cup (250 mL) each.*

Make ahead: Through step 3, cover and refrigerate for up to 1 day.

Per serving:

calories	**192**
protein	**18 g**
total fat	**6 g**
saturated fat	1 g
cholesterol	42 mg
carbohydrate	**17 g**
dietary fiber	**3 g**
sodium	**642 mg**

R.D.I. Vit A 25%, E 7%, C 8%,
Folate 8%, Ca 3% (37 mg), Iron 11%,
Zinc 17%.

Canada's Food Guide Serving:

1 🥕 ¾ 🍗

Quick Black Bean, Corn and Tomato Soup

*I developed this recipe for my children to cook at university.
It's homemade soup from a can — and it's a great fast and nutritious supper.
You can substitute red kidney beans for the black beans.*

2 tsp	olive oil	10 mL
2	onions, chopped	2
4 tsp	chili powder	20 mL
1	can (28 oz/796 mL) stewed tomatoes	1
1-3/4 cups	vegetable or chicken stock	425 mL
1	can (19 oz/540 mL) black beans, drained and rinsed	1
1-1/2 cups	corn kernels	375 mL
2 tbsp	coarsely chopped packed fresh coriander (cilantro)	25 mL

1 In large heavy saucepan, heat oil over medium heat; cook onions and chili powder, stirring often, for 5 to 8 minutes or until tender.

2 Coarsely chop tomatoes; add to onions along with stock, black beans and corn. Simmer, stirring often, for 5 to 10 minutes or until slightly thickened. Stir in coriander. *Makes 6 servings, about 1-1/3 cups (325 mL) each.*

Make ahead: Cover and refrigerate for up to 3 days.

Nutrition Tip

Black beans are very high in the B-vitamin folate, fiber and iron. They also contain some calcium.

Student's Supper Menu

Grilled Cheese Sandwich on Whole Wheat (or Cheese and Crackers)
Quick Black Bean, Corn and Tomato Soup (this page)
Raw Carrots
Orange

Per serving:

calories	187
protein	9 g
total fat	3 g
saturated fat	trace
cholesterol	0 mg
carbohydrate	36 g
dietary fiber	7 g
sodium	715 mg

R.D.I. Vit A 14%, E 8%, C 37%, Folate 52%, Ca 7% (78 mg), Iron 20%, Zinc 14%.

Canada's Food Guide Serving:

2 🥕 ½ 🫘

Onion and Potato Soup

*I made this thick soup one night when my shelves were
almost bare except for a large Spanish onion, some potatoes and Parmesan cheese.
The second time I made it, I added cabbage for an extra flavor dimension.
Serve with toast or sprinkle croutons onto each bowl.*

1 tbsp	olive oil	15 mL
1	large Spanish onion, coarsely chopped (2-1/2 cups/625 mL)	1
2	medium-large potatoes, peeled and diced (2-1/2 cups/625 mL)	2
1	can (10 oz/284 mL) chicken or vegetable broth	1
4 cups	water	1 L
3 cups	thinly sliced cabbage	750 mL
1 tsp	each salt and granulated sugar	5 mL
1/2 tsp	pepper	2 mL
1/2 cup	freshly grated Parmesan cheese	125 mL

1 In large heavy saucepan, heat oil over medium-low heat; cook onion, covered and stirring occasionally, for 10 to 15 minutes or until very tender.

2 Add potatoes; cook, uncovered and stirring frequently, for 2 minutes. Add broth and water; bring to boil. Cover, reduce heat and simmer for 10 to 15 minutes or until potatoes are tender.

3 Add cabbage; cover and simmer for 5 minutes or until cabbage is tender. Stir in salt, sugar and pepper.

4 Ladle into bowls; sprinkle with Parmesan. *Makes 8 servings, 1 cup (250 mL) each.*

Make ahead: Through step 3, cover and refrigerate for up to 3 days or freeze for up to 1 month. (Potatoes become mushy with freezing; purée soup or stir well.)

Per serving:

calories	**110**
protein	**6 g**
total fat	**4 g**
saturated fat	**2 g**
cholesterol	**5 mg**
carbohydrate	**13 g**
dietary fiber	**2 g**
sodium	**648 mg**

R.D.I. Vit A 1%, E 3%, C 17%,
Folate 7%, Ca 10% (111 mg), Iron 4%,
Zinc 6%.

Canada's Food Guide Serving:

1 🥕

Gazpacho

My daughter, Susie, learned this recipe at a restaurant in Spain where she once worked. She was told to add the vinegar just before serving. I added the tomato juice and reduced the amount of olive oil. It's the perfect soup for a hot summer's day. I also make this soup when I'm trying to lose a few pounds — it's filling and satisfying, full of good nutrients yet low in calories. I have it with toast, which I rub with a cut clove of garlic then cut into croutons.

2	cloves garlic	2
Half	onion, quartered	Half
1	sweet green or red pepper, seeded and quartered	1
4	tomatoes, quartered	4
1	cucumber (10-inch/25 cm) peeled, quartered and seeded	1
2 cups	tomato juice or 1 can (19 oz/540 mL) tomatoes, puréed	500 mL
1/4 cup	lightly packed coarsely chopped fresh basil or coriander (cilantro) or parsley or dill	50 mL
1/4 cup	balsamic or red wine vinegar*	50 mL
2 tbsp	extra-virgin olive oil	25 mL
1/2 tsp	each salt, pepper and hot pepper sauce	2 mL
1 cup	vegetable or chicken stock or water (optional)	250 mL

1 In food processor or blender, with machine running, drop garlic into feed tube, then onion; turn machine off. Add green pepper, tomatoes and cucumber; process until finely chopped. Transfer to large bowl.

2 Add tomato juice, basil, vinegar, oil, salt, pepper and hot pepper sauce. Add stock if mixture is too thick. Cover and refrigerate for 30 minutes. Serve cold.
Makes 8 servings, about 1 cup (250 mL) each.

Make ahead: Cover and refrigerate for up to 2 days.

* **Substitution Tip**

Vinegars vary in strength and flavor. You can substitute one kind for another in many recipes, but the amount you use might vary. To be on the safe side when substituting, add half the amount called for in a recipe, taste, then add more if desired.

Per serving:

calories	74
protein	2 g
total fat	4 g
saturated fat	1 g
cholesterol	0 mg
carbohydrate	10 g
dietary fiber	2 g
sodium	365 mg

R.D.I. Vit A 9%, E 13%, C 53%, Folate 14%, Ca 2% (20 mg), Iron 6%, Zinc 3%.

Canada's Food Guide Serving:
2 🥕

Pasta

Pasta with Chick-Peas and Spinach

Easy Creamy Turkey Fettuccine

Summer Corn and Tomato Pasta

Fettuccine with Pesto

Linguine with Shrimp and Fresh Basil

Pad Thai

Penne with Tomato, Tuna and Lemon

Thai Noodle and Vegetable Stir-Fry

Singapore-Style Noodles

Chinese Noodle and Shrimp Party Platter

Wild Mushroom and Spinach Lasagna

Grilled Italian Sausage and Red Peppers with Penne

Vegetable Tortellini Casserole with Cheese Topping

Penne with Sweet Red Peppers, Black Olives and Arugula

Skillet Pork Curry with Apples and Chinese Noodles

Lemon, Dill and Parsley Orzo

Beef, Tomato and Mushroom Rigatoni

Spicy Chicken with Broccoli and Chinese Noodles

Two-Cheese Pasta and Tomatoes

Nutrition Notes

Restaurant Food: "Dining Out in Good Health"

Calcium: "Bone Up with These Facts on Calcium"

Vitamin D: "Vitamin D: How To Get It"

Nutrition for Athletes: "Going for Gold with Healthy Eating"

Pasta with Chick-Peas and Spinach

This simple pasta dish is so delicious that you'll want to make it often.
Serve as a main course or side dish.

Nutrition Tip

Spinach and chick-peas are both high in the B vitamin folate (also called folacin or folic acid).

4 oz	medium pasta shells (1-2/3 cups/400 mL)	125 g
1	pkg (10 oz/284 g) fresh spinach, stemmed and coarsely chopped	1
1	can (19 oz/540 mL) chick-peas, drained and rinsed	1
1	clove garlic, chopped	1
1/2 cup	vegetable or chicken stock or water	125 mL
1 tsp	anchovy paste (optional)	5 mL
1/4 tsp	each salt and pepper	1 mL
	Grated rind or zest of half a medium lemon	

1 In large pot of boiling water, cook pasta until tender but firm. Add spinach and return to boil; drain.

2 Meanwhile, in food processor, purée half of the chick-peas with the garlic, stock, and anchovy paste (if using) until smooth; stir into drained pasta. Stir in remaining chick-peas, salt, pepper and lemon rind. *Makes 3 servings.*

Per serving:

calories	331
protein	16 g
total fat	3 g
saturated fat	trace
cholesterol	0 mg
carbohydrate	61 g
dietary fiber	8 g
sodium	634 mg

R.D.I. Vit A 68%, E 8%, C 22%, Folate 86%, Ca 14% (154 mg), Iron 34%, Zinc 24%.

Canada's Food Guide Serving:

1¼ 🌾 1½ 🥕 2

PASTA PRIMER

- Most pasta is made with fine semolina flour, which is made by grinding durum wheat and removing the bran and germ, leaving behind the endosperm. Because most of the vitamins and minerals are in the bran and the germ, the semolina flour may be enriched by adding niacin, thiamine, riboflavin, folate and iron. For a nutritional boost, buy pasta with added protein and fiber.

- To increase your fiber intake, choose pasta made from whole wheat flour, which includes the bran, germ and endosperm.

- For flavor and nutrients without a lot of extra fat, toss cooked pasta with cooked vegetables and a small amount of meat or fish or lower-fat cheese instead of cream, butter and regular cheese.

Easy Creamy Turkey Fettuccine

Here's a great way to use up leftover turkey, chicken or ham after the holidays.
Evaporated 2% milk has a cream-like thickness that works well in pasta dishes.

8 oz	fettuccine or spaghetti	250 g
2 tsp	olive oil	10 mL
2 cups	sliced mushrooms	500 mL
1 cup	each chopped red onion and sliced celery	250 mL
3	cloves garlic, minced	3
1-1/2 cups	cooked turkey strips*	375 mL
1 cup	2% evaporated milk	250 mL
1/4 cup	chopped fresh parsley	50 mL
1/4 cup	packed chopped fresh basil**	50 mL
1/4 cup	freshly grated Parmesan cheese	50 mL

1 In large pot of boiling water, cook fettuccine until tender but firm; drain.

2 Meanwhile, in large saucepan, heat oil over medium heat; cook mushrooms, onion, celery and garlic, stirring often, for 8 to 10 minutes or until tender.

3 Stir in turkey, milk, parsley, basil, cheese and hot pasta; simmer, stirring gently, for 3 minutes. Add salt and pepper to taste. *Makes 3 servings.*

LOWER-FAT PASTA SAUCES

- At home: Use a minimum of oil, butter and cream. Instead, use milk or evaporated skim milk, or ricotta cheese (whirl in blender or food processor for a creamy texture). Toss in ingredients such as garlic and hot peppers; they offer lots of flavor but little fat. Using strong cheeses such as Parmesan, allows you to use less.

- In stores: When purchasing a ready-made pasta sauce, check the ingredient list. If the first items are oil, butter, cream or cheese, it will be high in fat.

- In restaurants: If you are unsure about ingredients in a dish, ask your server. Go for dishes with lots of fresh vegetables and herbs.

Substitution Tips

* Instead of turkey, use cooked chicken, ham or shrimp or 1 can (6-1/2 oz/184 g) tuna or salmon.

** If fresh basil isn't available, substitute 2 tsp (10 mL) dried basil and cook it along with the onions.

Nutrition Tip

Evaporated milk has twice as much calcium as fresh milk.

Per serving:

calories	**584**
protein	**42 g**
total fat	**12 g**
saturated fat	**4 g**
cholesterol	**66 mg**
carbohydrate	**75 g**
dietary fiber	**5 g**
sodium	**338 mg**

R.D.I. Vit A 10%, D 31%, E 11%, C 30%, Folate 24%, Ca 39% (424 mg), Iron 27%, Zinc 53%.

Canada's Food Guide Serving:

2¾   2   ¾   1¼

Summer Corn and Tomato Pasta

This pasta makes a great main course or side dish for a casual summer dinner.
It also packs well for lunch or picnics. Any kind of cooked beans can be used, but black
beans look most attractive. Or for a change, substitute shrimp or tuna for the beans.

2 cups	cooked fresh or frozen corn kernels	500 mL
5	medium tomatoes, cut in chunks (5 cups/1.25 L)	5
1 cup	cooked or canned black beans, drained and rinsed	250 mL
1/2 cup	finely chopped fresh coriander (cilantro) or basil	125 mL
1 tbsp	extra-virgin olive oil	15 mL
1	jalapeño pepper, seeded and minced, or 2 cloves garlic, minced	1
4	green onions, finely chopped	4
1 tsp	each salt and pepper	5 mL
8 oz	penne (3 cups/750 mL) or other short pasta	250 g
1 cup	crumbled feta cheese (5 oz/150 g)	250 mL

1 In large bowl, stir together corn, tomatoes, beans, coriander, oil, jalapeño pepper, green onions, salt and pepper; let stand at room temperature for 15 minutes or for up to 2 hours.

2 In large pot of boiling water, cook pasta for 8 minutes or until tender but firm; drain and return to pot.

3 Add tomato mixture; stir over medium heat just until heated through. Serve sprinkled with feta. *Makes 6 main-course or 10 side servings.*

Make ahead: To serve cold, rinse hot pasta under cold water and add to tomato mixture; cover and refrigerate for up to 1 day.

Per side serving:

calories	**210**
protein	**8 g**
total fat	**6 g**
saturated fat	**3 g**
cholesterol	**13 mg**
carbohydrate	**34 g**
dietary fiber	**4 g**
sodium	**448 mg**

R.D.I. Vit A 9%, E 6%, C 38%, Folate 30%, Ca 9% (94 mg), Iron 11%, Zinc 13%.

Canada's Food Guide Serving:
¾ 🌾 1 🥕 ¼ 🥛

Fettuccini with Pesto

The most heavenly and, without a doubt, the very best pesto that I ever tasted was in the Cinque Terre on the Ligurian coast in Italy. I think they used a small-leafed basil, which when coupled with the bright sun, salty Mediterranean breezes, hillside soil and the local cheeses produced an unbelievably wonderful, fragrant dish. Prepared pesto sauce is easily available at most stores; however, I've yet to taste one as good as homemade pesto made with fresh basil. The ideal pesto isn't oozing with oil, yet has a full flavor and is moist enough when mixed with cooked pasta. For this light version, I add some white bread to stabilize the sauce and to allow water to be added for moisture.

12 oz	fettuccine or spaghetti	375 g
Pesto Sauce:		
3	cloves garlic	3
1-1/2 cups	packed fresh basil	375 mL
2	slices white bread, crusts removed	2
2 tbsp	olive oil	25 mL
2 tbsp	pine nuts (optional)	25 mL
1/2 tsp	salt	2 mL
1/4 cup	freshly grated Parmesan cheese	50 mL

1 In large pot of boiling water, cook pasta for 8 to 10 minutes or until tender but firm; drain, reserving about 1/2 cup (125 mL) cooking water. Transfer pasta to serving bowl.

2 Pesto Sauce: Meanwhile, with food processor on, drop garlic through tube and process until chopped. Add basil, bread, oil, pine nuts (if using) and salt; process until well mixed, scraping down sides once or twice. Add 1/2 cup (125 mL) of the reserved cooking liquid (or hot water); process until blended. Stir in cheese.

3 Spoon over hot pasta; toss to mix, adding more cooking liquid if too dry. *Makes 4 servings.*

Make ahead: Through step 2 (pesto sauce), cover and refrigerate for up to 4 days.

Freezing Pesto

It's great to have homemade pesto on hand. Just freeze it in ice cube trays, then transfer to airtight container and freeze for up to 6 months.

Using Pesto

Add a large spoonful of pesto to soups or stews; spread on pizza instead of tomato sauce; stuff under the skin of chicken or use in the Pesto Salmon Fillets recipe on page 204.

Per serving:

calories	441
protein	15 g
total fat	11 g
saturated fat	2 g
cholesterol	5 mg
carbohydrate	71 g
dietary fiber	4 g
sodium	467 mg

R.D.I. Vit A 1%, E 9%, C 2%, Folate 14%, Ca 13% (143 mg), Iron 11%, Zinc 18%.

Canada's Food Guide Serving:
3½ 🌾 ¼ 🥕

Dining Out in Good Health

In the overall scheme of things the occasional meal out isn't going to break a healthy eating pattern. But if you eat in restaurants frequently, you run the risk of consuming more fat than is healthy.

HEALTHY EATING TIPS: Dining Out

- Make your needs known. Good restaurants will accommodate your requests to grill rather than fry an entrée, to serve lighter salad dressings, to serve sauces on the side, or to prepare a tomato-based pasta dish even if it isn't on the menu.
- Watch out for these typical downfalls: butter on the bread, high-fat appetizers like Caesar salads or cream soups, deep-fried entrées and rich desserts.
- Make trade-offs: if you have Caesar salad, go light on the rest of the meal; or choose a very light meal so that you can enjoy one of the special desserts.
- Lower-fat choices in fast food restaurants are sometimes hard to come by but these types of foods are better if available:
  - a grilled rather than a fried chicken sandwich
  - a plain hamburger with lettuce and tomatoes rather than a burger with double patties, cheese, bacon and sauce
  - a vegetarian pizza rather than one with pepperoni, bacon and extra cheese
  - low-fat milk or juice instead of a milkshake
  - low-fat salad dressings rather than regular ones
  - cereal or a low-fat muffin instead of an egg-cheese-bacon on buttered toast or croissant
  - submarines or sandwiches on whole wheat bread without the butter or mayonnaise
  - chili or bean-based dishes

Linguine with Shrimp and Fresh Basil

*With shrimp in the freezer and canned tomatoes on the shelf, you can make this
any time of year. You can also use frozen and thawed cooked shrimp.
Serve with a crisp salad of tossed greens.*

1	can (28 oz/796 mL) tomatoes	1
1	can (5-1/2 oz/156 mL) tomato paste	1
1/2 cup	packed chopped fresh basil or 1 tbsp (15 mL) dried	125 mL
4	cloves garlic, minced	4
1	onion, chopped	1
1 tbsp	chopped fresh oregano or 1 tsp (5 mL) dried	15 mL
1 lb	large shrimp, peeled and deveined	500 g
12 oz	linguine, fettuccine or spaghetti	375 g
1/4 cup	freshly grated Parmesan cheese	50 mL

1 In saucepan, mash tomatoes with juice. Add tomato paste, half of the fresh basil
(all if using dried), garlic, onion and oregano; bring to boil. Reduce heat and simmer,
stirring occasionally, for 20 minutes or until onion is tender and sauce is thickened
slightly.

2 Add shrimp; cover and cook for about 3 minutes or just until shrimp are pink
and firm.

3 Meanwhile, in large pot of boiling water, cook linguine for 8 to 10 minutes or until
tender but firm; drain well. Toss with tomato sauce and remaining basil. Serve
sprinkled with Parmesan cheese. *Makes 4 servings.*

Make ahead: Through step 1, cover and refrigerate for up to 1 day.

Per serving:

calories	527
protein	35 g
total fat	6 g
saturated fat	2 g
cholesterol	134 mg
carbohydrate	85 g
dietary fiber	8 g
sodium	601 mg

R.D.I. Vit A 27%, E 27%, C 70%,
Folate 21%, Ca 19% (208 mg), Iron 39%,
Zinc 33%.

Canada's Food Guide Serving:
3 🌾 3¼ 🥕 1 🍖

Pad Thai

In Thailand, this noodle dish is eaten at any time or in any place — from restaurants to street stalls. Each cook adds a personal touch. My version is lower in fat and uses easily available ingredients.

Substitution Tip

For a more authentic Thai dish, substitute 3 tbsp (50 mL) dried chopped shrimp for the fresh. Pickled white radish or salted cabbage (1/4 cup/50 mL) is often added. Tamarind paste or juice is used instead of vinegar.

8 oz	medium-wide rice noodles	250 g
3 tbsp	fish sauce	50 mL
2 tbsp	rice vinegar or cider vinegar	25 mL
2 tbsp	granulated sugar	25 mL
1 tbsp	vegetable oil	15 mL
2	eggs, lightly beaten	2
3	large cloves garlic, finely chopped	3
1/4 tsp	red pepper flakes	1 mL
8 oz	large shrimp, peeled and deveined	250 g
4 oz	tofu, sliced in thin strips (about 1 cup/250 mL)	125 g
3 cups	bean sprouts	750 mL
6	green onions, chopped	6
1/2 cup	coarsely chopped fresh coriander (cilantro)	125 mL
1/4 cup	chopped unsalted peanuts	50 mL
1	lime, cut in wedges	1

1 Soak noodles in hot water for 20 minutes; drain. In small bowl, mix together fish sauce, rice vinegar and sugar; set aside.

2 In large nonstick wok or skillet, heat 1 tsp (5 mL) of the oil over medium-high heat; cook eggs, stirring, until scrambled. Cut into strips; transfer to side dish.

3 Wipe out pan; add remaining oil. Stir-fry garlic, red pepper flakes and shrimp for 2 minutes. Add tofu; stir-fry for 1 minute or until shrimp are pink and opaque.

4 Add noodles and 1/2 cup (125 mL) water; cook, stirring, for 2 to 3 minutes or until noodles are tender. Stir in fish sauce mixture, bean sprouts and half of the onions; toss to mix well. Transfer to serving dish. Top with eggs, remaining onions, coriander and peanuts. Garnish with lime. *Makes 4 servings.*

Per serving:

calories	459
protein	24 g
total fat	13 g
saturated fat	2 g
cholesterol	172 mg
carbohydrate	62 g
dietary fiber	3 g
sodium	680 mg

R.D.I. Vit A 9%, D 9%, E 16%, C 30%, Folate 45%, Ca 11% (117 mg), Iron 31%, Zinc 30%.

Canada's Food Guide Serving:
1½ ⁂ 1¾ ⁂ 1½ ⁑

Penne with Tomato, Tuna and Lemon

*Serve small portions of this dynamic, Italian-style pasta dish as
a first course or larger servings for a main course. Even when the fridge is bare,
you'll likely have these ingredients on hand.
The lemon rind adds a tremendous zing to the dish*

About Capers

Capers are the pickled bud of the caper bush, grown in the Mediterranean. They are available in jars at most supermarkets. Use them in sauces and salads and to garnish meats and fish.

Measuring Tip

A rough guide for the pasta serving sizes in this book is approximately 2 cups (500 mL) cooked pasta for a main course and 1 cup (250 mL) for a side dish.

8 oz	penne, rotini or rigatoni pasta	250 g
1 tbsp	olive oil	15 mL
4	cloves garlic, minced (2 tsp/10 mL)	4
1 tsp	fennel seeds, crushed	5 mL
1/4 tsp	crushed red pepper flakes	1 mL
1	can (19 oz/540 mL) chopped tomatoes or 3 cups (750 mL) coarsely chopped fresh	1
1	can (6.5 oz/184 g) water-packed tuna, drained	1
2 tbsp	drained capers	25 mL
1/4 cup	coarsely chopped fresh flat-leaf parsley	50 mL
	Grated rind of half a lemon (1/2 tsp/2 mL)	

1 In large pot of boiling water, cook pasta for 8 to 10 minutes or until tender but firm; drain well.

2 Meanwhile, in large nonstick skillet, heat oil over medium heat; cook garlic, fennel seeds and red pepper flakes, stirring, until garlic is softened, about 2 minutes.

3 Stir in tomatoes, tuna and capers; bring to boil. Reduce heat and simmer for 8 to 10 minutes or until thickened slightly.

4 Stir in cooked pasta, parsley, lemon rind, and salt and pepper to taste.

Makes 3 main-course or 6 first-course servings.

Per main-course serving:

calories	425
protein	24 g
total fat	7 g
saturated fat	1 g
cholesterol	15 mg
carbohydrate	67 g
dietary fiber	6 g
sodium	561 mg

R.D.I. Vit A 15%, E 13%, C 43%, Folate 15%, Ca 8% (90 mg), Iron 24%, Zinc 21%.

Canada's Food Guide Serving:
2¾ 🌾 1½ 🥕 1 🐟

Thai Noodle and Vegetable Stir-Fry

This quick and easy stir-fry with spunky Thai flavors makes a great quick supper.
Add shrimp, scallops, chicken, meat or tofu for a heartier dish.
Consider broccoli, bok choy, cauliflower, carrots, mushrooms, celery, zucchini,
cabbage or green beans for the stir-fry vegetables.

4 oz	rice vermicelli noodles*	125 g
4 cups	chopped stir-fry vegetables or 1 pkg (500 g) frozen mixed Chinese vegetables, thawed	1 L
1 tbsp	vegetable oil	15 mL
2	cloves garlic, minced	2
1	fresh red chili pepper, seeded and chopped, or 1/4 tsp (1 mL) red pepper flakes	1
3 tbsp	oyster sauce	50 mL
2 tbsp	fresh lime or lemon juice	25 mL
1 tbsp	each fish sauce (or soy sauce) and minced gingerroot	15 mL
1 tsp	granulated sugar	5 mL
3	green onions, chopped	3
2 tbsp	toasted sesame seeds	25 mL

1 Soak noodles in hot water for 15 minutes; drain.

2 In large pot of boiling water, cook vegetables for 2 minutes. Add noodles; cook for 1 minute or until tender. Drain well.

3 Meanwhile, in wok or large nonstick skillet, heat oil over medium heat; stir-fry garlic for 1 minute. Stir in chili pepper, oyster sauce, lime juice, fish sauce, ginger and sugar; cook for 1 minute.

4 Mix noodle mixture into wok; cook, stirring, for 1 minute. Sprinkle with green onions and sesame seeds. *Makes 4 servings.*

* Substitution Tip

Instead of rice vermicelli noodles, cook 6 oz (175 g) spaghettini or other very thin noodle in saucepan of boiling water for 6 minutes. Add vegetables; bring to boil. Reduce heat and simmer for 2 to 4 minutes or until just tender; drain and continue with step 3.

Per serving:

calories	210
protein	8 g
total fat	7 g
saturated fat	1 mg
cholesterol	0 mg
carbohydrate	31 g
dietary fiber	4 g
sodium	995 mg

R.D.I. Vit A 78%, E 12%, C 60%, Folate 24%, Ca 6% (14 mg), Iron 14%, Zinc 14%.

Canada's Food Guide Serving:

1 🌾 2 🥕

Singapore-Style Noodles

Although it looks long, this vegetarian dish can be made in less than half an hour.

*Substitution Tip

If rice noodles are unavailable, substitute 6 oz (175 g) very thin noodles and cook for 8 to 10 minutes in large pot of boiling water.

Singapore-Style Noodles with Shrimp and Chicken

Omit egg and tofu. Instead, after step 2, add 6 oz (175 g) boneless, skinless chicken, cut in strips, and 8 oz (250 g) peeled, deveined medium-to-large shrimp; stir-fry for about 5 minutes or until chicken is no longer pink inside and shrimp is bright pink. Continue with step 3.

6 oz	rice vermicelli noodles*	175 g
2 tsp	vegetable oil	10 mL
2	eggs, lightly beaten	2
2	large cloves garlic, minced	2
1	onion, thinly sliced	1
1 tbsp	minced gingerroot	15 mL
2 tsp	each curry powder and granulated sugar	10 mL
3/4 tsp	each ground cumin and ground coriander	4 mL
1/2 tsp	pepper or hot chili sauce or hot pepper sauce	2 mL
3/4 cup	vegetable stock	175 mL
1	each sweet green and red pepper, cut in thin strips	1
6 oz	firm tofu, cubed	175 g
2 cups	bean sprouts (5 oz/150 g)	500 mL
1/2 cup	sliced green onions	125 mL
1/4 cup	coarsely chopped fresh basil and/or coriander (cilantro)	50 mL
1/4 cup	sodium-reduced soy sauce	50 mL
1 tbsp	fresh lime juice	15 mL

1 Soak noodles in hot water for 20 minutes; drain. Meanwhile, in large nonstick skillet or wok, heat 1 tsp (5 mL) of the oil over medium heat; cook egg, stirring, until scrambled and set. Remove to plate. Cut into strips and keep warm.

2 In same skillet, heat remaining oil over medium-high heat; stir-fry garlic, onion, ginger, curry powder, sugar, cumin, ground coriander, pepper and 2 tbsp (25 mL) of the stock for 2 minutes. Add sweet peppers, tofu and 2 tbsp (25 mL) more of the stock; stir-fry for 2 to 3 minutes or until peppers are slightly softened.

3 Add drained noodles, remaining stock, half of the bean sprouts, the green onions, half of the basil, the soy sauce and lime juice; stir-fry until well coated. Stir in egg strips. Serve garnished with remaining bean sprouts and basil. *Makes 4 servings.*

Per serving:

calories	352
protein	17 g
total fat	10 g
saturated fat	2 g
cholesterol	108 mg
carbohydrate	52 g
dietary fiber	3 g
sodium	762 mg

R.D.I. Vit A 19%, D 9%, E 8%, C 135%, Folate 34%, Ca 15% (163 mg), Iron 51%, Zinc 23%.

Canada's Food Guide Serving:
1 🌾 2¾ 🥕 ¾ 🍗

Chinese Noodle and Shrimp Party Platter

I served this at a summer buffet party for my daughter, Susie, and her student friends. The menu included grilled flank steak, sliced tomatoes with fresh basil and chèvre and Black Bean and Corn Salad (page 45). They all raved about this dish.

1	pkg (375 g) thin egg noodles or precooked (steamed) Chinese noodles	1
2 cups	coarsely shredded carrots	500 mL
2 cups	julienned seeded peeled cucumbers (1-1/2-inch/4 cm strips)	500 mL
5 cups	bean sprouts (12 oz/375 g)	1.25 L
1/2 cup	chopped fresh coriander	125 mL
1/4 cup	chopped fresh mint	50 mL
1 lb	large cooked peeled shrimp	500 g
1/4 cup	chopped peanuts (optional)	50 mL
Dressing:		
1/2 cup	sodium-reduced soy sauce	125 mL
1/4 cup	rice vinegar	50 mL
1 tbsp	sake or rice wine or scotch	15 mL
2 tbsp	granulated sugar	25 mL
2 tbsp	dark roasted sesame oil	25 mL
1/4 tsp	hot chili paste or hot pepper sauce	1 mL

1 Cook noodles according to package directions until tender yet firm; drain and rinse with water until cold. Drain well and transfer to center of very large platter.

2 Dressing: In small bowl, mix together soy sauce, vinegar, sake, sugar, oil and hot chili paste until sugar dissolves. Pour half of the dressing over noodles and toss to mix.

3 Arrange carrots and cucumber around noodles. Place bean sprouts on top of noodles; sprinkle with coriander and mint. Top with shrimp, and peanuts (if using).

4 Just before serving, drizzle with remaining dressing and toss lightly.
Makes 10 servings (1-1/2 cups /375 mL each).

Make ahead: Through step 3, cover and refrigerate for up to 6 hours.

Per serving:

calories	281
protein	20 g
total fat	6 g
saturated fat	1 g
cholesterol	130 mg
carbohydrate	37 g
dietary fiber	4 g
sodium	761 mg

R.D.I. Vit A 67%, E 3%, C 20%, Folate 23%, Ca 4% (47 mg), Iron 20%, Zinc 18%.

Canada's Food Guide Serving:
1¼ 🌾 1½ 🥕 1 🍖

Bone Up with These Facts on Calcium

How Much Calcium Do You Need?

In 1997 higher recommendations for calcium intake were released. Meeting these higher levels is a challenge, particularly for women, many of whom get less than 700 mg daily.

1997 Daily Calcium Recommendations*

Ages 9 to 18	1300 mg
Ages 19 to 50	1000 mg
Age 50 plus	1200 mg

*These recommendations were made by a Calcium Review Committee of the Food and Nutrition Board of the U.S. National Academy of Science, which included Canadian representatives. Health Canada plans to consider these recommendations when updating Canadian Nutrient Recommendations in the future.

The recipes in this book include a variety of calcium-rich foods — milk, cheese, yogurt, beans and dark green vegetables — because many Canadians, particularly women, aren't getting enough calcium, a crucial component of life-long bone health. In Canada, one in four women and one in eight men are at risk of developing osteoporosis, a debilitating disease in which bones become thin and porous and fracture easily. And there's mounting evidence that calcium is important for healthy blood pressure as well.

The Best Sources of Calcium

Milk products are the best dietary sources of calcium not only because they contain large amounts of calcium but also because of the vitamin D found in milk. Vitamin D is closely linked to the proper absorption and utilization of calcium. (See page 97.)

Other foods contribute to calcium intake but few can deliver the calcium of milk products. The calcium in spinach, for instance, is of little benefit because spinach contains a lot of oxalate, a substance that binds with the calcium making it largely unavailable. The same goes for the calcium in beet greens, sweet potatoes and rhubarb. However, the calcium in other plant sources like broccoli, kale and bok choy is well absorbed. It is difficult to meet the new calcium recommendations unless you consume 2 to 3 servings of milk products daily.

Don't Do Dairy?

If you can't or choose not to eat or drink milk products, include as many servings of non-dairy sources of calcium as possible and consider taking a calcium supplement.

Calcium Supplement Guide

- Calcium pills are sold as calcium carbonate, calcium gluconate or calcium lactate. These pills contain varying amounts of pure or elemental calcium. Always buy according to elemental calcium content, not the weight of the whole pill.
- Take only what you think you need to top up your diet, probably not more than 500 to 1000 mg of elemental calcium daily.

- Extra calcium is best obtained from a separate calcium supplement, not a multi-vitamin preparation. Don't take two or three multi-vitamin tablets for extra calcium as you run the risk of getting too much of other nutrients such as vitamin D. While it's a good idea to include extra vitamin D when you take a separate calcium supplement, don't exceed 400 IU per day.
- Drink extra water to reduce risk of developing kidney stones and prevent excess calcium settling in soft tissues.
- Take supplements between meals to increase absorption and to avoid interference with iron absorption.
- Avoid taking calcium along with bulk-forming laxatives. They interfere with calcium absorption.

Top Food Choices for Calcium

Dairy Sources	mg calcium
• milk, 1 cup (250 mL)	300
• evaporated skim milk, 1 cup (250 mL)	746
• cheese, 1-1/2 oz (45 g)	325
• yogurt, 3/4 cup (175 mL) 1% to 2%, plain	300
• yogurt, 2% fruit-flavored, 3/4 cup (175 mL)	250
• processed cheese, 45 g or 2 thin slices	225
• cottage cheese, 2% MF, 1/2 cup (125 mL)	75

Non-Dairy Sources	mg calcium
• tofu set with calcium sulphate, 1/2 cup (125 mL)	110
• salmon with crushed bones, half 213 g can	225
• 8 small sardines, 3 oz (90 g)	165
• 7 large scallops, 3 oz (90 g)	30

Non-Dairy Sources (continued)	mg calcium
1/2 c (125 mL) cooked	
• bok choy	80
• kale	45
• green cabbage	26
• broccoli	38
• brussels sprouts	30
• cauliflower	17
• rutabaga	36
• almonds, 1/4 cup, (50 g)	95
• sesame seeds, 1/4 cup, (50 g)	50
• sunflower seeds, 1/4 cup, (50 g)	40
• baked beans, navy beans, 3/4 cup (175 mL)	100
• pinto beans, chick-peas, kidney beans, 3/4 cup (175 mL)	50

Wild Mushroom and Spinach Lasagna

This lasagna is my favorite, probably because of the woodsy, gutsy flavor of porcini mushrooms, combined with an abundance of regular mushrooms. Porcini are available, dried, in some supermarkets and many specialty food stores.

2	pkg (300 g each) frozen spinach, thawed	2
9	lasagna noodles	9
1/4 cup	freshly grated Parmesan cheese	50 mL
Mushroom Filling:		
1 oz	dried porcini mushrooms (about 1-1/2 cups/375 mL)	30 g
1 tsp	olive oil	5 mL
1	medium onion, finely chopped	1
3	cloves garlic, minced	3
1 tsp	dried thyme	5 mL
1/4 tsp	each salt and pepper	1 mL
2 lb	fresh mushrooms, thickly sliced	1 kg
Cheese Sauce:		
4 cups	1% milk	1 L
1/2 cup	all-purpose flour	125 mL
1/2 tsp	each salt and pepper	2 mL
Pinch	ground nutmeg	Pinch
2 cups	grated part-skim mozzarella cheese	500 mL

Per serving:

calories	447
protein	28 g
total fat	12 g
saturated fat	6 g
cholesterol	30 mg
carbohydrate	60 g
dietary fiber	7 g
sodium	706 mg

R.D.I. Vit A 68%, D 28%, E 12%, C 25%, Folate 53%, Ca 60% (656 mg), Iron 31%, Zinc 47%.

Canada's Food Guide Serving:
2 🌾 3 🥕 1½ 🥛

1 Remove stems from spinach; squeeze out liquid and coarsely chop. Set aside.

2 Mushroom Filling: Quickly rinse dried mushrooms in sieve under cold water to remove any grit; place in bowl. Cover with 1 cup (250 mL) very hot water; let stand for 20 to 30 minutes or until very soft. Reserve liquid; chop large mushrooms.

3 Meanwhile, in large nonstick skillet, heat oil over medium heat; cook onion, garlic, thyme, salt and pepper for 3 minutes, stirring. Increase heat to high. Add fresh mushrooms; cook, stirring often, for 15 to 20 minutes or until all liquid is evaporated and mushrooms are golden. Stir in soaked porcini mushrooms. Set aside.

4 Cheese Sauce: Pour 1 cup (250 mL) of the milk into nonstick saucepan. Whisking

constantly, slowly sprinkle flour over milk. Stir in remaining milk, salt, pepper and nutmeg; whisk over medium-high heat until boiling. Reduce heat to low; stir until thickened. Stir in mozzarella and 1/2 cup (125 mL) reserved mushroom liquid.

5 Meanwhile, in large pot of boiling water, cook lasagna noodles for about 10 minutes or until almost tender; drain and refresh under cold running water. Drain again.

6 Line bottom of lightly greased 13- x 9-inch (3 L) baking dish with 3 noodles. Top with one-third of the cheese sauce. Arrange half of the mushroom filling over top. Layer with 3 lasagna noodles, half of the remaining sauce, then all the spinach. Top with final layer of noodles, remaining mushroom filling and remaining sauce. Sprinkle Parmesan evenly over top.

7 Bake in 375°F (190°C) oven for 45 minutes or until golden on top and bubbling. Let stand for 10 minutes before serving. *Makes 6 servings.*
Make ahead: Through step 6, cover and refrigerate for up to 1 day. Remove from refrigerator 30 minutes before baking.

Vitamin D: How To Get It

Vitamin D plays a crucial role in the development and protection of healthy bones since it is absolutely essential for the absorption of calcium. It is different from most vitamins, however, in that it doesn't all have to come from food. Most of your daily requirement for vitamin D can be made from a reaction in your skin upon exposure to sunlight. During the summer months, 15 to 20 minutes of sun exposure on your hands and face, using no sunscreen, can produce adequate vitamin D.

Trouble is, between November and March in Canada, the sun's rays are not strong enough to produce vitamin D. And sun exposure in the warmer months is limited now that sunscreens and cover-up clothing are widely used.

It is therefore now more important than ever that we get vitamin D from foods. Unfortunately, the list of vitamin D-containing foods is short. Milk and margarine are the most widely used food sources. If you don't eat either of these, consider taking a supplement.

Daily Vitamin D Recommendations From Food

Recommendations for vitamin D intake released in 1997 doubled the amount previously recommended for adults.

1997 Vitamin D Recommendations*

Birth to 50	5 mcg (200 IU)
Age 51 to 70	10 mcg (400 IU)
Age 71 plus	15 mcg (600 IU)

*These recommendations were made by a Vitamin D Review Committee of the Food and Nutrition Board of the U.S. National Academy of Science, which included Canadian representatives. Health Canada plans to consider these recommendations when updating Canadian Nutrient Recommendations.

Dietary Sources of Vitamin D

Excellent Sources
(at least 1.25 mcg or 50 IU)
- milk (cow's),* 1 cup (250 mL)
- margarine, 2 tsp (10 mL)
- salmon, 3 oz (90 g)

Sources (at least 0.25 mcg or 10 IU)
- egg yolk, 1

*Vitamin D is not added to the milk used to make ice cream, yogurt and cheese.

Vitamin D Supplements

Vitamin D is one of the more toxic vitamins. As a general guide, don't supplement in excess of 400 IU daily. Multivitamin preparations commonly contain between 200 and 400 IU.

Grilled Italian Sausage and Red Peppers
with Penne

I came upon this winning flavor combination one Labour Day when using up what was left in our cottage refrigerator. Grilling the sausages and peppers adds extra flavor. However, you can also cook them in a skillet.

*Substitution Tip

Instead of fresh dill or basil, add 1 tsp (5 mL) dried basil with the garlic and 1/2 cup (125 mL) fresh parsley with the salt.

Lower-Fat Tip

The fat content of sausages varies considerably. An average was used in this recipe. Here 12 grams of fat in each serving is from the sausages. This can be reduced by half if you use leaner sausages.

Per serving:

calories	604
protein	29 g
total fat	19 g
saturated fat	6 g
cholesterol	42 mg
carbohydrate	80 g
dietary fiber	7 g
sodium	909 mg

R.D.I. Vit A 44%, E 6%, C 262%, Folate 21%, Ca 12% (136 mg), Iron 24%, Zinc 25%.

Canada's Food Guide Serving:

3 🌾 3 🥕 1 🍗

12 oz	hot Italian sausages	375 g
2	large sweet red peppers	2
1 tbsp	olive oil	15 mL
1 cup	chopped onion	250 mL
12 oz	penne	375 g
4	large cloves garlic, finely chopped	4
3	large tomatoes, chopped	3
1/2 cup	chopped fresh dill or basil*	125 mL
1/2 tsp	each salt and pepper	2 mL
1/3 cup	grated light (19%) old Cheddar-style or Parmesan cheese	75 mL

1 Prick sausages all over. Quarter and seed peppers. Place peppers on greased grill over medium heat; close lid and cook for 5 minutes. Move peppers to upper rack if possible. Place sausages on grill; close lid and cook for 20 minutes or until sausages are no longer pink in center, turning peppers and sausages after 10 minutes. Slice sausages; cut peppers into chunks.

2 Meanwhile, in large nonstick skillet, heat oil over medium heat; cook onion for 10 to 15 minutes or until tender, stirring occasionally.

3 Meanwhile, in large pot of boiling water, cook penne until tender but firm; drain well.

4 Add garlic to onion; increase heat to high. Add tomatoes; cook, stirring occasionally, for about 2 minutes or until heated through. Add dill, red peppers, sausages, penne, salt and pepper; toss to mix. Serve sprinkled with cheese.
Makes 4 servings (3 cups/750 mL each).

Make ahead: Through step 2, cover and refrigerate for up to 4 hours.

Vegetable Tortellini Casserole
with Cheese Topping

Consider this casserole when you want a quick dish that all ages will enjoy. It's perfect for entertaining families and is a good choice when you want a change from lasagna.

1 tbsp	olive oil	15 mL
2	cloves garlic, minced	2
1	each medium onion and carrot, chopped	1
1	each sweet green and red pepper, chopped	1
1 tsp	each dried basil and oregano	5 mL
1/4 tsp	each salt and pepper	1 mL
1	can (28 oz/796 mL) stewed tomatoes	1
1	can (5-1/2 oz/156 mL) tomato paste	1
1 cup	corn kernels	250 mL
1 lb	cheese-filled tortellini	500 g
1 cup	grated part-skim mozzarella cheese	250 mL
1/4 cup	freshly grated Parmesan cheese	50 mL
2 tbsp	chopped fresh parsley	25 mL

1 In large nonstick skillet, heat oil over medium heat; cook garlic, onion, carrot, sweet peppers, basil, oregano, salt and pepper, stirring, for 5 minutes or until softened.

2 Stir in tomatoes and tomato paste; bring to boil. Reduce heat and simmer, uncovered, for 15 to 20 minutes or until thickened. Stir in corn.

3 Meanwhile, in large pot of boiling water, cook tortellini for 8 to 10 minutes or according to package directions. Drain and add to tomato sauce; pour into 13- x 9-inch (3 L) shallow baking dish.

4 Toss together mozzarella, Parmesan and parsley; sprinkle over casserole. Bake, uncovered, in 400°F (200°C) oven for 15 minutes or until bubbling and golden. *Makes 6 servings.*

Make ahead: Through step 3, cover and refrigerate for up to 2 days; remove from refrigerator 45 minutes before baking.

Menu Suggestion

Serve with Spinach Salad (page 38) and/or Indonesian Coleslaw (page 43) or asparagus.

Freezing Instructions

Wrap and freeze the cooked casserole for up to 2 weeks. Thaw in the refrigerator for up to 48 hours.

Per serving:

calories	499
protein	25 g
total fat	14 g
saturated fat	6 g
cholesterol	75 mg
carbohydrate	72 g
dietary fiber	8 g
sodium	1085 mg

R.D.I. Vit A 75%, E 26%, C 162%, Folate 24%, Ca 41% (453 mg), Iron 32%, Zinc 33%.

Canada's Food Guide Serving:

2½ 4 ¾

Penne with Sweet Red Peppers, Black Olives and Arugula

Penne, the tubular pasta with a quill-shaped end, or rigatoni, the very fat tubular pasta, or large shell pasta work well in this dish. Serve hot or at room temperature.

2	sweet red peppers	2
8 oz	penne or rigatoni (about 3-1/2 cups/875 mL)	250 g
2	cloves garlic, minced	2
2 tbsp	olive oil	25 mL
3 cups	arugula or watercress leaves (about 1 bunch)	750 mL
12	pitted black olives	12
	Pepper	
1/2 cup	freshly grated Parmesan cheese	125 mL

1 Broil red peppers, turning often, for 20 minutes or until charred. Let cool. Holding peppers over bowl to catch juices, peel off blackened skin. Core and seed; cut into strips. Set aside.

2 In large pot of boiling water, cook rigatoni for 8 to 10 minutes or until tender but firm; drain well.

3 Meanwhile, in small microwaveable dish, microwave garlic with oil on High for 1 minute. In large bowl, combine garlic mixture, red peppers, arugula and olives. Add pasta; toss well. Add enough reserved pepper juice to moisten pasta. Season with pepper to taste and sprinkle with Parmesan; toss to mix. *Makes 4 servings.*

Per serving:

calories	371
protein	14 g
total fat	13 g
saturated fat	4 g
cholesterol	10 g
carbohydrate	49 g
dietary fiber	4 g
sodium	361 mg

R.D.I. Vit A 33%, E 15%, C 163%, Folate 22%, Ca 24% (267 mg), Iron 12%, Zinc 17%.

Canada's Food Guide Serving:

2 🌾 1¾ 🥕 ¼ 🥛

Skillet Pork Curry with Apples and Chinese Noodles

I usually have a package of precooked, steamed (not fried) Chinese or chow mein noodles in my refrigerator because they cook in less than 3 minutes (not to mention the fact that my son John loves them!). They are available in the produce section of most supermarkets. Any other very thin egg or regular noodle also works well, as does pasta. You could even serve this over rice instead of the noodles. Choose Red Delicious or Northern Spy apples.

Nut Alert

Avoid nuts that show signs of mold or shriveling on the shell. Moldy peanuts harbor aflatoxin, a cancer-causing agent.

1-1/2 lb	pork tenderloin or boneless fast-fry chops	750 g
1 tbsp	vegetable oil	15 mL
1 tsp	each ground coriander, ground cumin and turmeric	5 mL
1/2 tsp	each salt and red pepper flakes	2 mL
1/2 tsp	fennel seeds, crushed	2 mL
1	large onion, sliced	1
2	cloves garlic, minced	2
1 tbsp	minced gingerroot	15 mL
2	red-skinned apples, cored and cubed	2
1 cup	chicken stock	250 mL
1 tbsp	all-purpose flour	15 mL
1 cup	1% or 2% plain yogurt	250 mL
1 tbsp	liquid honey	15 mL
1	pkg (350 g) precooked Chinese noodles	1
1/3 cup	chopped fresh coriander (cilantro) or parsley	75 mL
1/4 cup	each raisins and chopped peanuts	50 mL

1 Trim fat from pork; cut across the grain into 3/4-inch (2 cm) wide strips.

2 In nonstick skillet, heat 1 tsp (5 mL) of the oil over high heat; brown half of the pork. Transfer to plate. Repeat with another 1 tsp (5 mL) oil and remaining pork.

3 Reduce heat to medium-low. Add remaining oil, ground coriander, cumin, turmeric, salt, red pepper flakes and fennel seeds; cook, stirring, for 1 minute. Add onion, garlic and ginger; cook, stirring often, for 5 minutes.

Per serving:

calories	478
protein	39 g
total fat	11 g
saturated fat	2 g
cholesterol	105 mg
carbohydrate	56 g
dietary fiber	4 g
sodium	411 mg

R.D.I. Vit A 2%, E 13%, C 7%, Folate 14%, Ca 10% (115 mg), Iron 22%, Zinc 44%.

Canada's Food Guide Serving:

1½ 🌾 1 🥕 ¼ 🥛 2 🍖

4 Add apples; cook, stirring often, for 5 minutes or until onion is tender. Pour in stock and bring to boil; reduce heat and stir in pork. Cover and simmer for about 3 minutes or until pork is barely pink inside.

5 Sprinkle flour over yogurt; add honey and stir to mix well. Stir into pork mixture.

6 Meanwhile, in large pot of boiling water, cook noodles for 1 to 2 minutes or until tender; drain and add to pork mixture, tossing to mix. Transfer to large platter. Sprinkle with coriander, raisins and peanuts. *Makes 6 servings.*

Lemon, Dill and Parsley Orzo

Tiny rice-shaped pasta adds novelty
to the meal and makes a great side dish for chicken and fish.

1 cup	orzo pasta	250 mL
2 tbsp	each chopped fresh dill and parsley	25 mL
2 tbsp	chopped green onions	25 mL
1 tbsp	olive oil	15 mL
1/2 tsp	grated lemon rind	2 mL
1 tbsp	fresh lemon juice	15 mL

1 In large pot of boiling salted water, cook orzo for 8 to 10 minutes or until tender but firm; drain well.

2 Toss with dill, parsley, onions, oil, lemon rind and juice. Season with salt and pepper to taste. *Makes 4 servings.*

Make ahead: Best served immediately. For a make-ahead dish, use rice instead of orzo. Cook long-grain white rice for 20 minutes, brown rice for 40 minutes.

Wild and Basmati Rice with Lemon and Herbs

Substitute 1/2 cup (125 mL) each brown basmati rice or long-grain brown rice and wild rice for pasta. Cook wild and brown rice in large saucepan of boiling water for 35 to 40 minutes or until wild rice splays and brown is tender; drain well. Continue with step 2. *Make ahead:* Cover and refrigerate for up to 1 day.

Per serving:	
calories	191
protein	5 g
total fat	4 g
saturated fat	1 g
cholesterol	0 mg
carbohydrate	32 g
dietary fiber	2 g
sodium	114 mg

R.D.I. Vit A 1%, E 4%, C 8%, Folate 6%, Ca 1% (14 mg), Iron 5%, Zinc 7%.

Canada's Food Guide Serving:
1½ 🌾

Going for Gold with Healthy Eating

Healthy eating can contribute to a child's success at sports, but sports nutrition is fraught with misinformation.

HEALTHY EATING TIPS: Sports Nutrition for Kids

- The pre-game or pre-event meal isn't what wins the game. It's what the athlete eats, day in and day out, all year round that makes the most difference. And what should this be? The same healthy eating pattern we all should be eating. (See page 1.)
- Sufficient protein is easily obtained through healthy eating; protein supplements are not needed except in a few specialized situations.
- Fluid is important for maintaining strength and stamina. Dehydration can debilitate an athlete quickly, especially in hot and humid conditions. Don't wait until a child is thirsty to provide fluid. The child should start sipping water at least 2 hours before an event. Have water available during and after the event too. The amount varies from child to child, but 4 to 8 glasses of extra water is a good guideline.
- Water is the best fluid to keep a person hydrated. Cold water is okay; it is absorbed more quickly, and contrary to myth, it does not cause cramps.
- Sports drinks are recommended in events lasting more than an hour.
- The main purpose of a pre-competition meal is to prevent the discomfort of hunger and to keep blood sugars from falling to a point where tiredness and poor concentration set in. Plan a small meal of easily digested foods, eaten at least 2 hours before an event. Since fat and protein slow down digestion, the meal should consist mostly of carbohydrate-rich foods such as bread, cereal, pasta, rice, vegetables and fruit.
- Tournaments present extra problems, especially if they are out of town and there are long waits between games or events. Resist the temptation to rely on higher-fat fast foods for meals and to nibble on typical ball park or arena snacks such as donuts, chips, chocolate bars and pop.

Beef, Tomato and Mushroom Rigatoni

I updated my family's favorite beef and tomato spaghetti sauce by adding lots of mushrooms, garlic and chopped fresh basil. For a vegetarian version, omit the beef and add tofu, chick-peas or cooked beans. You could also add dried mushrooms, sun-dried tomatoes and/or a sweet green pepper.

1 lb	extra-lean ground beef	500 g
2	onions, chopped	2
6	cloves garlic, minced	6
1 lb	thickly sliced mushrooms (6 cups/1.5 L)	500 g
2 tsp	dried Italian herb seasoning or dried oregano	10 mL
1	can (5-1/2 oz/156 mL) tomato paste	1
1	can (28 oz/796 mL) tomatoes	1
1 tsp	granulated sugar	5 mL
1/2 cup	chopped fresh basil or 1 tsp (5 mL) dried	125 mL
1/4 cup	chopped fresh flat-leaf parsley	50 mL
1 tsp	each salt and pepper	5 mL
12 oz	rigatoni (6 cups/1.5 L)*	375 g
1	bag (10 oz/284 g) fresh spinach, chopped (optional)	1
1/3 cup	freshly grated Parmesan cheese	75 mL

* Substitution Tip

Rigatoni, the fat tubular pasta, works well in this recipe, but any kind can be used.

1 In large nonstick skillet, brown beef over medium heat; pour off all fat. Stir in onions, garlic, mushrooms and Italian seasoning; cook, stirring occasionally, until onions are softened, about 8 minutes.

2 Stir in tomato paste, tomatoes (breaking up with back of spoon), sugar and half of the basil (or dried if using); bring to boil. Reduce heat and simmer for 10 minutes. Add water if too thick. Stir in remaining fresh basil, parsley, salt and pepper.

3 Meanwhile, in large pot of boiling water, cook rigatoni until tender but firm, 8 to 10 minutes. Add spinach (if using): cook for 1 minute. Drain well and toss with sauce. Sprinkle each serving with Parmesan cheese. *Makes 6 servings.*

Make ahead: Refrigerate up to one day. Reheat, stirring in hot water if mixture is dry.

Per serving:

calories	434
protein	28 g
total fat	9 g
saturated fat	3 g
cholesterol	44 mg
carbohydrate	62 g
dietary fiber	7 g
sodium	770 mg

R.D.I. Vit A 17%, E 19%, C 55%, Folate 22%, Ca 15% (164 mg), Iron 37%, Zinc 57%.

Canada's Food Guide Serving:

2 🌾 3½ 🥕 ¾ 🍗

Spicy Chicken with Broccoli and Chinese Noodles

This meal-in-one dish looks pretty served on a platter garnished with fresh coriander.

2 tbsp	minced gingerroot	25 mL
2 tbsp	rice wine, sake or scotch	25 mL
1 tbsp	cornstarch	15 mL
1 tsp	sesame oil	5 mL
1-1/2 lb	boneless skinless chicken cut in 1-inch (2.5 cm) pieces	750 g
6 cups	broccoli pieces (1-inch/2.5 cm), 1 lb (500 g)	1.5 L
1	pkg (10 oz/284 g) precooked Chinese noodles	1
1 tbsp	each vegetable oil and minced garlic (3 cloves)	15 mL
1/2 tsp	crushed red pepper flakes	2 mL
1	can (10 oz/284 mL) water chestnuts, drained and sliced (about 1 cup/250 mL) or celery	1
1/4 cup	chopped fresh coriander (cilantro)	50 mL
Seasoning Sauce:		
3/4 cup	chicken stock	175 mL
1/4 cup	soy sauce	50 mL
2 tbsp	rice vinegar	25 mL
1 tbsp	granulated sugar	15 mL
2 tsp	each sesame oil and cornstarch	10 mL

1 In bowl, stir together ginger, rice wine, cornstarch and sesame oil until smooth. Stir in chicken; cover and refrigerate for 20 minutes or for up to 2 hours.

2 In saucepan of boiling water, cook broccoli for 2 minutes; drain and set aside.

3 Seasoning Sauce: Meanwhile, in small bowl, combine chicken stock, soy sauce, rice vinegar, sugar, sesame oil and cornstarch; set aside.

4 In large pot of boiling water, cook noodles for 3 minutes or according to package directions or until tender yet firm; drain and arrange on heated platter.

5 Meanwhile, in wok, heat oil over high heat; stir-fry chicken mixture for 5 minutes or until chicken is no longer pink inside. Add garlic and red pepper flakes; stir-fry for 30 seconds.

Per serving:
calories	381
protein	35 g
total fat	8 g
saturated fat	1 g
cholesterol	101 mg
carbohydrate	42 g
dietary fiber	4 g
sodium	878 mg

R.D.I. Vit A 11%, E 22%, C 87%, Folate 24%, Ca 5% (52 mg), Iron 19%, Zinc 21%.

Canada's Food Guide Serving:
1¼ 🌾 1¾ 🥕 1 🍗

6 Add water chestnuts and broccoli. Stir sauce; add to chicken mixture. Bring to boil, stirring constantly. Pour over noodles and toss. Sprinkle with coriander. *Makes 6 servings.*

Make ahead: Through step 3 for up to 2 hours.

Two-Cheese Pasta and Tomatoes

Here's an updated and lighter version of the traditional macaroni and cheese.
Keep some in your freezer: it's satisfying on nights when you're too
tired to cook. If you don't have tarragon on hand, use 1/2 tsp (2 mL) dried thyme
plus 1 tsp (5 mL) dried sage.

8 oz	macaroni (2-1/4 cups/550 mL) or penne (3 cups/750 mL)	250 g
1 cup	grated reduced fat (19%) old Cheddar-style cheese	250 mL
1 cup	chopped green onions	250 mL
1/2 cup	freshly grated Parmesan cheese	125 mL
1/3 cup	all-purpose flour	75 mL
1 tbsp	dry mustard	15 mL
1 tsp	dried tarragon	5 mL
1/2 tsp	each salt, pepper and paprika	2 mL
3 cups	1% milk	750 mL
2	tomatoes, chopped (2 cups/500 mL)	2
2 tbsp	chopped fresh parsley (optional)	25 mL

1 In large pot of boiling water, cook macaroni for 10 minutes or until tender but firm; drain.

2 Meanwhile, in bowl, combine Cheddar cheese, onions, Parmesan cheese, flour, mustard, tarragon, salt, pepper and paprika.

3 In large saucepan, heat milk until hot; gradually add cheese mixture, whisking constantly until well combined. Cook over medium heat, stirring constantly, until thickened and bubbly. Stir in macaroni; cook for 2 minutes. Stir in tomatoes. Add parsley (if using). *Makes 6 servings.*

Make ahead: Cover and refrigerate for up to 2 days or freeze for up to 2 weeks.

Two-Cheese Pasta and Tomato Casserole

Prepare through step 2, but add only 1/3 cup (75 mL) of the Parmesan cheese. Continue through step 3, but after stirring in macaroni, transfer to lightly greased 8-inch (2 L) square or 11- x 7-inch (2 L) baking dish. Place tomatoes over top; sprinkle with remaining Parmesan cheese. Bake in 375°F (190°C) oven for 10 minutes. Broil for 5 minutes or until cheese melts and tomatoes are hot. Sprinkle with parsley (if using).

Per serving:

calories	335
protein	20 g
total fat	9 g
saturated fat	5 g
cholesterol	23 mg
carbohydrate	44 g
dietary fiber	3 g
sodium	557 mg

R.D.I. Vit A 13%, D 21%, E 4%, C 23%, Folate 13%, Ca 40% (437 mg), Iron 13%, Zinc 16%.

Canada's Food Guide Serving:

1¾ 🌾 ½ 🥕 1 🥛

Vegetarian Main Dishes

Mediterranean Vegetable Stew

Vegetarian Paella

Artichoke, Goat Cheese, Fresh Tomato and Onion Pizza

Leek and Rice Pilaf

Potato Vegetable Curry

Sweet Potato, Squash and Bulgur

Mushroom Lentil Burgers

Chick-Pea Burgers

Sunflower Veggie Tofu Burgers

Grilled Portobello Mushroom Burgers

Coconut Rice

Mexican Brown Rice with Tomatoes and Corn

Couscous with Tomato and Basil

Tuscan White Kidney Beans with Sage

Quinoa Pilaf

Tofu Vegetable Shish Kebabs

Lentil and Vegetable Curry

Barley and Black Bean Casserole

Nutrition Notes

Vegetarians: "Key Issues for Vegetarians"

Soybeans: "Soybeans Anyone?"

Gas: "Take a Pass on Gas"

Heartburn: "Put a Stop to Heartburn"

Key Issues for Vegetarians

Kinds of Vegetarian Eating

- Vegan diets are the most limited, excluding all foods of animal origin, including animal by-products like gelatin and honey.
- Lacto-vegetarian diets allow for the use of milk products.
- Lacto-ovo vegetarian diets are more liberal, allowing milk and egg products.

Interest in vegetarian eating is growing, even among people who aren't vegetarians. Since vegetarian meals consist primarily of the foods most often recommended for good health, this trend is a positive one. However, vegetarian diets are no guarantee for good health. What you eat matters as much as what you don't eat. And at certain times — especially during childhood, adolescence and pregnancy — vegan diets are not appropriate because it is difficult to get sufficient calories, calcium and iron on such a diet.

HEALTHY EATING TIPS: Vegetarians

- Vegetarian diets should be based on the same principles of healthy eating as meat-based diets, with lower-fat, higher-fiber foods emphasized.
- If you include milk, yogurt, cheese and/or eggs in your diet, there is no need to worry about either the quantity or quality of protein. Only vegans need to ensure they eat a variety of vegetable proteins throughout the day (but not necessarily at each meal) to provide complete protein. Tofu and legumes (dried beans, peas and lentils) are some of the best sources of vegetable protein.
- Children, adolescents, pregnant and breast-feeding women are advised to include milk products and/or eggs in their diet.
- Include a source of vitamin C at each meal to help you absorb the non-heme iron in grains, legumes (dried beans, peas and lentils), vegetables, dried fruit and enriched products like cereal and pasta. (See page 214 for sources of vitamin C.)
- If you eat no animal products whatsoever, make sure you get enough calcium and vitamin D (see page 97) and vitamin B12. Vegans should consume a supplement of at least 1 microgram of vitamin B12 a day or the equivalent in vitamin B12-fortified foods.
- To ensure sufficient intake of zinc, particularly if folic acid and iron supplements are taken, be sure to eat nuts, legumes (dried beans, peas and lentils), whole grains, milk and egg yolk.

Mediterranean Vegetable Stew

Potatoes are often taken for granted, but in this stew they not only balance the acidity of the tomatoes, their skins add color and flavor, as do the zucchini and eggplant skins. Therefore, peel them only if the skins are tough or blemished.

1 tbsp	olive oil	15 mL
Half	onion, sliced	Half
3	tomatoes, coarsely chopped	3
1 tsp	each dried basil, salt and pepper	5 mL
4	red potatoes, cut in 1/2-inch (1 cm) cubes	4
1	sweet red or green pepper, chopped	1
2 cups	each cubed eggplant and zucchini	500 mL
1/4 cup	chopped fresh basil or parsley	50 mL
1/4 cup	freshly grated Parmesan cheese	50 mL

1 In large nonstick skillet, heat oil over medium heat; cook onion, stirring occasionally, for 5 minutes or until softened. Add tomatoes, basil, salt and pepper; cover and cook for 5 minutes.

2 Add potatoes and red pepper (and 1/4 cup/50 mL water if necessary). Reduce heat to medium-low; simmer, covered, for 10 minutes. Add eggplant; simmer, covered, for 10 minutes, stirring occasionally. Add zucchini; simmer, covered, for 5 minutes or until vegetables are tender.

3 Stir in basil. Top each serving with cheese. *Makes 4 servings.*

Make ahead: Through step 2, cover and refrigerate for up to 1 day; reheat to serve.

Per serving:

calories	240
protein	8 g
total fat	6 g
saturated fat	2 g
cholesterol	5 mg
carbohydrate	42 g
dietary fiber	6 g
sodium	709 mg

R.D.I. Vit A 24%, E 6%, C 140%, Folate 20%, Ca 12% (132 mg), Iron 18%, Zinc 11%.

Canada's Food Guide Serving:
4 🥕

111

Vegetarian Paella

This special dish is chock full of colorful vegetables and saffron. Paella is typically made with short-grain rice, which has a creamy texture, but it can be made with long-grain rice, which doesn't stick together. If making ahead of time, use long-grain rice. You might like to add asparagus and green beans, too; just add along with the chick-peas.

1 tsp	saffron threads	5 mL
2 tbsp	olive oil	25 mL
5	cloves garlic, minced	5
2	carrots, peeled and thickly sliced on the diagonal	2
1	large onion, chopped	1
2 cups	short-grain rice (Valencia or Arborio) or long-grain converted rice	500 mL
2	large tomatoes, coarsely chopped (or 1 can 19 oz/540 mL tomatoes, undrained and chopped)	2
4 cups	vegetable stock	1 L
1/2 cup	dry white wine	125 mL
10	dry-packed sun-dried tomato halves, coarsely chopped	10
2	bay leaves	2
1	can (19 oz/540 mL) chick-peas, drained and rinsed	1
1	can (14 oz/398 mL) artichokes, drained and quartered	1
1	sweet red pepper, roasted and sliced	1
1 cup	each frozen peas and corn kernels	250 mL
1/4 cup	black olives, pitted and halved (optional)	50 mL
1/2 cup	coarsely chopped fresh coriander (cilantro) or parsley	125 mL
1/4 tsp	each salt and pepper	1 mL

1 Soak saffron threads in 2 tbsp (25 mL) very hot water for at least 15 minutes or for up to 1 hour.

2 In large nonstick skillet, heat oil over medium heat; cook garlic, carrots and onion, stirring occasionally, for 5 minutes or until softened. Stir in rice.

Sodium-Reduced Cooking

To reduce sodium by nearly half, use water or homemade stock with no added salt in place of the vegetable stock.

Cooking Tip

For roasted red pepper, see Cooking Tip on page 32.

Per serving:

calories	491
protein	15 g
total fat	7 g
saturated fat	1 g
cholesterol	0 mg
carbohydrate	94 g
dietary fiber	9 g
sodium	900 mg

R.D.I. Vit A 78%, E 8%, C 77%, Folate 42%, Ca 7% (76 mg), Iron 21%, Zinc 24%.

Canada's Food Guide Serving:

1¾ 🌾 3 🥕 1 🫘

113

Lower-Fat Tip

Lower-Fat Tip

Plan more meatless meals. Chick-peas and other legumes (dried beans, peas and lentils) are low in fat and a good source of vegetable protein, complex carbohydrates and fiber.

3 Add tomatoes, stock, wine, sun-dried tomatoes, bay leaves and saffron; bring to boil. Reduce heat to low; cover and cook for 15 minutes, stirring occasionally.

4 Add chick-peas, artichokes, red pepper, peas (if serving immediately), corn, and olives (if using); cook, stirring, over low heat for 5 minutes or until vegetables are heated through. Discard bay leaves.

5 Stir in coriander, salt and pepper. (If using long-grain rice, cover loosely with foil and let stand for 20 minutes to absorb some of the liquid.) *Makes 6 servings.*

Make ahead: Through step 4, omitting peas, cover and refrigerate for up to 2 days. Reheat gently, adding peas.

Seafood Paella: Omit chick-peas and corn. Add 1 lb (500 g) shelled and deveined large shrimp (raw or cooked) and 1 lb (500 g) scrubbed mussels in step 3; cover and cook until shrimp are opaque and mussels open. Discard any mussels that don't open.

Vegetarian Dinner Party

Mango Salsa in Mini Phyllo Tarts (page 11)
Roasted Red Pepper and Arugula Spirals (page 32)
Sesame Wasabi Spirals (page 31)
Porcini Mushroom Bisque (page 73)or Sweet Potato and Ginger Soup (page 66)
or Thai Vegetarian Salad (page 44)
Vegetarian Paella (previous page)
Apple Berry Crisp (page 271) or Peach Blueberry Pie (page 279)

Artichoke, Goat Cheese, Fresh Tomato and Onion Pizza

Any kid will tell you that leftover pizza makes a great breakfast. I like this particular combination of toppings for any meal. However, other toppings work well. Frozen pizza dough is available at most supermarkets or make your own crust using the Focaccia recipe on page 246. A pizza base or toasted tortilla can also be used.

12 oz	frozen or homemade pizza dough	375 g
1 cup	grated part-skim mozzarella cheese	250 mL
1 cup	thinly sliced Spanish onion	250 mL
1	can (14 oz/398 mL) artichokes, drained and quartered	1
2	tomatoes, sliced	2
1	sweet red or green pepper, roasted and sliced*	1
1/4 cup	chopped fresh basil or 2 tsp (10 mL) dried	50 mL
1 oz	soft goat cheese (chèvre), crumbled	30 g
Pinch	red pepper flakes	Pinch

1 On lightly floured surface, roll out pizza dough to fit 17- x 11-inch (45 x 28 cm) baking sheet.

2 Sprinkle with mozzarella cheese, onion and artichokes. Top with tomatoes and roasted pepper. Sprinkle with basil, chèvre and red pepper flakes.

3 Bake on bottom rack of 500°F (260°C) oven for 15 minutes or until cheese is bubbly and crust is golden. *Makes 6 servings.*

Make ahead: Through step 2, cover and refrigerate for up to 4 hours.

*Use bottled roasted red peppers or grill or broil red or green peppers, turning often, for 20 to 25 minutes or until charred. Let cool slightly; peel and slice.

Pesto Pizza

Spread 1/3 cup (75 mL) Pesto Sauce (page 85) over pizza base. Top with any combination of pizza toppings, including roasted vegetables, goat cheese, mushrooms and sliced fresh tomatoes; bake as in step 3.

Cooking Tip

Create your own pizza by adding all sorts of toppings. For instance, try blanched green beans or asparagus or cooked sliced potatoes.

Per serving:

calories	256
protein	12 g
total fat	7 g
saturated fat	3 g
cholesterol	16 mg
carbohydrate	38 g
dietary fiber	4 g
sodium	530 mg

R.D.I. Vit A 14%, E 6%, C 53%, Folate 22%, Ca 17% (191 mg), Iron 16%, Zinc 10%.

Canada's Food Guide Serving:
1¾ 🌾 1¼ 🥕 ¼ 🧈

Leek and Rice Pilaf

To Cook Rice

Follow package instructions when available. Rinse rice only if bought in bulk or if using jasmine rice. For each cup (250 mL) of long-grain rice, bring 2 cups (500 mL) water or stock to a boil. Stir in rice; reduce heat, cover and simmer for about 20 minutes for white, 40 minutes for brown, or until water is absorbed and rice is tender. Fluff with a fork. One cup (250 mL) of raw rice yields about 3 cups (750 mL) when cooked. For best results use a heavy saucepan with a tight-fitting lid.

The delicate flavors of leek and fresh dill combined with rice make a satisfying dish.
For a simple meal, serve with sliced tomatoes, feta cheese and crusty bread.

1 tbsp	olive oil	15 mL
4 cups	coarsely chopped leeks (white and light green parts only)	1 L
1 cup	long-grain converted white or brown rice	250 mL
2 cups	boiling water	500 mL
1/2 cup	coarsely chopped fresh dill	125 mL
1/4 tsp	each salt and pepper	1 mL

1 In large heavy saucepan, heat oil over medium heat; cook leeks, stirring often, until translucent and almost tender, about 5 minutes. Stir in rice, then water; bring to boil.

2 Reduce heat, cover and simmer for 20 minutes for white rice (40 minutes for brown rice) or until rice is tender and water absorbed. Stir in dill, salt and pepper.
Makes 4 servings.

Make ahead: Cover and refrigerate for up to 1 day. Add a few tablespoonfuls (15 mL) of water when reheating.

KINDS OF RICE

- White rice is the most common kind. During processing, the bran is removed.
- Brown rice is the most nutritious because it is whole grain and contains the bran. It's higher in fiber and B vitamins than other rice. Regular brown rice takes about 40 minutes to cook. You can also buy a partially cooked whole-grain brown rice that cooks in 25 minutes.
- Instant or pre-cooked rice is white rice that has been cooked then dehydrated. In Canada it can be enriched. It cooks the fastest but doesn't have the texture of regular rice.
- Parboiled rice, often referred to as converted rice, has been processed to force the nutrients from the bran into the center (endosperm) of the rice. It is more nutritious than white rice. When cooked, the grains are firm and separate. White and brown rice can be parboiled.
- Aromatic rices are brown or white long-grain rice with a fragrant nut-like aroma and flavor. The most popular are basmati rice from India and Pakistan and jasmine rice from Thailand.
- Arborio is a short- to medium-grain rice imported from Italy used in risotto. It is cooked by gradually adding liquid while stirring. The cooked rice is creamy on the outside and firm on the inside. Look for the top grade, called superfino.
- Short-grain rice is stickier than long-grain.

Per serving:

calories	221
protein	4 g
total fat	4 g
saturated fat	1 g
cholesterol	0 mg
carbohydrate	42 g
dietary fiber	2 g
sodium	155 mg

R.D.I. Vit E 10%, C 5%, Folate 10%, Ca 5% (50 mg), Iron 7%, Zinc 6%.

Canada's Food Guide Serving:
1¾ 🌾   1 🥕

Potato Vegetable Curry

This curry makes a hearty main course or a tasty side dish. Instead of (or even with) the potatoes, I sometimes use cauliflower. Serve this with basmati rice.

1-1/2 cups	cubed peeled potatoes	375 mL
1 tbsp	vegetable oil	15 mL
2 tsp	cumin seeds	10 mL
2	cloves garlic, minced	2
1	medium onion, thinly sliced	1
2 tsp	minced gingerroot	10 mL
2 tbsp	medium curry paste or 2 tsp (10 mL) curry powder	25 mL
1	small eggplant, diced (about 3 cups/750 mL)	1
1-1/4 cups	cut green beans (2-inch/5 cm lengths), about 4 oz (125 g)	300 mL
1	can (19 oz/540 mL) tomatoes, chopped (undrained)	1
1	pkg (10 oz/284 mL) fresh spinach, stems removed	1
1/4 cup	chopped fresh coriander (cilantro), optional	50 mL
2 tbsp	plain yogurt (preferably extra-thick or Greek-style)	25 mL

1 In saucepan of boiling water, cook potatoes for 6 minutes or until just tender; drain.

2 Meanwhile, in nonstick skillet or wok, heat oil over high heat; stir-fry cumin seeds for 30 seconds. Reduce heat to medium. Add garlic, onion and ginger; stir-fry for 2 minutes. Stir in curry paste; cook for 1 minute.

3 Add eggplant and beans; cook, stirring often, for 2 minutes. Stir in tomatoes; cover and simmer for 10 minutes. Add potato and spinach; cook, covered, for 4 minutes or until vegetables are tender.

4 Remove from heat. Stir in coriander and yogurt. Season with salt and pepper to taste. *Makes 4 main-course or 6 side-dish servings.*

Make ahead: Through step 3, omitting beans and spinach; cover and refrigerate for up to 4 hours. Reheat. Blanch beans in boiling water for 5 minutes; drain and add with spinach; cook until spinach wilts.

Per main-course serving:	
calories	178
protein	7 g
total fat	5 g
saturated fat	1 g
cholesterol	1 mg
carbohydrate	32 g
dietary fiber	7 g
sodium	284 mg

R.D.I. Vit A 62%, E 20%, C 48%, Folate 59%, Ca 17% (186 mg), Iron 36%, Zinc 14%.

Canada's Food Guide Serving:
4¾ 🥕

Sweet Potato, Squash and Bulgur

Thick but juicy, this vibrantly colored dish has a pleasant balance of textures and seasonings. For a main course, top each serving with a spoonful of yogurt, shredded cheese and fresh coriander. As a side dish, serve with roasts or chicken or turkey. This casserole is a great buffet dish.

*Substitution Tip

Instead of fresh tomatoes, you can use 1 can (19 oz/540 mL) chopped tomatoes, drained.

Nutrition Tip

Sweet potatoes and squash are very high in beta carotene, which the body converts to vitamin A. Sweet red peppers are very high in vitamin C.

1/2 cup	bulgur	125 mL
1 tbsp	olive oil	15 mL
1	onion, sliced	1
2	cloves garlic, chopped	2
1 tsp	each cumin seeds, dried oregano and paprika	5 mL
3 cups	cubed peeled butternut or winter squash (10 oz/320 g)	750 mL
1-1/2 cups	cubed peeled sweet potato (8 oz/250 g)	375 mL
1	sweet red or green pepper, chopped	1
2 cups	chopped tomatoes*	500 mL
3/4 cup	vegetable or chicken stock	175 mL
2 tbsp	balsamic vinegar	25 mL

1 In bowl, cover bulgur with 2 cups (500 mL) hot water; let stand for 15 minutes. Drain.

2 Meanwhile, in large nonstick wok or pan, heat oil over medium-high heat; cook onion and garlic, stirring often, for 5 minutes or until onion is softened. Add cumin seeds, oregano and paprika; cook, stirring, for 2 minutes. Add squash, sweet potato and red pepper; cook, stirring, for 2 minutes.

3 Add tomatoes and stock; bring to simmer. Cover and cook for 15 minutes or until vegetables are tender-crisp.

4 Stir in bulgur; simmer for 5 minutes. Stir in vinegar; season with salt and pepper to taste. *Makes 4 main-course or 8 side-dish servings.*

Make ahead: Cover and refrigerate for up to 1 day.

Per main-course serving:

calories	241
protein	6 g
total fat	4 g
saturated fat	1 g
cholesterol	0 mg
carbohydrate	49 g
dietary fiber	7 g
sodium	136 mg

R.D.I. Vit A 191%, E 5%, C 150%, Folate 25%, Ca 8% (91 mg), Iron 21%, Zinc 11%.

Canada's Food Guide Serving:
1 🌾 3½ 🥕

Mushroom Lentil Burgers

Fresh coriander and ground cumin enliven these quick-to-prepare burgers.
Serve with Skillet Sweet Potatoes (page 147) and Spinach with Tomatoes and Cumin (page 139).
Or treat them as a burger and serve in a bun with roasted vegetables and tzatziki
or with the traditional trimmings.

Mushroom Lentil Tortilla Wrap

Spoon unshaped Mushroom Lentil Burger mixture down center of 4 large soft flour tortillas. Cover with sliced tomato, diced avocado and shredded lettuce or spinach leaves. Fold one side, then ends over filling and roll up. *Makes 4 servings.*

Nutrition Tip

Lentils are very high in folate and fiber, and are a good source of protein.

Per serving:

calories	207
protein	11 g
total fat	3 g
saturated fat	trace
cholesterol	0 mg
carbohydrate	35 g
dietary fiber	6 g
sodium	478 mg

R.D.I. Vit A 63%, E 7%, C 8%, Folate 89%, Ca 6% (64 mg), Iron 34%, Zinc 19%.

Canada's Food Guide Serving:
¼ 🌾 1 🥕 1 🫘

2 tsp	vegetable oil	10 mL
2	cloves garlic, minced	2
1	onion, finely chopped (1 cup/250 mL)	1
1/2 tsp	each ground cumin and ground coriander	2 mL
1-1/2 cups	diced mushrooms (about 3 oz/90 g)	375 mL
1	can (19 oz/540 mL) lentils, drained and rinsed	1
1	carrot, grated (about 1 cup/250 mL)	1
1/3 cup	fine dry bread crumbs	75 mL
1/4 cup	chopped fresh coriander (cilantro)	50 mL
1/4 tsp	each salt and pepper	1 mL

1 In nonstick skillet, heat 1 tsp (5 mL) of the oil over medium heat; cook garlic, onion, cumin and ground coriander, stirring, for 2 minutes. Add mushrooms; cook, stirring, for about 8 minutes or until just golden. Let cool.

2 In food processor, coarsely mash lentils. Using pulsing motion, add mushroom mixture and carrot; transfer to bowl. Stir in bread crumbs, coriander, salt and pepper; pressing firmly, shape into 4 patties.

3 In nonstick skillet, heat remaining oil over medium heat; cook burgers for 4 minutes on each side or until heated through. *Makes 4 servings.*

Make ahead: Through step 2, wrap well and refrigerate for up to 2 days or freeze for up to 1 month. Thaw before proceeding.

Chick-Pea Burgers

Hot pickled peppers add zing to these burgers.
Tuck them into pita pockets or buns with yogurt, fresh coriander, lettuce and tomatoes.
Or serve the mixture wrapped in a soft tortilla as in the tortilla wraps.

2 tsp	vegetable oil	10 mL
3	green onions (including tops), chopped	3
2	cloves garlic, minced	2
1 tsp	each dried oregano and chili powder	5 mL
1 cup	diced sweet red or green pepper and/or 1/4 to 1/2 cup (50 to 125 mL) chopped pickled hot peppers	250 mL
Half	tomato, chopped	Half
1	can (19 oz/540 mL) chick-peas, drained and rinsed	1
1/3 cup	fine dry bread crumbs	75 mL
2 tbsp	chopped fresh coriander (cilantro) or parsley	25 mL

1 In nonstick skillet, heat 1 tsp (5 mL) of the oil over medium heat; cook onions, garlic, oregano and chili powder, stirring, for 2 minutes. Add red pepper and tomato; cook, stirring, for about 3 minutes or until pepper is tender and liquid is evaporated.

2 In food processor, mix pepper mixture with chick-peas; transfer to bowl. Stir in bread crumbs, parsley, and salt and pepper to taste until well combined; pressing firmly, shape into 4 burgers.

3 In nonstick skillet, heat remaining oil over medium heat; cook burgers for 4 minutes on each side or until heated through. *Makes 4 servings.*

Make ahead: Through step 2, wrap well and refrigerate for up to 3 days or freeze for up to 1 month. Thaw before proceeding.

Chick-Pea, Tomato, Coriander Tortilla Wraps

Omit bread crumbs. Spoon unshaped Chick-Pea Burger mixture down center of 4 large soft flour tortillas. Top with diced tomato, drizzle of yogurt, chopped fresh coriander and shredded lettuce or spinach. Fold one side, then ends over filling and roll up. *Makes 4 servings.*

Per serving:

calories	199
protein	9 g
total fat	5 g
saturated fat	trace
cholesterol	0 mg
carbohydrate	32 g
dietary fiber	4 g
sodium	293 mg

R.D.I. Vit A 13%, E 6%, C 82%, Folate 27%, Ca 5% (60 mg), Iron 14%, Zinc 11%.

Canada's Food Guide Serving:
¼ 🌾 ¾ 🥕 1 🫘

Soybeans Anyone?

Once a neglected ingredient on North American menus, soybeans are now recognized as a food that may offer unique health benefits. Soybeans are rich in isoflavones, plant chemicals that during digestion convert to estrogen-like compounds called phytoestrogens.

Some Potential Benefits

Although far from proved just yet, these are some of the potential health benefits linked with plant estrogens:

- They may reduce the risk of estrogen-dependent breast and prostate cancers, perhaps by competing with real estrogen for receptor sites, thereby reducing cells' exposure to estrogen.
- They may discourage the growth of cancer cells.
- They may lower blood cholesterol and reduce the risk of cholesterol build-up along artery walls.
- They may reduce the risk of osteoporosis by promoting calcium retention in bones.
- They may relieve menopausal discomforts such as hot flashes.

HEALTHY EATING TIPS: Soybeans

- Add tofu or tempeh to soups, stews, stir-frys and salads.
- Use tofu or textured vegetable protein in place of cheese and meat in casseroles, chili, tacos and spaghetti sauce.
- Mix soy flour with other flours to make muffins or pancakes.
- Use some soy milk in cooking.

Sunflower Veggie Tofu Burgers

Homemade veggie burgers have a fresher flavor than store-bought.
You can vary the vegetables according to preferences: raw beet adds a meat-like color
and crunchy texture; corn adds juiciness and yellow color. Chopped green onions,
sweet red peppers and fresh coriander would also be wonderful additions.

2 tsp	vegetable oil	10 mL
1	onion, chopped	1
3	cloves garlic, minced	3
1/2 cup	brown or white long-grain converted rice	125 mL
1 cup	water	250 mL
1-1/2 cups	extra-firm tofu, drained and coarsely grated (6 oz/175 g)	375 mL
3/4 cup	each grated peeled raw beet and carrot	175 mL
1/2 cup	fine dry bread crumbs	125 mL
1/2 cup	grated part-skim mozzarella cheese	125 mL
1/4 cup	each corn kernels and soy sauce	50 mL
3 tbsp	sunflower seeds or pine nuts, chopped	50 mL
1 tsp	grated gingerroot	5 mL
1/2 tsp	hot pepper sauce or chili paste	2 mL

1 In heavy or nonstick saucepan, heat 1 tsp (5 mL) of the oil over medium heat; cook onion and garlic, stirring, for 3 minutes or until softened. Stir in rice. Pour in water and bring to boil; reduce heat, cover and simmer for 40 minutes for brown (20 minutes for white) or until rice is tender and liquid is absorbed. Let cool enough to handle.

2 Stir in tofu, beet, carrot, bread crumbs, cheese, corn, soy sauce, sunflower seeds, ginger, hot pepper sauce, and salt and pepper to taste, mashing together until well combined. Pressing firmly, shape into 4 burgers.

3 In nonstick skillet, heat remaining oil over medium heat; cook burgers for about 6 minutes per side or until heated through. *Makes 4 servings.*

Make ahead: Through step 3, wrap well and refrigerate for up to 2 days or freeze for up to 1 month. Thaw before proceeding.

Herbed Sunflower Tofu Veggie Burgers

Omit ginger and hot pepper sauce. Add 1 tsp (5 mL) each dried basil and oregano or 2 tbsp (25 mL) each chopped fresh and 2 tbsp (25 mL) chopped fresh parsley.

Per serving:

calories	329
protein	18 g
total fat	10 g
saturated fat	2 g
cholesterol	8 mg
carbohydrate	42 g
dietary fiber	6 g
sodium	830 mg

R.D.I. Vit A 50%, E 47%, C 7%, Folate 23%, Ca 25% (270 mg), Iron 17%, Zinc 19%.

Canada's Food Guide Serving:

1¼ 🌾 1 🥕 ¼ 🍞 ½ 🫘

Grilled Portobello Mushroom Burgers

This is my choice for a vegetarian burger. I buy portobello mushrooms weighing about 4 oz (125 g) each because they are meaty and juicy. I often add other grilled vegetables, such as sliced eggplant, sweet red, green or yellow peppers or sliced sweet onions.

	Grilled Marinated Portobello Mushrooms (page 154)	
4 oz	part-skim mozzarella or Swiss cheese, sliced	125 g
8	slices (3 inches/8 cm long x 1/4-inch/5 mm thick) zucchini	8
4	hamburger buns	4
1/2 cup	Creamy Coriander Mint Dip, page 20 (optional)*	125 mL
4	each tomato slices and lettuce leaves	4

1 Prepare Grilled Marinated Portobello Mushrooms as on page 154.

2 Meanwhile, brush zucchini with remaining marinade; grill for 6 minutes per side or until tender and golden.

3 Spread buns with Creamy Coriander Mint Dip. Top with mushrooms, zucchini, tomato and lettuce. *Makes 4 servings.*

PORTOBELLO MUSHROOMS

Portobello mushrooms are large (4 to 6 inch/10 to 15 cm caps) cremini mushrooms (the brown version of the regular white button mushrooms) that are grown an extra three days before harvesting. Store them unwashed, in a paper bag in refrigerator.

To prepare: Cut off stem, wipe with a damp cloth.

To grill: Brush lightly with olive oil then sprinkle with salt, pepper and thyme; grill over medium heat for 3 to 6 minutes per side or until tender.

To bake: Place on nonstick pan, sprinkle with grated cheese and oregano and bake in 350°F (180°C) oven for 12 to 15 minutes or until tender.

To sauté: Slice in thick strips. Cook in nonstick pan over medium-high heat in small amount of olive oil with garlic and pepper for 5 to 7 minutes, stirring often.

---

*Substitution Tip

Instead of the Coriander Mint Dip, you can use Dijon mustard mixed with light mayonnaise, or any of the traditional hamburger fixings.

Lower-Fat Cooking

For a lower-fat version, grill whole mushrooms without marinating, and omit the cheese.

Per serving:

calories	332
protein	15 g
total fat	13 g
saturated fat	4 g
cholesterol	15 mg
carbohydrate	40 g
dietary fiber	4 g
sodium	492 mg

R.D.I. Vit A 10%, E 9%, C 20%, Folate 21%, Ca 28% (313 mg), Iron 25%, Zinc 21%.

Canada's Food Guide Serving:

2 🌾 2 🥕 ½ 🥛

Coconut Rice

Thai or jasmine rice is a fragrant, flavorful rice. When combined with coconut milk and ginger, it is heavenly. Look for it at food markets or Asian grocery stores. Serve with stir-frys or Asian dishes such as the Chinese Barbecued Pork Tenderloin (page 190).

1 tbsp	minced garlic	15 mL
2 tsp	minced gingerroot	10 mL
1/3 cup	chopped green onion	75 mL
1 cup	Thai, jasmine or long-grain white rice	250 mL
1 cup	each light coconut milk* and water	250 mL
1/4 tsp	salt	1 mL
2 tbsp	chopped fresh coriander (cilantro), optional	25 mL

1 In saucepan, combine 1 tbsp (15 mL) water, garlic, ginger and half of the onion; cook over medium heat, stirring, for 2 minutes.

2 Stir in rice, coconut milk and water; bring to boil. Reduce heat to low; cover and simmer for 20 minutes. Remove from heat and let stand for 5 minutes.

3 Sprinkle with salt; fluff with fork. Garnish with remaining onion and coriander (if using). *Makes 4 servings (1 cup/250 mL each).*

To Cook Jasmine Rice
Wash 1 cup (250 mL) jasmine rice then drain well. Put in saucepan and add 1-3/4 cups (425 mL) cold water; bring to boil. Reduce heat to very low; cover and cook for 15 minutes. Remove from heat and let stand for 5 minutes. Makes about 2-1/2 cups (625 mL).

*COCONUT MILK

Coconut milk is available canned or as a powder. If using canned, look for light coconut milk. It has 12 to 20 grams of fat per 1 cup (250 mL); the regular is 75% higher in fat. If light isn't available and the amount of fat is a concern, dilute regular coconut milk with an equal amount of water. Stir canned coconut milk well before using.

Powdered coconut milk has excellent flavor and is easy to use, but is very high in fat. You can make your own light version by mixing less of the powder than called for with the water. For example, if you mix 5 tbsp (75 mL) powder with 1 cup (250 mL) water, you will have 20 grams of fat, the same amount of fat as in some brands of canned coconut milk. I use 3 tbsp (50 mL) of powder with 1 cup (250 mL) of warm water.

Per serving:

calories	213
protein	4 g
total fat	3 g
saturated fat	3 g
cholesterol	0 mg
carbohydrate	41 g
dietary fiber	1 g
sodium	168 mg

R.D.I. Vit C 3%, Folate 4%, Ca 2% (25 mg), Iron 3%, Zinc 7%.

Canada's Food Guide Serving:
1¼

Mexican Brown Rice with Tomatoes and Corn

This is a handy dish to make ahead and keep in the refrigerator ready
for a quick supper. I often top it with grated cheese and chopped fresh coriander.
Brown rice is higher in fiber than white, but long-grain white rice works well.
Use Mexican-style tomatoes, if available.

*Substitution Tip

Regular brown rice instead of
converted can be used in
Mexican Brown Rice, but
cook it with the tomatoes and
water for about 35 minutes.

1 tbsp	olive oil	15 mL
4	cloves garlic, minced	4
1	large onion, chopped (1-1/3 cups/325 mL)	1
1 tbsp	chili powder	15 mL
1-1/2 tsp	each ground cumin and dried oregano	7 mL
1-1/3 cups	long-grain converted brown rice*	325 mL
1	can (19 oz/540 mL) stewed tomatoes	1
1/4 tsp	hot pepper sauce	1 mL
1 cup	each frozen corn and peas	250 mL
1/2 tsp	each salt and pepper	2 mL

1 In saucepan, heat oil over medium heat; cook garlic and onion, stirring,
for 3 minutes or until softened. Stir in chili powder, cumin and oregano; cook for
1 minute. Stir in rice until well coated.

2 Stir in 1 cup (250 mL) water, tomatoes and hot pepper sauce; bring to boil, breaking
up tomatoes with back of spoon. Reduce heat to low; cover and simmer for
20 minutes. Stir in corn and peas; simmer, covered, for 5 to 10 minutes or until rice
and vegetables are tender. Stir in salt and pepper. *Makes 4 servings.*

Make ahead: Cover and refrigerate for up to 3 days; reheat gently.

Per serving:

calories	404
protein	11 g
total fat	6 g
saturated fat	1 g
cholesterol	0 mg
carbohydrate	81 g
dietary fiber	5 g
sodium	738 mg

R.D.I. Vit A 18%, E 11%, C 45%,
Folate 23%, Ca 10% (111 mg), Iron 27%,
Zinc 11%.

Canada's Food Guide Serving:

2 🌾 2½ 🥕

Mexican Brown Rice with Beans: Add 1 can (19 oz/540 mL) red kidney or
black beans, drained and rinsed, and 1/2 cup (125 mL) water when adding corn and
peas; simmer, covered, for about 10 minutes. *Makes 4 servings.*

Couscous with **Tomato and Basil**

Couscous is a great convenience food. It is fast to prepare and can be used in many ways.
I like to add chopped tomato for color, texture and juiciness without extra fat or calories.
Fresh mint instead of basil is also tasty in this dish. For a more substantial meal, add currants
or raisins and chick-peas, then top with toasted pine nuts or sunflower seeds.

2 tsp	vegetable or olive oil	10 mL
2	cloves garlic, minced	2
2 tsp	dried basil** or 1/2 cup (125 mL) chopped fresh	10 mL
1-1/4 cups	water or vegetable or chicken stock	300 mL
1 cup	couscous	250 mL
1 cup	finely chopped tomatoes*	250 mL
1/4 cup	chopped fresh parsley	50 mL
	Salt and pepper	

1 In nonstick saucepan, heat oil over medium heat; cook garlic for 2 minutes or until softened.

2 Add basil (if using dried) and water; bring to boil. Stir in couscous. Cover and remove from heat. Let stand for 5 minutes. Fluff with fork. Stir in tomatoes, basil (if using fresh), parsley, and salt and pepper to taste. *Makes 4 servings.*

Make ahead: Cover and refrigerate for up to 1 day.

Cooking Tips

*Couscous is truly versatile. Instead of tomatoes, try stirring in sautéed mushrooms, toasted almonds or peanuts, shredded arugula or fresh or roasted sweet peppers.

**If you are using dried basil and it has been around for a year or so, increase the amount to 1 tbsp (15 mL).

Cholesterol-Lowering Tip

Don't be taken in by labels that claim the food is cholesterol-free. Many cholesterol-free foods, such as oil, margarine, potato chips and shortening, are high in fat and should be used sparingly. Fat, particularly saturated and trans fat (partially hydrogenated fat), does more to raise blood cholesterol than does the cholesterol in food.

Per serving:

calories	205
protein	6 g
total fat	3 g
saturated fat	trace
cholesterol	0 mg
carbohydrate	39 g
dietary fiber	3 g
sodium	14 mg

R.D.I. Vit A 7%, E 5%, C 17%, Folate 14%, Ca 3% (30 mg), Iron 9%, Zinc 6%.

Canada's Food Guide Serving:
1½ 🌾 ¼ 🥕

Take a Pass on Gas

Gassy Foods

Legumes (dried beans, peas and lentils), certain vegetables and, to a lesser extent, grains contain complex sugars called oligosaccharides that we can't properly digest because we lack the right enzyme. Left undigested, these complex sugars ferment in the large intestine, producing gas.

Many people shy away from beans, lentils and vegetables like broccoli or Brussels sprouts for fear of the cramping, bloating and explosive gas that these foods can cause.

If the fear or discomfort of gas is preventing you from taking advantage of these very nutritious foods, ask your pharmacist for a gas-reducing product like Beano™ that contains alpha-d-galactosidase. It works by breaking the gas-producing oligosaccharides down into simple sugars like glucose and fructose, which are quickly absorbed and utilized for energy.

HEALTHY EATING TIPS: Less Wind

In addition to alpha-d-galactosidase, try these ways to reduce gas:
- A major cause of gas is swallowing too much air. Eat more slowly. Avoid chewing gum and drink fewer carbonated beverages such as pop and beer.
- Eating more fiber helps prevent gas by keeping foods moving through the intestinal tract but it's a source of gas, too. To minimize fiber's gassy effects, don't eat huge amounts of high-fiber foods at once. Instead, gradually increase your intake over time.
- To reduce the gassy effects of legumes, always rinse canned beans well before using or soak dried beans twice, discarding the water before cooking.
- Be active. Exercise doesn't stop gas production but it does help to pass it and lessen the discomfort.

Put a Stop to Heartburn

If you regularly suffer heartburn after eating, it's a sign that stomach contents are backing up (refluxing) into the esophagus. Reflux can be a symptom of several conditions: hiatus hernia, an impaired esophageal sphincter, or high abdominal pressure caused by obesity or pregnancy.

The symptoms of food reflux mimic some of the warning signs of heart attack. If heartburn is sudden and uncommon, seek medical attention immediately.

HEALTHY LIFESTYLE AND EATING TIPS: Heartburn

While antacids are useful in relieving the discomfort of heartburn, here are some ways to help prevent it:
- Lose weight if overweight.
- Avoid bending after eating.

- Sleep with upper body elevated; put 4 to 6 inch (10 to 15 cm) blocks under the head of your bed.
- Avoid tight-fitting clothes.
- Stop smoking.
- Eat small, healthy, low-fat meals. Don't overeat. Small meals are less likely to back up.
- Avoid foods that relax the sphincter and encourage reflux: fatty foods, spicy foods, onion, garlic, chocolate, excessive alcohol, peppermint and spearmint.
- Avoid foods that tend to irritate an inflamed esophagus: citrus juices, pepper, tomato products, tea, cola, regular and decaffeinated coffee.
- Avoid food and drink for 2 hours prior to lying down.

Tuscan White Kidney Beans with Sage

I first tasted the splendid combination of fresh sage and white beans when we rented a little house in the region of Tuscany one summer. I've made it many times since for my family.
Serve hot, warm or at room temperature as part of a buffet, or with a dinner of grilled vegetables, polenta and a salad. Garnish with extra chopped fresh sage, if desired.

2	tomatoes, coarsely chopped	2
1 tbsp	chopped fresh sage or 1 tsp (5 mL) crumbled dried	15 mL
1	clove garlic, minced	1
1	can (19 oz/540 mL) white kidney beans, drained and rinsed	1
1 tbsp	red wine vinegar	15 mL
1 tbsp	extra-virgin olive oil	15 mL
Pinch	each salt and pepper	Pinch

1 In large saucepan, stir together tomatoes, sage and garlic; simmer over medium heat for about 20 minutes or until liquid is evaporated.

2 Add beans; cook, stirring occasionally, for about 5 minutes or until heated through. Remove from heat.

3 Stir together vinegar, oil, salt and pepper; stir into bean mixture. *Makes 4 servings.*

Make ahead: Cover and refrigerate for up to 2 days.

Zinc

Zinc is an essential mineral. It functions as part of more than 100 enzyme systems that control many of the body's major metabolic reactions. Zinc is not generally lacking in our diets since it can be obtained from a wide variety of foods, including meat, fish, poultry, eggs, milk, cheese, whole grain and fortified cereals. Generally only vegans and people on long-term iron supplementation are at risk of zinc deficiency. Claims that zinc supplements can bolster the immune system, soothe a swollen prostate or delay macular degeneration of the eyes remain unproved.

Per serving:

calories	157
protein	8 g
total fat	4 g
saturated fat	1 g
cholesterol	0 mg
carbohydrate	23 g
dietary fiber	9 g
sodium	315 mg

R.D.I. Vit A 4%, E 6%, C 22%, Folate 25%, Ca 3% (28 mg), Iron 11%, Zinc 6%.

Canada's Food Guide Serving:
½ 🥕 1 🍴

129

Quinoa Pilaf

Quinoa (pronounced Keen-wha) is available in health food stores and some supermarkets. It has a mild flavor, making it a pleasant substitute for rice or other grains with meats, stir-frys or in salads.

Quinoa Squash Pilaf

Add 1 cup (250 mL) diced peeled butternut squash along with water.

Nutrition Tip

Quinoa is higher in iron and potassium than other grains. It is also high in magnesium and is a source of zinc, vitamin B6, riboflavin and niacin.

Kitchen Tip

To store grains, seal in air-tight container and keep in cool dark place.

1 tbsp	olive oil	15 mL
Half	onion, chopped	Half
1	stalk celery (including leaves), diced	1
2	carrots, finely chopped	2
1/2 cup	quinoa	125 mL
1 cup	hot water or vegetable stock	250 mL
1	bay leaf	1
	Grated rind from 1 medium lemon	
1 tbsp	fresh lemon juice	15 mL
1/2 cup	frozen peas, thawed	125 mL

1 In nonstick saucepan, heat oil over medium heat; cook onion, celery and carrots, stirring occasionally, for 10 minutes.

2 In strainer, rinse quinoa under cold water; drain well and add to pan. Cook, stirring, for 1 minute.

3 Add water, bay leaf and lemon rind and juice; bring to boil. Reduce heat to medium-low; cover and simmer for 15 to 20 minutes or until liquid is absorbed and quinoa is tender. Discard bay leaf. Stir in peas; season with salt and pepper to taste.
Makes 3 servings.

Per serving:

calories	199
protein	6 g
total fat	6 g
saturated fat	1 g
cholesterol	0 mg
carbohydrate	31 g
dietary fiber	5 g
sodium	80 mg

R.D.I. Vit A 123%, E 9%, C 18%, Folate 16%, Ca 5% (51 mg), Iron 25%, Zinc 15%.

Canada's Food Guide Serving:

1 🌾 1¼ 🥕

Tofu Vegetable Shish Kebabs

The longer the tofu marinates, the more flavorful it will be.
I use wooden skewers which I soak in water for at least 15 minutes before
using to prevent them from charring.

2 tbsp	each cider vinegar and soy sauce	25 mL
1 tbsp	each sesame oil and minced gingerroot	15 mL
1-1/2 tsp	granulated sugar	7 mL
1/2 tsp	hot chili paste or hot pepper sauce	2 mL
10 oz	extra-firm tofu, cut into 16 pieces (about 1/2-inch/1 cm)	300 g
1	red onion, quartered and separated into pieces	1
1	sweet red, yellow or green pepper, cut in 1-inch (2.5 cm) pieces	1
1	yellow or green zucchini, cut in 3/4-inch (2 cm) thick slices	1
	Coriander (cilantro) leaves (optional)	

1 In large bowl, combine vinegar, soy sauce, sesame oil, ginger, sugar and hot chili paste; add tofu and stir to coat. Let stand for at least 1 hour or cover and refrigerate for up to 1 day.

2 Add onion, red pepper and zucchini to tofu mixture; stir to coat with marinade. Reserving marinade, alternately thread pieces of tofu, then coriander leaf (if using), zucchini, pepper and onion onto each of 4 skewers.

3 Place on greased grill over medium-high heat; close lid and cook, turning once and basting occasionally with reserved marinade, for 8 to 10 minutes or until browned. *Makes 4 servings.*

Make ahead: Through step 1, cover and refrigerate for up to 1 day. Through step 2, cover and set aside for up to 2 hours, basting with marinade occasionally.

More Ways To Use Tofu

- Marinate 1/2-inch (1 cm) thick slices or cubes of firm tofu in this marinade or in soy sauce, sesame oil and chopped gingerroot; bake in 375°F (190°C) oven for 15 minutes, grill or barbecue or add to stir-frys.

- Add small chunks of plain or marinated firm tofu to pasta sauces, chili, tacos, soups, stews and salads.

- Mix chopped medium tofu with onion, celery, light mayonnaise and fresh herbs or a touch of curry or cumin. Use as a sandwich filling.

- Add soft tofu to spreads, dips or salad dressings.

Per serving:

calories	131
protein	12 g
total fat	4 g
saturated fat	1 g
cholesterol	0 mg
carbohydrate	13 g
dietary fiber	4 g
sodium	390 mg

R.D.I. Vit A 12%, E 2%, C 88%, Folate 8%, Ca 16% (180 mg), Iron 4%, Zinc 2%.

Canada's Food Guide Serving:
1¾ 🌱 ½ 🥩

Lentil and Vegetable Curry

Spicy Lentil and Vegetable Tortilla Wraps

For each serving, warm large flour tortilla on paper towel in microwave on High for 15 seconds. Spoon 2/3 cup (150 mL) lentil mixture down center; top with 1 tbsp (15 mL) plain yogurt and sprinkling of fresh coriander. Fold one side over filling, then ends and roll up.

Nutrition Tip

Lentils are very high in folate, fiber, and are a good source of vegetable protein. They also contain some calcium.

Top this curry with yogurt and a sprinkle of fresh coriander and serve with a spinach salad and crusty bread. I particularly like the mild combination of spices here. However, you may prefer to increase the amount of hot pepper. You could substitute 1 tbsp (15 mL) curry powder or 2 tbsp (25 mL) curry paste for the spices.

1 tbsp	vegetable oil	15 mL
1	onion, chopped	1
2	cloves garlic, minced	2
1 tbsp	minced gingerroot	15 mL
1/2 tsp	each ground cumin, turmeric and coriander	2 mL
1/4 tsp	each cinnamon and hot pepper flakes	1 mL
2 cups	water or vegetable stock	500 mL
1 cup	green lentils	250 mL
1	large potato, peeled and cubed	1
1 cup	each chopped carrots and corn kernels	250 mL
2	tomatoes, coarsely chopped (2 cups/500 mL)	2
1/4 cup	chopped fresh parsley or coriander (cilantro)	50 mL

1 In large heavy or nonstick saucepan, heat oil over medium heat; cook onion and garlic, stirring often, for 5 minutes or until softened.

2 Stir in ginger, cumin, turmeric, coriander, cinnamon and hot pepper flakes; cook, stirring, for 1 minute. Add water and lentils; bring to boil. Cover, reduce heat and simmer for 25 minutes.

3 Add potato and carrots; cover and cook for 15 minutes or until lentils and vegetables are tender. Stir in corn and tomatoes; cover and cook for 5 minutes or until heated through. Stir in parsley, and salt and pepper to taste. *Makes 6 servings.*

Make ahead: Cover and refrigerate for up to 2 days or freeze for up to 1 month.

Per serving:

calories	206
protein	11 g
total fat	3 g
saturated fat	trace
cholesterol	0 mg
carbohydrate	37 g
dietary fiber	7 g
sodium	24 mg

R.D.I. Vit A 55%, E 15%, C 30%, Folate 87%, Ca 4% (44 mg), Iron 30%, Zinc 18%.

Canada's Food Guide Serving:

2 ⍦ ¾ ⍭

Barley and Black Bean Casserole

Not only is this healthy dish packed with vitamins and fiber,
it is also tasty and satisfying. Serve with Greek Marinated Leg of Lamb (page 195)
or with any grilled meats or fish. It's also perfect with tofu and
roasted or grilled vegetables.

1 tbsp	vegetable oil	15 mL
1	onion, chopped	1
3	large cloves garlic, minced	3
1 cup	pearl or pot barley	250 mL
3 cups	vegetable or chicken stock	750 mL
2 cups	corn kernels	500 mL
1	can (19 oz/540 mL) black beans, drained and rinsed	1
1/2 cup	chopped fresh parsley or basil	125 mL
2 tbsp	fresh lemon or lime juice	25 mL
1	tomato, diced	1

1 In casserole, heat oil over medium heat; cook onion and garlic for 5 minutes or until softened. Stir in barley; pour in stock. Cover and bake in 350°F (180°C) oven for 1 hour. Stir in corn and black beans.

2 Bake for 5 minutes longer or until heated through and barley is tender. Stir in parsley, lemon juice and tomato. *Makes 10 servings.*

Make ahead: Through step 1, cover and refrigerate for up to 1 day. Add 2 tbsp (25 mL) stock or water, reheat in microwave and continue.

For more Vegetarian Main Dishes see also Pasta, Soup, Salad and Brunch sections.

Barley

Barley does not require pre-soaking. Generally, pearl and pot barley can be used interchangeably, requiring about 1 hour of cooking.

- Do not confuse pearl or pot barley with whole hulled barley, which is brownish and more fibrous (generally found at health food stores). Although whole hulled barley is somewhat higher in nutrients, because only the outer husk has been removed (pearl barley has also had the bran removed), it needs to be soaked and is considerably tougher.

- Barley is a very high source of soluble fiber (the same kind as in oat bran), which may reduce blood cholesterol.

Per serving:

calories	171
protein	6 g
total fat	2 g
saturated fat	trace
cholesterol	0 mg
carbohydrate	34 g
dietary fiber	5 g
sodium	282 mg

R.D.I. Vit A 3%, E 4%, C 15%, Folate 37%, Ca 2% (26 mg), Iron 14%, Zinc 12%.

Canada's Food Guide Serving:
¾ 🌾 ½ 🥕 ¼ 🫘

Vegetable Side Dishes

Spanish-Style Asparagus

Roasted Asparagus with Parmesan

Asparagus with Shaved Parmesan

Make-Ahead Cumin-Spiced Broccoli

Spiced Cabbage and Spinach

Spinach with Tomatoes and Cumin

Beet Greens with Lemon and Almonds

Tomato Gratin

Tomatoes Provençal

New Potatoes with Mint Pesto

Sesame-Spiced Oven-Fried Potatoes

Herb Roasted Potatoes and Onions

Skillet Sweet Potatoes

Carrots Provençal

Two-Potato Scallop

Broccoli Carrot Stir-Fry

Carrot and Squash Purée with Citrus

Braised Fennel with Parmesan

Grilled Marinated Portobello Mushrooms

Roasted Eggplant Slices with Roasted Garlic Purée

Roasted Winter Vegetables

Nutrition Notes

Phytochemicals: "Phyto...What?"

Menopause: "Menopause on the Menu"

Nutrition Tip

Asparagus is an excellent source of folate, a B vitamin.

Spanish-Style Asparagus

The idea for this recipe came from editor Doug Pepper. Other tasty additions would include sesame oil and soy sauce, or grated lemon or orange rind.

1 lb	asparagus	500 g
1 tbsp	each olive oil and balsamic vinegar	15 mL
1	small clove garlic, minced	1
1/4 tsp	each paprika, granulated sugar, salt and pepper	1 mL

1 Snap off tough ends of asparagus. Cook in saucepan of boiling water for 5 minutes or steam until tender-crisp; drain well. Place in shallow serving dish.

2 Whisk together oil, vinegar, garlic, paprika, sugar, salt and pepper; pour over hot asparagus, turning to coat. *Makes 4 servings.*

Roasted Asparagus with Parmesan

This amazing way to cook asparagus is my husband's favorite. I prefer thick asparagus for roasting. However, very thin asparagus is also scrumptious. It may take a minute less.

1 lb	asparagus	500 g
2 tsp	olive oil	10 mL
1/4 tsp	each salt and pepper	1 mL
2 tbsp	freshly grated Parmesan cheese	25 mL

1 Arrange asparagus in single layer on baking sheet; drizzle with oil; turn to coat. Sprinkle with salt and pepper. Bake in 500°F (260°C) oven for 8 minutes or until tender and slightly charred in places.

2 Transfer to shallow serving dish; sprinkle with Parmesan. *Makes 4 servings.*

Asparagus with Shaved Parmesan

Buy a chunk of the best Parmesan (Parmigiano-Reggiano) and grate it yourself.

1 lb	asparagus	500 g
1 tbsp	balsamic vinegar	15 mL
1/4 cup	coarsely grated Parmesan cheese	50 mL

1 Snap off tough ends of asparagus. Cook in saucepan of boiling water for 5 minutes or steam until tender-crisp; drain well. Place in shallow serving dish.

2 Sprinkle with vinegar; turn to coat. Sprinkle with Parmesan. *Makes 4 servings.*

Per serving:

calories	51
protein	5 g
total fat	2 g
saturated fat	1 g
cholesterol	5 mg
carbohydrate	5 g
dietary fiber	1 g
sodium	125 mg

R.D.I. Vit A 5%, E 4%, C 15%, Folate 53%, Ca 9% (102 mg), Iron 4%, Zinc 6%.

Canada's Food Guide Serving:
1¼ 🥕

Make-Ahead Cumin-Spiced Broccoli

My friend Sandra Lawrence gave me this recipe for cumin-spiced broccoli with ginger. Use tender peeled broccoli stalks and florets, or use only the florets and save the stalks for soup or coleslaw.

6 cups	broccoli chunks (1 lb/500 g)	1.5 L
4 tsp	butter or soft margarine	20 mL
1 tsp	cumin seeds or ground cumin	5 mL
1 tbsp	grated gingerroot	15 mL
1/3 cup	milk (2% or whole)	75 mL
1 tbsp	cornstarch	15 mL

1 In saucepan of boiling water, cover and cook broccoli until fork-tender, about 5 minutes; drain well. Pulse in food processor until finely chopped but not smooth.

2 Meanwhile, in nonstick skillet, melt butter over medium heat; cook cumin seeds for about 1 minute or until lightly browned. Stir in hot broccoli and ginger.

3 Whisk milk with cornstarch; pour into broccoli and cook, stirring, for 2 minutes. Season with salt and pepper to taste. *Makes 4 servings, about 2/3 cup (150 mL) each.*

Make ahead: Cover and refrigerate for up to 2 hours or freeze for up to 2 weeks (cumin and ginger flavors strengthen with freezing).

Nutrition Tip

Broccoli is very high in vitamin C, beta carotene and folate.

Per serving:

calories	81
protein	4 g
total fat	5 g
saturated fat	3 g
cholesterol	12 mg
carbohydrate	8 g
dietary fiber	2 g
sodium	74 mg

R.D.I. Vit A 17%, D 4%, E 16%, C 110%, Folate 20%, Ca 7% (72 mg), Iron 9%, Zinc 5%.

Canada's Food Guide Serving:
2 🥕

Spiced Cabbage and Spinach

Nutrition Tip

Cabbage is a good source of vitamin C. Spinach is a good source of folate. Both contain fiber.

Vitamin C

Vitamin C is destroyed by prolonged cooking, and it also leaches into cooking liquid. To get the most vitamin C from vegetables, bring water to a boil before adding them and cook for a short time. Raw fruits and vegetables have the most vitamin C. Since vitamin C is water-soluble and is not stored by the body, you need to eat vitamin-C rich fruits and vegetables every day. If you take in too much, it is simply excreted.

Per serving:

calories	**74**
protein	**3 g**
total fat	**4 g**
saturated fat	**trace**
cholesterol	**0 mg**
carbohydrate	**9 g**
dietary fiber	**3 g**
sodium	**326 mg**

R.D.I. Vit A 35%, E 11%, C 43%, Folate 36%, Ca 9% (101 mg), Iron 15%, Zinc 5%.

Canada's Food Guide Serving:

2¼

Spices, garlic, red pepper flakes and lemon add terrific flavor to this quick vegetable dish. My husband prefers it with 1/4 tsp (1 mL) red pepper flakes. However, he likes most dishes hotter than I do.

1 tbsp	vegetable oil	15 mL
1 tsp	cumin seeds	5 mL
4	cloves garlic, minced	4
1 tsp	ground coriander	5 mL
1/4 cup	water	50 mL
1 tbsp	fresh lemon juice	15 mL
1 tsp	granulated sugar	5 mL
1/2 tsp	salt	2 mL
Pinch	red pepper flakes	Pinch
6 cups	thinly sliced cabbage	1.5 L
3 cups	thinly sliced spinach	750 mL

1 In heavy saucepan, heat oil over medium heat. Add cumin seeds; cook until sizzling. Stir in garlic and coriander; cook, stirring, for 30 seconds. Add water, lemon juice, sugar, salt and red pepper flakes.

2 Stir in cabbage and bring to simmer; cover and simmer for 15 to 20 minutes or until cabbage is tender.

3 Stir in spinach; cook for 2 minutes or until wilted. *Makes 4 servings.*

Make ahead: Through step 2 for up to 2 hours.

Spinach with Tomatoes and Cumin

*The dynamic flavors of cumin, ground coriander and fresh ginger
liven up spinach. This side dish goes well with grilled or roasted meats,
chicken or fish and mashed potatoes or rice dishes.*

1 lb	fresh spinach (or 10 oz/300 g bag), trimmed	500 g
1-1/2 tsp	butter	7 mL
1/2 tsp	ground cumin or cumin seeds	2 mL
1/4 tsp	ground coriander	1 mL
2 tbsp	chopped onion	25 mL
1	clove garlic, minced	1
1 tsp	grated gingerroot	5 mL
1	small tomato, seeded and finely chopped	1
Pinch	salt	Pinch
2 tbsp	1% sour cream	25 mL

1 Remove tough stems from spinach; rinse and shake off excess water. In saucepan, cover and cook spinach over medium heat, with just the water clinging to leaves, for 3 minutes or until wilted; drain well and chop.

2 Meanwhile, in nonstick skillet, melt butter over medium heat; cook cumin and coriander, stirring, for 1 minute. Add onion and garlic; cook, stirring occasionally, for 2 minutes or until tender.

3 Add ginger, tomato and salt; cook for 1 minute or until heated through. Stir in spinach, then sour cream. *Makes 3 servings.*

Make ahead: Through step 2 for up to 2 hours.

Per serving:

calories	59
protein	4 g
total fat	2 g
saturated fat	1 g
cholesterol	6 mg
carbohydrate	7 g
dietary fiber	3 g
sodium	90 mg

R.D.I. Vit A 73%, E 9%, C 22%,
Folate 56%, Ca 13% (142 mg), Iron 24%,
Zinc 8%.

Canada's Food Guide Serving:
1¾

Beet Greens with
Lemon and Almonds

When I was growing up in Vancouver, my father always had a vegetable garden in the backyard. Just-picked and cooked beet greens as well as the tender young beets were a summer treat. Cook beet greens as you would spinach or Swiss chard.

8 oz	beet greens (2 bunches)	250 g
2 tbsp	toasted slivered almonds	25 mL
2 tsp	butter	10 mL
1/2 tsp	grated lemon rind	2 mL

1 Wash beet greens; coarsely chop to make about 6 cups (1.5 L).

2 In saucepan with small amount of boiling water, cook greens until wilted and tender, about 3 minutes; drain well.

3 Stir in almonds, butter, lemon rind, and salt and pepper to taste; cook, stirring, over medium heat for 1 minute. *Makes 3 servings.*

BEETS

To prepare: Wash beets to remove any grit. Cut off green tops, leaving an inch (2.5 cm) of stem. Don't cut or peel beets before boiling or steaming because they will bleed into the liquid and lose color and flavor.

To steam or boil: Cook beets in or over boiling water for 25 to 40 minutes, depending on size, or until tender and the skin slips off easily.

To roast: Wrap beets in foil and roast in a 375°F to 400°F (190°C to 200° C) oven (depending on what else is in the oven) for about 1-1/2 hours.

To peel cooked beets: Hold hot beet with a fork or place it under cold water then slip skin off with a knife. Trim ends. Beets prepared in advance can be reheated in the microwave.

To serve cooked beets: Serve hot or cold. Slice, dice or coarsely grate cold beets then drizzle with balsamic vinegar or toss with Herb and Ginger Vinaigrette (page 57).

Per serving:

calories	67
protein	2 g
total fat	5 g
saturated fat	2 g
cholesterol	7 mg
carbohydrate	4 g
dietary fiber	2 g
sodium	155 mg

R.D.I. Vit A 30%, E 13%, C 23%, Folate 5%, Ca 7% (75 mg), Iron 9%, Zinc 5%.

Canada's Food Guide Serving:
1 🌱

Tomato Gratin

This delicious fall and winter side dish is tasty with omelets,
roasts or grilled meats. For the bread cubes, use a crusty French or Italian bread.

1-1/2 cups	small fresh bread cubes	375 mL
1	can (28 oz/796 mL) tomatoes, drained	1
1 tbsp	olive oil	15 mL
3	cloves garlic, minced	3
1/4 cup	coarsely chopped fresh parsley	50 mL
2 tbsp	chopped fresh basil or 1/2 tsp (2 mL) dried	25 mL
1/4 tsp	pepper	1 mL
3 tbsp	freshly grated Parmesan cheese	50 mL

1 Spread bread cubes on baking sheet; bake in 375°F (190°C) oven for about 5 minutes or until crisp and lightly browned.

2 Meanwhile, cut tomatoes into quarters. In shallow 6-cup (1.5 L) baking dish or casserole, combine tomatoes, oil, garlic, parsley, basil and pepper.

3 Stir in bread; sprinkle cheese over top. Bake, uncovered, in 375°F (190°C) oven for 20 minutes or until heated through. *Makes 4 servings.*

Make ahead: Through step 2 for up to 3 hours.

Vegetarian Supper

Tomato Gratin (this page)
Lentil and Vegetable Curry (page 132)
Spinach Salad with Walnut Vinaigrette (page 38)
Focaccia (page 246)

Per serving:

calories	117
protein	5 g
total fat	6 g
saturated fat	1 g
cholesterol	4 mg
carbohydrate	13 g
dietary fiber	2 g
sodium	380 mg

R.D.I. Vit A 10%, E 9%, C 27%, Folate 7%, Ca 11% (119 mg), Iron 11%, Zinc 6%.

Canada's Food Guide Serving:
¼ 🌾 1¼ 🥕

Tomatoes Provençal

One of my ever-lasting favorites, this dish is colorful, juicy, easy to make and goes well with most meats, fish, poultry, egg or vegetarian dishes. It's best in tomato season. However, if making in winter, buy local hothouse tomatoes, which are more flavorful than any imported ones.

6	medium tomatoes	6
	Salt and pepper	
1 cup	fresh homemade whole wheat bread crumbs	250 mL
2	large cloves garlic, minced	2
1/4 cup	each chopped fresh parsley and basil*	50 mL
1 tbsp	olive oil	15 mL

1 Cut tomatoes in half crosswise. Sprinkle cut side with salt and pepper to taste; place in baking dish.

2 In small bowl, combine crumbs, garlic, parsley, basil and oil. Spoon on top of tomatoes.

3 Bake in 400°F (200°C) oven for 15 to 20 minutes or until heated through.
Makes 6 servings.

Make ahead: Through step 2 for up to 6 hours.

---

*Substitution Tip

If fresh basil is unavailable, use 1/2 cup (125 mL) coarsely chopped fresh parsley and 1/2 tsp (2 mL) dried basil leaves

Make Your Own Bread Crumbs

It's a snap to make your own bread crumbs. For 1 cup (250 mL) crumbs, process about 2 slices day-old whole wheat bread in a food processor. However, if you want to use store-bought fine dry bread crumbs in this recipe, use about 1/3 cup (75 mL).

Per serving:

calories	64
protein	2 g
total fat	3 g
saturated fat	trace
cholesterol	0 mg
carbohydrate	9 g
dietary fiber	2 g
sodium	49 mg

R.D.I. Vit A 14%, E 3%, C 33%, Folate 6%, Ca 2% (22 mg), Iron 7%, Zinc 4%.

Canada's Food Guide Serving:
1/4 🌾 1 🥕

New Potatoes with Mint Pesto

I try to make enough of these potatoes to have leftovers. They are equally tasty the next day hot, cold or tossed with a little vinaigrette or balsamic vinegar. If you want to serve two to four more people, just add extra potatoes. Almonds can be used instead of pine nuts.

1	small clove garlic	1
1/2 cup	fresh mint leaves	125 mL
1/4 cup	fresh parsley leaves	50 mL
1 tbsp	pine nuts, toasted	15 mL
1 tbsp	each olive oil and water	15 mL
1/2 tsp	salt	2 mL
1-1/2 lb	tiny new potatoes (about 6 cups/1.5 L)	750 g

1 Prepare mint pesto: in food processor, chop garlic. Add mint, parsley, pine nuts, oil, water and salt; process until nearly smooth.

2 Scrub potatoes; cut any larger ones in half. In saucepan of boiling water, cook potatoes until tender; drain well. Heat potatoes in pan over low heat for 2 minutes to dry. Transfer to serving bowl; toss with pesto. *Makes 6 servings.*

Make ahead: Through step 1, cover and refrigerate for up to 24 hours.

Cooking Tips

Toast pine nuts in a skillet over medium heat for 3 to 5 minutes or until golden.

To prevent the nut oil from going rancid, store pine nuts and sesame seeds in the freezer.

Per serving:

calories	113
protein	2 g
total fat	3 g
cholesterol	0 mg
carbohydrate	20 g
dietary fiber	2 g
sodium	197 mg

R.D.I. Vit A 4%, E 4%, C 28%, Folate 6%, Ca 2% (18 mg), Iron 10%, Zinc 4%.

Canada's Food Guide Serving:
1 🥕

Sesame-Spiced Oven-Fried Potatoes

My kids really like these potatoes and have them with burgers, meat loaf or chicken.
My husband loves sweet potatoes cooked this way. For extra fiber and flavor,
leave skins on the regular potatoes.

Nutrition Tip

Potatoes are a source of
fiber and vitamin C.

4	medium potatoes or 2 sweet potatoes (1-1/2 lb/750 g)	4
1 tbsp	vegetable oil	15 mL
2 tbsp	sesame seeds	25 mL
1/2 tsp	each paprika and crushed fennel seeds	2 mL
1/4 tsp	each cayenne pepper and salt	1 mL

1 Peel sweet potatoes; peel regular potatoes only if skin is tough or blemished. Cut lengthwise into eighths. Place in bowl and toss with oil. Combine sesame seeds, paprika, fennel seeds and cayenne; sprinkle over potatoes and toss to mix.

2 Spread on baking sheet. Bake in 400°F (200°C) oven, turning once, for 40 minutes for sweet potatoes, 60 minutes for regular, or until tender. (Time will vary depending on size of pieces. Check after 30 minutes.) Sprinkle with salt. *Makes 4 servings.*

Make ahead: For sweet potatoes only, prepare through step 1 and refrigerate for up to 2 hours.

Per serving (regular potatoes):

calories	214
protein	5 g
total fat	6 g
saturated fat	1 g
cholesterol	0 mg
carbohydrate	37 g
dietary fiber	3 g
sodium	157 mg

R.D.I. Vit A 3%, E 9%, C 32%,
Folate 9%, Ca 2% (24 mg), Iron 17%,
Zinc 11%.

Canada's Food Guide Serving:

1

Foil-Roasted or Barbecued Vegetables

These are as delicious and even moister than dry-roasted vegetables. Prepare vegetables as directed; add 3 cloves of chopped garlic. Arrange on greased foil; fold foil over and secure tightly. Cook in oven or on barbecue for 30 to 40 minutes or until vegetables are tender.

Per serving:

calories	168
protein	3 g
total fat	7 g
saturated fat	1 mg
cholesterol	0 mg
carbohydrate	25 g
dietary fiber	3 g
sodium	8 mg

R.D.I. Vit E 16%, C 22%, Folate 8%, Ca 3% (29 mg), Iron 9%, Zinc 4%.

Canada's Food Guide Serving: 1¼ 🥕

Herb-Roasted Potatoes and Onions

For extra flavor and variety, I often add carrots and parsnips (peeled and cut into 1-1/2 inch/4 cm lengths) and whole cloves of garlic.

12	small red-skinned potatoes, halved	12
3	onions, quartered	3
2 tbsp	vegetable or olive oil	25 mL
2 tsp	dried Italian herb seasoning or herbs de Provence	10 mL

1 In bowl, sprinkle unpeeled potatoes and onions with oil, Italian seasoning, and salt and pepper to taste; toss to coat well. Transfer to large rimmed baking sheet. Bake in 400°F (200°C) oven, stirring 3 or 4 times, for 55 to 65 minutes or until golden and tender. *Makes 4 servings.*

Phyto...What?

In addition to vitamins and minerals, vegetables and fruits contain various plant chemicals called phytochemicals that are thought to confer some health benefits. While the potential health benefits are far from proven, you can't go wrong eating more of these foods.

A Guide to Some of the Best-Known Phytochemicals

- Indoles and isothiocyanates may protect against colon cancer. They are found in broccoli, brussels sprouts, cabbage, cauliflower, kale, bok choy and rutabaga.
- Isoflavones such as genistein may offset the effects of estrogen in breast and ovarian cancer. They are found in soybean products.
- Limonene helps produce enzymes that in turn get rid of cancer-causing substances. They are found in citrus fruits.
- Allicin, the chemical that gives garlic and onions their typical odor, reduces blood cholesterol and blood pressure.
- Phytosterols may help prevent colon cancer and prevent cholesterol absorption from foods. They are found mainly in soybeans.

Skillet Sweet Potatoes

Sautéed mellow onions and sweet potatoes make a wonderful combination of flavor and texture.

2 tsp	olive oil	10 mL
1 cup	thinly sliced onions	250 mL
2	medium sweet potatoes (about 1 lb/500 g)	2
1/2 cup	vegetable stock	125 mL

1 In nonstick skillet, heat oil over medium heat; cook onions, stirring occasionally, until softened and golden, about 5 minutes.

2 Peel sweet potatoes; cut into 1/2- x 1/2-inch (1 x 1 cm) thick strips. Add to skillet along with stock. Cover tightly and simmer, stirring every 5 minutes, for about 15 minutes or until tender. Season with salt and pepper to taste. *Makes 3 servings.*

Nutrition Tip

Sweet potatoes are packed with vitamin C, beta carotene and fiber.

Per serving:

calories	162
protein	3 g
total fat	3 g
saturated fat	trace
cholesterol	0 mg
carbohydrate	31 g
dietary fiber	4 g
sodium	124 mg

R.D.I. Vit A 238%, E 4%, C 48%, Folate 14%, Ca 4% (41 mg), Iron 4%, Zinc 5%.

Canada's Food Guide Serving:
1¼

Carrots Provençal

Perk up carrots with fresh parsley, basil and garlic in this simple dish. You can also use chopped fresh dill to taste instead of the other herbs.

5	medium carrots (1 lb/500 g), peeled and cut in sticks	5
1/4 cup	water	50 mL
1 tbsp	olive oil	15 mL
3	cloves garlic, minced (about 1 tbsp/15 mL)	3
1/4 cup	chopped fresh parsley	50 mL
1 tbsp	chopped fresh basil or tarragon	15 mL
1/4 tsp	each salt and pepper	1 mL

1 In nonstick or heavy saucepan, combine carrots, water, oil and half of the garlic; cover and simmer over medium-low heat for 15 minutes or until carrots are crisp-tender.

2 Stir in parsley, basil, remaining garlic, salt and pepper; cover and cook for 5 minutes or until carrots are tender. *Makes 4 servings.*

Fiber-Booster

All fruits and vegetables contain fiber but dried fruits, pears, apples, corn and peas are exceptional choices.

Per serving:

calories	77
protein	1 g
total fat	4 g
saturated fat	1 g
cholesterol	0 mg
carbohydrate	11 g
dietary fiber	3 g
sodium	207 mg

R.D.I. Vit A 229%, E 8%, C 10%, Folate 8%, Ca 4% (40 mg), Iron 6%, Zinc 4%.

Canada's Food Guide Serving:
1¼

Sweet Potatoes

To prepare: Wash, trim ends; don't peel if baking or microwaving whole, otherwise peel.

To bake: Prick in several places; bake on baking sheet in 400°F (200°C) oven for 40 to 50 minutes or until soft when pressed.

To microwave: Prick in several places; microwave 2 medium on High power for 8 minutes or until tender.

To boil: Cut in half; boil covered in water for 20 minutes or until tender.

To steam: Cut in half; steam for 25 to 30 minutes or until tender.

To season: Mash cooked potatoes and add orange or lemon juice or grated rind and/or sherry. Spice with ginger or nutmeg.

Two-Potato Scallop

Sweet potatoes and Yukon Gold potatoes cooked with chicken stock, garlic and Parmesan make a delicious dish. We tested these with various combinations of milk, sour cream and stock and liked this version the best. You can use one chopped onion instead of the garlic. The amount of stock will vary depending on the variety of potato. Don't worry about a little extra liquid in the pan because this adds sauce to the dish.

3 cups	each sliced (1/4-inch/5 mm thick) peeled sweet potatoes and white potatoes (e.g., Yukon Gold)	750 mL
2	large cloves garlic, minced (2 tsp/10 mL)	2
1/3 cup	freshly grated Parmesan cheese	75 mL
2 tbsp	all-purpose flour	25 mL
1/4 tsp	each salt, pepper and dried thyme	1 mL
1-1/2 cups	chicken or vegetable stock	375 mL

1 In large bowl, mix together sweet and white potatoes, garlic, cheese, flour, salt, pepper and thyme. Transfer to 8-inch (2 L) square or 11- x 7-inch (2 L) baking dish sprayed with nonstick cooking spray.

2 Pour in stock. Cover with foil and bake in 375°F (190°C) oven for 50 minutes. Uncover and bake for 30 to 40 minutes longer or until golden brown and potatoes are tender. *Makes 4 servings.*

Make ahead: Through step 1 for up to 2 hours. Through step 2 for up to 4 hours; reheat to serve.

Two-Potato Mash: In separate saucepans, boil equal amounts of regular and sweet potatoes in water; drain well. Heat in pan over low heat for 2 minutes to dry. Mash together with buttermilk, salt and pepper.

Broccoli Carrot Stir-Fry

Sesame oil, ginger and garlic are my choice flavors to add to broccoli, cabbage and carrots. This easy vegetable stir-fry is a terrific side dish with most meat, fish or poultry.

1 tbsp	vegetable oil	15 mL
1 tbsp	minced gingerroot	15 mL
2 tsp	minced garlic	10 mL
1/4 tsp	red pepper flakes	1 mL
2 tbsp	soy sauce	25 mL
2 tbsp	sherry or chicken stock	25 mL
2 tsp	granulated sugar	10 mL
8	small carrots, diagonally sliced (2 cups/500 mL)	8
4 cups	shredded cabbage, cut in 1-inch (2.5 cm) long strips	1 L
2 cups	broccoli florets	500 mL
2 tsp	sesame oil	10 mL

Sesame Oil

This dark, strong-flavored oil is made from roasted sesame seeds. Don't buy the light sesame oil as it is light in flavor, not in fat; instead buy ones from Asia, preferably roasted sesame oil.

1 In wok or skillet, heat oil over high heat; stir-fry ginger, garlic and red pepper flakes for a few seconds or until fragrant. Add 1/3 cup (75 mL) water, soy sauce, sherry and sugar; bring to boil.

2 Add carrots; cover and simmer for 2 minutes. Add cabbage and broccoli; cover and simmer for 2 minutes. Uncover and cook, stirring, until vegetables are tender-crisp, about 5 minutes. Stir in sesame oil, and salt and pepper to taste. *Makes 4 servings.*

Per serving:

calories	136
protein	3 g
total fat	6 g
saturated fat	1 g
cholesterol	0 mg
carbohydrate	18 g
dietary fiber	4 g
sodium	593 mg

R.D.I. Vit A 231%, E 16%, C 57%, Folate 18%, Ca 6% (66 mg), Iron 8%, Zinc 6%.

Canada's Food Guide Serving:
2½

Carrot and Squash Purée with Citrus

Puréed squash and carrots with a kick of citrus makes an appealing side dish.
For a special occasion, top with toasted slivered almonds, pine nuts or pecans.
Serve with turkey, fish or meats.

Squash

To prepare: Cut squash in half or in chunks; with spoon, scrape out seeds and fibers.

To bake: Place cut side down in oiled baking dish. Bake in 400°F (200°C) oven for about 45 minutes or until tender.

To steam: Place in steamer. Cover and steam for 10 to 20 minutes or until tender.

Nutrition Tip

Winter Squashes are high in beta carotene and a source of folate and vitamin C.

2 cups	chopped carrots (12 oz/375 g)	500 mL
2 cups	cubed peeled butternut or other squash	500 mL
1/2 cup	chicken or vegetable stock	125 mL
1 tsp	granulated sugar	5 mL
1 tsp	grated orange rind	5 mL
1/4 tsp	salt	1 mL
Pinch	each nutmeg and pepper	Pinch
1/2 cup	1% or 2% plain low-fat yogurt or 1% sour cream	125 mL

1 In saucepan, bring carrots, squash and stock to boil; cover and simmer for 15 minutes or until vegetables are tender and most liquid is absorbed.

2 Purée in food processor or blender. Stir in sugar, orange rind, salt, nutmeg and pepper; stir in yogurt. *Makes 4 servings.*

Make ahead: Cover and refrigerate for up to 2 days.

Per serving:

calories	83
protein	4 g
total fat	1 g
saturated fat	trace
cholesterol	1 mg
carbohydrate	17 g
dietary fiber	3 g
sodium	302 mg

R.D.I. Vit A 193%, E 3%, C 23%, Folate 12%, Ca 10% (105 mg), Iron 6%, Zinc 6%.

Canada's Food Guide Serving:
1½

Braised Fennel with Parmesan

I love the mild licorice or anise flavor of this Italian vegetable and actually prefer it cooked rather than raw in salads. This dish goes well with fish, meat or poultry

3	medium fennel bulbs (1 lb/500 g)	3
1 tsp	extra-virgin olive oil	5 mL
	Salt and pepper	
1/4 cup	freshly grated Parmesan cheese	50 mL

1 Cut off and discard feathery top of fennel. Trim base; discard tough or bruised outer layers. Cut bulbs lengthwise into quarters.

2 In saucepan of simmering water, cook fennel just until tender when tested with fork, about 10 minutes; drain.

3 Drizzle oil into shallow baking dish just large enough to hold fennel in single layer. Add fennel and turn to coat with oil; sprinkle with salt and pepper to taste. Cover and bake in 375°F (190°C) oven for 20 minutes. Sprinkle with Parmesan; broil, uncovered, until cheese melts, 3 to 5 minutes. *Makes 6 servings.*

Make ahead: Let stand at room temperature for up to 2 hours.

Fennel

In some stores, fennel is labeled sweet anise or finocchio. It adds flavor to fish stews and soups as well as vegetable dishes.

Per serving:

calories	43
protein	2 g
total fat	2 g
saturated fat	1 g
cholesterol	3 mg
carbohydrate	4 g
dietary fiber	2 g
sodium	106 mg

R.D.I. Vit A 1%, E 1%, C 8%, Folate 5%, Ca 8% (84 mg), Zinc 3%.

Canada's Food Guide Serving:

1¼ 🥕

Menopause on the Menu

If you are a woman in your forties or early fifties and are suffering from the discomforts of mid-life menstrual and menopausal symptoms, you may have wondered if therapies like vitamin B6, dong quai and oil of evening primrose can help. The symptoms associated with perimenopause (the years before menstruation ceases) stem primarily from fluctuating levels of estrogen. Most therapies either directly replace the estrogen or treat the symptoms brought on by its decline.

The Soybean Connection

The fact that Japanese women don't suffer from the menopausal complaints of American women has been linked to their diet, which is high in soybean foods. Soybeans contain compounds known as isoflavones, which are converted during digestion to phytoestrogens or plant estrogens. Preliminary evidence suggests that these plant estrogens may be useful in relieving the discomfort of hot flashes, night sweats and vaginal dryness.

Herbs such as fenugreek, gotu kola, sarsaparilla, licorice root and wild yam root are also said to contain estrogen-like substances, but there is little evidence to confirm or challenge the usefulness of these therapies.

HEALTHY EATING TIPS: Help for the Symptoms of PMS and Menopause

Women today have a variety of therapies, both traditional and alternative, available to help them through the perimenopause and the menopausal years. Whatever therapies you try, these diet and lifestyle tips are bound to help you cope with some of the common symptoms and discomforts.

- Adopt a healthy eating pattern.
- Include more vegetarian dishes in your meals, especially more soybean-based products such as tofu.
- Avoid caffeine if you are experiencing sleep problems or breast tenderness.
- Limit your salt intake. Recent evidence concludes that water isn't retained premenstrually but simply shifts around, a phenomena unrelated to the influences of salt. However, eating less salt is still a healthy choice.

- Avoid alcohol, especially red wine, beer, rum, rye, brandy and sherry if you suffer from headaches and depression. These symptoms may also improve by avoiding chocolate, aged cheese, nuts, aspartame, onions, tomatoes, mushrooms, nitrites and monosodium glutamate.
- Eat smaller and more frequent meals.

Other Nutrition-Related Therapies

Other nutrition-related therapies are thought to act by increasing levels of neurotransmitters in the brain, particularly serotonin. Low levels of serotonin have been linked to hot flashes, mood swings, irritability, sleep problems and fluid retention. At this time, none of these therapies has proved effective. They are discussed here only as a caution against popular self-help therapies.

- Vitamin B6: This vitamin can cause nerve damage. Long-term use of 50 to 100 mg daily is likely safe; never take more than 200 mg daily.
- Vitamin A: Vitamin A is relatively safe up to 8000 Retinol Equivalents except during pregnancy. Excess vitamin A causes birth defects and should never be taken if there is any chance of pregnancy occurring.
- Vitamin E: Vitamin E in dosages of 300 IU is relatively safe but should not be taken when on anticoagulant (blood thinner) medication. Never self-medicate with amounts in excess of 800 IU.
- Calcium and magnesium: Both calcium and magnesium are relatively safe when taken sensibly. For premenstrual and menopausal symptoms, calcium supplements of 1000 mg daily are common. If you take magnesium, limit the supplement to 300 to 600 mg daily.
- Oil of evening primrose: Oil of evening primrose is safe but costly and sometimes causes diarrhea.
- Dong quai: The active ingredients in dong quai are coumarins, naturally occurring chemicals that are harmful in larger doses. For this reason, it is not advisable to use dong quai.
- Ginseng: Some types of ginseng can increase the risk of the very symptoms women are trying to avoid: nervousness, sleeplessness, diarrhea, hypertension, even uterine bleeding.

Grilled Marinated Portobello Mushrooms

This is memorable as a vegetable side dish, as a first course or as a burger.
For an appetizer, serve with Caramelized Onion and Basil Dip (page 13) or Creamy
Coriander Mint Dip (page 20). The mushrooms can also be sliced and served with
grilled sweet peppers, eggplant and/or zucchini and chèvre cheese.
Garnish with watercress or fresh basil.

Grilled Portobello Mushroom Hors d'oeuvres

Slice mushrooms 3/8 inch (1 cm) thick before marinating. Grill or sauté for 2 to 3 minutes per side, then coarsely chop. Use to fill Mini Phyllo Tart Shells (page 10) or tiny toast cups; top with a sprinkling of grated Parmesan cheese.

4	portobello mushrooms (1 lb/500 g)	4
1/4 cup	balsamic vinegar	50 mL
2 tbsp	olive oil	25 mL
1 tsp	each dried basil and oregano or 1 tbsp (15 mL) each chopped fresh	5 mL
1	clove garlic, minced	1
Pinch	each salt and pepper	Pinch
4 oz	thinly sliced part-skim cheese (optional)	125 g

1 Cut stems off mushrooms; place, smooth side up, in single layer in shallow dish.

2 Whisk together vinegar, oil, basil, oregano, garlic, salt and pepper; pour over mushrooms. Let stand at room temperature for 15 minutes, turning twice.

3 Reserving marinade, place mushrooms, smooth side up, on grill over medium-high heat; cook for 5 to 8 minutes on each side or until tender, brushing occasionally with marinade. Top with cheese for last 2 minutes of grilling (if using).
Makes 4 servings.

Make ahead: Through step 2 for up to 4 hours.

Per serving (no cheese):

calories	**63**
protein	**1 g**
total fat	**4 g**
saturated fat	**1 g**
cholesterol	**0 mg**
carbohydrate	**7 g**
dietary fiber	**1 g**
sodium	**1 mg**

R.D.I. Vit E 5%, C 5%, Folate 5%, Ca 1% (8 mg), Iron 8%, Zinc 6%.

Canada's Food Guide Serving:
1¼

Roasted Eggplant Slices with Roasted Garlic Purée

Rich and smoky, eggplant slices are delectable as a side dish, or in a sandwich or pita with tomatoes and fresh basil. Or serve as a first course drizzled with balsamic vinegar and freshly grated Parmesan cheese.

1	eggplant (1 lb/500 g)	1
4 tsp	olive oil	20 mL
2 tbsp	Roasted Garlic Purée (see below)	25 mL
1-1/2 tsp	dried Italian herb seasoning	7 mL
Pinch	each salt and pepper	Pinch

1 Trim ends from eggplant; cut crosswise into 3/4-inch (2 cm) thick slices. Arrange in single layer on greased baking sheet. Brush oil over slices. Spread with garlic purée; sprinkle with Italian herbs, salt and pepper.

2 Roast in 400°F (200°C) oven for about 20 minutes or until very tender and undersides are browned. *Makes 4 servings.*

Make ahead: Through step 1, cover and refrigerate for up to 2 hours.

Roasted Garlic Purée

Use to flavor salad dressings, pasta sauces, soups or stews or to spread on crackers or toasted French bread.

2	large heads garlic	2
1/2 tsp	fresh lemon juice	2 mL
Pinch	each salt and pepper	Pinch

1 Cut off 1/4 inch (5 mm) from top of each head of garlic.

2 Loosely wrap in double thickness foil. Bake in 400°F (200°C) oven for about 1 hour or until extremely soft and golden brown. Let cool slightly.

3 Squeeze out pulp from skin of each clove into bowl. Mash. Stir in lemon juice, salt and pepper. *Makes about 1/4 cup (50 mL).*

Make ahead: Cover and refrigerate for up to 3 days.

Grilled Eggplant

To cook eggplant on barbecue or grill, cut into 1/2-inch (1 cm) thick slices; brush with olive oil and sprinkle with herbs, salt and pepper. Grill over medium heat, with lid down, for 15 to 20 minutes, turning once or twice or until very tender.

Per serving:

calories	**84 g**
protein	**1 g**
total fat	**5 g**
saturated fat	1 g
cholesterol	0 mg
carbohydrate	**10 g**
dietary fiber	**5 g**
sodium	**5 mg**

R.D.I. Vit A 1%, E 6%, C 7%, Folate 7%, Ca 3% (28 mg), Iron 5%, Zinc 3%.

Canada's Food Guide Serving:
1½

Per tbsp (15 mL):

calories	**27**
protein	**1 g**
total fat	**trace**
cholesterol	0 mg
carbohydrate	**6 g**
dietary fiber	**trace**
sodium	**3 mg**

R.D.I. Vit C 10%, Ca 3% (33 mg), Iron 2%, Zinc 2%.

Canada's Food Guide Serving:
¼

GRILLING VEGETABLES

Lower-Fat Tip

With a few exceptions (like avocados and coconuts), vegetables and fruit are fat-free foods. Keep them that way by not serving them with butter, margarine or cream sauces. Instead, dress them up with ginger, garlic, mushrooms, lemon juice, 1% sour cream, wine, juice or sugar.

Grilled Onions

Peel onions; cut crosswise into 1/2-inch (1 cm) thick slices, keeping the rounds intact. Place slices on lightly greased vegetable rack or barbecue grill (to place directly on barbecue grill, cut onions into wedges with root ends attached). Grill over medium heat, with lid closed and turning once, for about 20 minutes or until very tender and golden.

For oven grilling, arrange slices in single layer on greased, rimmed baking sheet. Broil about 8 inches (20 cm) from heat for about 10 minutes or until very tender and browned, checking carefully during last few minutes to make sure thinner slices do not overbrown.

Grilled Sweet Peppers

Seed and cut into quarters. Brush lightly with olive oil if desired. Grill on top rack of barbecue over medium-low heat, with lid closed, until tender and slightly browned, 20 to 30 minutes.

Grilled Zucchini

I think most zucchini dishes tend to be bland. However, grilled zucchini is totally different because it takes on a rich smoky flavor and soft creamy texture that is fabulous. Slice unpeeled zucchini lengthwise into 1/2-inch (1 cm) thick slices; drizzle with olive oil and sprinkle with salt and pepper. Grill over medium-low heat, with lid closed and turning every 5 minutes, until lightly browned and soft inside, 15 to 20 minutes.

Grilled Mixed Vegetables

Cut onion, zucchini, sweet peppers and eggplant into 1/2-inch (1 cm) thick same-size pieces (about 1-1/2-inch/4 cm). Place in bowl and drizzle with a little olive oil, salt and pepper, tossing to mix. Place in grill basket and grill over medium heat, with lid closed and turning occasionally, for 20 to 30 minutes or until tender.

Roasted Winter Vegetables

*My mother taught me to roast vegetables. She just added them to the pan
when roasting beef, pork or a chicken. They soaked up all the fat and drippings and were
absolutely delicious. This lightened-up method uses stock and a little olive oil
and is just as delicious. What's more, you don't need to cook a roast or a whole chicken to
enjoy them. Roast extra vegetables and use the leftovers on pizza, or in
a pasta, salad, sandwich or soup. You can also roast regular potatoes, any color
of peppers, carrots, onions, rutabagas and turnips.*

2 cups	cubed (1-1/2-inch/4 cm) peeled butternut squash (8 oz/250 g)	500 mL
2 cups	cubed (1-1/2-inch/4 cm) peeled sweet potato (12 oz/375 g)	500 mL
3	medium leeks, trimmed and halved lengthwise	3
1	large fennel, trimmed and cut lengthwise in sixths	1
3	medium parsnips (4 oz/125 g), peeled and cut in 1-1/2 inch (4 cm) lengths	3
1	sweet red pepper, seeded and cut lengthwise in sixths	1
3 tbsp	olive or vegetable oil	50 mL
2 tbsp	chopped fresh rosemary or 2 tsp (10 mL) dried	25 mL
1-1/2 cups	vegetable or chicken stock	375 mL

1 In roasting pan, toss together squash, sweet potato, leeks, fennel, parsnips,
red pepper, oil, rosemary, and salt and pepper to taste. Spread out in single layer.

2 Add stock; cover tightly with foil. Roast in 400°F (200°C) oven for 20 to 30 minutes
or until liquid has evaporated and vegetables are almost tender.

3 Remove foil and turn vegetables. Reduce heat to 375°F (190°C); roast, uncovered,
for 15 to 30 minutes or until vegetables are very tender and golden.
Makes 8 servings.

Make ahead: Through step 1 for up to 4 hours.

Nutrition Tip
This dish is particularly high
in vitamins and fiber.

Per serving:

calories	171
protein	3 g
total fat	6 g
saturated fat	1 g
cholesterol	0 mg
carbohydrate	30 g
dietary fiber	6 g
sodium	154 mg

R.D.I. Vit A 90%, E 16%, C 80%,
Folate 28%, Ca 7% (80 mg), Iron 10%,
Zinc 5%.

Canada's Food Guide Serving:
3 🥕

Poultry and Meat

Ginger Chicken

Asian Chicken

Mexican Chicken with Cumin and Garlic

Spicy Baked Chicken with Tomato Salsa

Thai Chicken Curry in Coconut Milk

Baked Chicken Breasts with Mango Chutney Sauce

Chicken, Italian Sausage and Sweet Pepper Skewers

Chicken, Spinach and Dried Cranberry Phyllo Pie

Sesame Herb Chicken

Provençal Saffron Chicken

Romaine Salad with Grilled Lemon Chicken

Roasted Chicken, Fennel and Sweet Potatoes

Cornish Hens with Porcini Mushrooms and Basil Stuffing

Cranberry-Glazed Turkey Breast

Turkey Potato Patties

Grilled Turkey Scaloppini in Citrus Ginger Sauce

Turkey Scaloppini with Tomato and Herbs

Ginger Beef and Broccoli Stir-Fry

Szechuan Green Beans and Beef with Rice

Salsa Meat Loaf

Picadillo

Beef Fajitas

Mexican Pork Loin Roast

Chinese Barbecued Pork Tenderloin

Thai Pork and Vegetable Curry with Fresh Basil

Rack of Lamb with Wine Sauce and Cucumber Mint Raita

Greek Marinated Leg of Lamb

Nutritional Notes

Cholesterol: "Help! The Doctor Says My Cholesterol Is Too High"

Red Meats: "Red Meat and Health"

Iron: "Iron-Clad Advice"

Ginger Chicken

Fresh ginger and coriander turn everyday chicken into a dish fit for company.
Serve with basmati rice and herbed carrots.

1 lb	boneless skinless chicken breasts	500 g
1 tbsp	vegetable oil	15 mL
2	cloves garlic, minced	2
1	sweet green or red pepper, cut in thin strips	1
1 cup	thinly sliced mushrooms	250 mL
2 tbsp	each minced gingerroot and soy sauce	25 mL
1 tbsp	oyster sauce	15 mL
1 tsp	granulated sugar	5 mL
1/2 tsp	cornstarch	2 mL
1/4 tsp	cayenne pepper	1 mL
1/4 cup	fresh coriander (cilantro) leaves	50 mL

1 Cut chicken into 2- x 1-inch (5 x 2.5 cm) thin strips.

2 In large nonstick skillet or wok, heat oil over high heat; stir-fry chicken and garlic for 2 minutes. Add sweet pepper and mushrooms; stir-fry for 1 minute.

3 Stir together ginger, soy sauce, oyster sauce, 1 tbsp (15 mL) water, sugar, cornstarch and cayenne pepper; add to skillet and stir-fry for 1 minute or until chicken is no longer pink inside and sauce is thickened. Sprinkle with coriander. *Makes 4 servings.*

Per serving:

calories	**185**
protein	**27 g**
total fat	**5 g**
saturated fat	1 g
cholesterol	67 mg
carbohydrate	**7 g**
dietary fiber	**1 g**
sodium	**687 mg**

R.D.I. Vit A 3%, E 10%, C 38%,
Folate 6%, Ca 1% (15 mg), Iron 8%,
Zinc 11%.

Canada's Food Guide Serving:
¾ 🥕 1 🍗

Asian Chicken

I've updated one of my favorite ways to cook chicken by adding five-spice powder and hot chili paste. Sometimes I add chopped garlic. I like to serve this over precooked chow-mein-type Chinese noodles (not the canned fried ones) that I mix with bean sprouts and green onions and either the sauce in this recipe (I often make extra) or hoisin sauce.

1/3 cup	hoisin sauce	75 mL
2 tbsp	rice wine, scotch or sherry	25 mL
1 tbsp	soy sauce	15 mL
1 tbsp	minced gingerroot	15 mL
1 tsp	chili paste or 1/2 tsp (2 mL) hot pepper sauce	5 mL
1 tsp	sesame oil	5 mL
1 tsp	five-spice powder	5 mL
3 lb	skinless chicken legs and thighs	1.5 kg
4	green onions, chopped	4

1 In small bowl, mix hoisin sauce, rice wine, soy sauce, ginger, chili paste, sesame oil and five-spice powder. Place chicken in baking dish; brush with hoisin mixture. Cover and refrigerate for 1 hour or for up to 24 hours.

2 Bake in 350°F (180°C) oven, basting occasionally, for 40 minutes or until juices run clear when chicken is pierced. Serve sprinkled with green onions. *Makes 6 servings.*

Make ahead: Through step 1, cover and refrigerate for up to 1 day.

Barbecued Asian Chicken: Prepare through step 1. Grill over medium heat with closed lid, turning occasionally, for 25 to 35 minutes or until juices run clear when chicken is pierced.

Five-Spice Powder
This pungent seasoning is a mixture of star anise, Szechuan peppercorns, fennel, cloves and cinnamon. Found in many supermarkets and in Chinese grocery stores, it is used in marinades and sauces.

Per serving:

calories	246
protein	30 g
total fat	9 g
saturated fat	2 g
cholesterol	112 mg
carbohydrate	8 g
dietary fiber	1 g
sodium	474 mg

R.D.I. Vit A 4%, E 3%, C 3%, Folate 9%, Ca 3% (30 mg), Iron 14%, Zinc 39%.

Canada's Food Guide Serving:
1½ 🍗

161

Mexican Chicken with Cumin and Garlic

You can use chicken legs, thighs or breasts in this recipe. If you like more heat, increase the hot pepper flakes. Serve with fresh corn.

Lower-Fat Tip

Removing the skin from chicken parts before cooking significantly reduces fat.

1 tsp	ground cumin	5 mL
1/4 tsp	each salt, pepper and red pepper flakes	1 mL
1 tbsp	vegetable oil	15 mL
2 lb	skinless chicken pieces	1 kg
3	cloves garlic, minced	3
2	whole cloves (optional)	2
2 tsp	fresh lemon or lime juice	10 mL
1/4 cup	chopped fresh coriander (cilantro) or parsley	50 mL

1 Combine cumin, salt, pepper and red pepper flakes; set aside.

2 In large nonstick skillet, heat oil over medium-high heat; brown chicken on all sides. Sprinkle cumin mixture over chicken; add 1 cup (250 mL) water, garlic, whole cloves (if using) and lemon juice. Reduce heat, cover and simmer for 15 minutes.

3 Discard cloves. Remove chicken and keep warm. Boil liquid for about 5 minutes or until reduced to about 1/4 cup (50 mL). Stir in coriander. Spoon over chicken.
   Makes 4 servings.

Per serving:

calories	240
protein	36 g
total fat	9 g
saturated fat	2 g
cholesterol	112 mg
carbohydrate	1 g
sodium	248 mg

R.D.I. Vit A 3%, E 11%, C 2%, Folate 4%, Ca 2% (23 mg), Iron 12%, Zinc 26%.

Canada's Food Guide Serving:
1½)

Spicy Baked Chicken with Tomato Salsa

Wonderful cold as well as hot, this is also great for a picnic.

2 tsp	chili powder	10 mL
1 tsp	each ground cumin and paprika	5 mL
1/4 tsp	turmeric	1 mL
1 tsp	dried oregano	5 mL
1/2 tsp	each salt and pepper	2 mL
1/4 tsp	cayenne pepper	1 mL
2	cloves garlic, minced	2
2 tbsp	fresh lemon juice	25 mL
1 tbsp	vegetable oil	15 mL
4	skinless chicken pieces (legs and breasts), about 2 lb (1 kg)	4
Tomato Salsa:		
2	tomatoes, diced	2
1/2 cup	chopped fresh coriander (cilantro)	125 mL
1/4 tsp	each salt and pepper	1 mL

1 In small nonstick skillet, toast chili powder, cumin, paprika and turmeric over medium heat for about 20 seconds or until it begins to darken. Remove from heat. Stir in oregano, salt, pepper, cayenne, garlic, lemon juice and oil; brush over chicken.

2 Arrange chicken on rimmed baking sheet. Bake in 375°F (190°C) oven, uncovered, turning halfway through and basting twice with juices, for 30 to 40 minutes or until juices run clear when chicken is pierced.

3 Tomato Salsa: Meanwhile, in small bowl, stir together tomato, coriander, salt and pepper. Serve with chicken. *Makes 4 servings.*

Make ahead: Through step 1, cover and refrigerate for up to 8 hours.

Per serving:

calories	**260**
protein	**37 g**
total fat	**10 g**
saturated fat	**2 g**
cholesterol	**111 mg**
carbohydrate	**6 g**
dietary fiber	**1 g**
sodium	**552 mg**

R.D.I. Vit A 14%, E 14%, C 25%, Folate 8%, Ca 3% (33 mg), Iron 17%, Zinc 27%.

Canada's Food Guide Serving:
½ 🥕 1½ 🍗

Thai Chicken Curry in Coconut Milk

I absolutely love the combination of flavors in this easy-to-make yet exotic dish. You can use Thai or Indian curry paste in this recipe and simply add a little more to make this saucy chicken dish hotter and spicier. Serve with basmati rice and a green vegetable.

1 tbsp	vegetable oil	15 mL
4 tsp	red curry paste (medium)	20 mL
1-1/4 lb	boneless skinless chicken, cut in thin strips	625 g
1	onion, coarsely chopped	1
1	sweet red pepper, cut in thin strips	1
	Grated rind of 1 medium lemon	
1 cup	light coconut milk	250 mL
2 tbsp	fish sauce or soy sauce	25 mL
1 tbsp	fresh lemon juice	15 mL
1/3 cup	chopped fresh coriander (cilantro)	75 mL

1 In large nonstick skillet, heat oil over high heat; stir-fry curry paste for 30 seconds.

2 Add chicken; stir-fry for 3 minutes. Stir in onion; stir-fry for 1 minute.

3 Add red pepper and lemon rind; stir-fry for 1 minute or until onion is softened.

4 Stir in coconut milk, fish sauce and lemon juice; bring to boil. Cook for about 2 minutes or until liquid is reduced slightly. Stir in coriander. *Makes 4 servings.*

CHOICE CHICKEN

I prefer chicken labeled air-chilled for its flavor and texture. The surface is drier (it doesn't glisten) than that of water-chilled, and the skin looks slightly yellow. Although a little more expensive, it has a firmer texture because there is less water in the bird; it doesn't "weep" in the package and shrinks less during cooking.

Curry Paste

Curry paste is available in many supermarkets. It keeps its fresh flavor better than curry powder, which loses intensity over time. Pastes bought in a jar keep well for months in the refrigerator. If paste is unavailable substitute curry powder to taste.

Coconut Milk

Canned light coconut milk is available in some supermarkets. If it's unavailable, use 1/2 cup (125 mL) regular coconut milk (which is thicker and about 75% higher in fat than the light) mixed with an equal amount of water.

Per serving:

calories	251
protein	34 g
total fat	9 g
saturated fat	3 g
cholesterol	83 mg
carbohydrate	9 g
dietary fiber	1 g
sodium	478 mg

R.D.I. Vit A 12%, E 11%, C 90%, Folate 8%, Ca 2% (24 mg), Iron 7%, Zinc 12%.

Canada's Food Guide Serving:
1 🍴 1¼ 🍗

Baked Chicken Breasts
with Mango Chutney Sauce

This easy-to-make chicken dish is incredibly moist, tender and delicious. You can dress up the plate with a slice of fresh mango and a sprig of watercress. Serve with chutney and basmati rice cooked in chicken stock and a teaspoon or two of chopped fresh gingerroot.

1/3 cup	mango chutney	75 mL
1/3 cup	1% or 2% plain yogurt	75 mL
1 tbsp	each Dijon mustard and minced gingerroot	15 mL
2 tsp	all-purpose flour	10 mL
2 lb	skinless chicken breasts (about 4, bone-in)	1 kg

1 In small bowl, stir together chutney, yogurt, mustard, ginger and flour. Arrange chicken, bone side down, in single layer in baking dish; spoon chutney mixture over chicken.

2 Bake, uncovered, in 350°F (180°C) oven for 45 minutes or until chicken is no longer pink in center. Remove from oven; let stand for 5 minutes. Spoon any baking juices over top before serving. *Makes 4 servings.*

Make ahead: Through step 1, cover and refrigerate for up to 3 hours.

SAFE HANDLING OF POULTRY

After working with raw or partly cooked chicken, wash the cutting board, counter and utensils with hot, soapy water; rinse. Mix 1 tbsp (15 mL) chlorine bleach in 4 cups (1 L) water; scrub all items, leaving solution on surfaces for at least 45 seconds before rinsing.

Per serving:

calories	258
protein	41 g
total fat	3 g
saturated fat	1 g
cholesterol	103 mg
carbohydrate	15 g
dietary fiber	1 g
sodium	198 mg

R.D.I. Vit A 7%, E 3%, C 15%, Folate 4%, Ca 5% (57 mg), Iron 9%, Zinc 16%.

Canada's Food Guide Serving:
1½

Help! The Doctor Says My Cholesterol Is Too High

Unhealthy levels of cholesterol or triglycerides in the blood are right up there with smoking, high blood pressure and lack of physical activity as risk factors for heart disease and stroke. Fortunately, changes in your diet can significantly lower the risk.

A Primer on Blood Fats: Cholesterol and Triglycerides

- LDL-C, or Low Density Lipoprotein Cholesterol, is the so-called bad kind of cholesterol. It clogs arteries, causes high blood pressure, heart attacks and stroke. The lower LDL-C, the better.
- HDL-C, or High Density Lipoprotein Cholesterol, is a good form of cholesterol. A high reading is a sign that cholesterol is being delivered to the liver, where it is processed and excreted as it should be. The higher HDL-C, the better.
- TC, or Total Cholesterol, is the sum of LDL-C and HDL-C. Although a low TC is generally good news, you can still be at increased risk for heart attack and stroke if your HDL-C is low as well.
- TG, or triglycerides, are a type of blood fat that, like LDL-C, can increase the risk of heart disease, particularly in women. High triglyceride levels tend to go hand in hand with being overweight, alcohol consumption, high blood pressure, low HDL-C levels and diabetes.

HEALTHY EATING TIPS: Lowering High Blood Cholesterol

- Cut back on total amount of fat in your diet, particularly saturated and trans fat (hydrogenated or partially hydrogenated vegetable oil), by following the Lower-Fat Tips throughout this cookbook. To lower elevated blood fats, no more than 25% of your day's calories should come from fat. To get 25% or less of the day's calories from fat, most men should limit fat intake to 75 grams or less, and most women should limit fat intake to 53 grams or less.
- Eat lots of fiber, especially soluble fiber, which helps to lower LDL cholesterol. Whole grain foods, vegetables, fruits and legumes (dried beans, peas and lentils) are high in fiber. (See page 266.)

What's Healthy?

These are commonly accepted benchmarks for healthy blood levels of cholesterol and triglycerides:

- **LDL-C**   less than 3.4 mmol\L
- **HDL-C**   more than 0.9 mmol\L
- **TC**   less than 5.2 mmol\L
- **TG**   less than 2.3 mmol\L

Levels of TC, LDL-C and TG above these levels or a HDL-C below this level are associated with increasing risk for heart disease.

- When a recipe calls for fat, use a little soft margarine or an oil high in either polyunsaturates or monounsaturates instead of butter or shortening. Good choices in oil are olive, canola, safflower, sunflower and corn.
- Restrict the cholesterol in your diet to less than 250 mg a day. The main foods to avoid are organ meats, such as liver, and whole eggs. Eat no more than 2 whole eggs per week, although cholesterol-free egg whites can be used in food preparation. Two egg whites combined with 1 tsp (5 mL) oil can replace 1 whole egg in most recipes.
- If your triglycerides are high as well, avoid all forms of sugar (white and brown sugar, honey, syrup) and alcohol since sugar and alcohol, once digested, are readily converted to triglycerides. Eating more fish rich in omega-3 fat (see page 203) may also help lower blood triglycerides.
- If you are overweight, lose weight. Even small losses can make a big difference. (See page 16.)

HEALTHY EATING TIPS: Raising the Good HDL-Cholesterol

Raising HDL-C is more difficult than lowering TC and LDL-C but it's worth trying if your HDL-C is too low. Follow the same advice for lowering LDL-C with special attention to these points and exceptions:

- Exercise every day. It's more important than ever.
- Choose margarines and oils like olive and canola oil that contain mostly monounsaturated fat rather than oils like safflower, sunflower and corn oil that contain mostly polyunsaturates. Monounsaturated fat doesn't lower HDL-C, whereas polyunsaturates do.
- Women who are at menopause might consider hormone replacement therapy since estrogen raises HDL-C levels.
- Some people may benefit from an alcoholic drink. See page 34 for more details.

Lower-Fat Tip
To reduce fat intake from meat and poultry, reduce portion sizes. Have a 4-oz (125 g) steak instead of an 8-oz (250 g) steak. Have one pork chop or chicken kebab, not two. Make smaller hamburger patties.

Chicken, Italian Sausage and Sweet Pepper Skewers

The sausages in this great summer barbecue dish complement the chicken and colorful vegetables. I usually serve this over rice.

3	small hot Italian sausages (12 oz/375 g)	3
1 lb	boneless skinless chicken breasts	500 g
2	medium sweet peppers (red, yellow or green)	2
2	small yellow or green zucchini	2
Half	red onion or one-quarter Spanish onion	Half
1/4 cup	balsamic vinegar	50 mL
1 tbsp	Dijon mustard	15 mL
2	cloves garlic, minced	2
1/4 tsp	each dried thyme, basil and pepper	1 mL
1 tbsp	olive oil	15 mL

1 Prick sausages all over with sharp knife. Place in saucepan and pour in enough water to cover; bring to boil. Reduce heat and simmer for 15 minutes or until firm; drain. Cut sausages and chicken into 1-inch (2.5 cm) pieces.

2 Core and seed sweet peppers; cut into 1-inch (2.5 cm) pieces. Remove ends from zucchini; cut into 3/4-inch (2 cm) thick slices. Cut onion into 3 or 4 pieces; separate into 1-1/2-inch (4 cm) thick wedges.

3 In shallow dish, combine sausages, chicken, peppers, zucchini and onion. In measuring cup, whisk together vinegar, mustard, garlic, thyme, basil and pepper; whisk in oil. Pour over chicken mixture and toss to mix. Cover and refrigerate for at least 2 hours or for up to 8 hours.

4 Alternating ingredients, thread sausage, chicken, peppers, onion and zucchini onto six 12-inch (30 cm) soaked wooden skewers.

5 Place on greased grill over medium heat. Baste with any remaining marinade. Close lid and cook, turning occasionally, for 10 to 15 minutes or until chicken is no longer pink inside. *Makes 6 servings.*

Make ahead: Through step 3 for up to 8 hours. Through step 4 for up to 1 hour.

Chicken, Spinach and Dried Cranberry Phyllo Pie

This is a favorite recipe of Toronto caterers Caroline McRobbie and Laurien Trowell of C'est Cheese Encore. Serve for brunch, luncheon or dinner along with a salad and warm breads.

* Cooking Tip

For 2 cups (500 mL) cooked cubed chicken, microwave 2 large skinless chicken breasts (1-1/4 lb/625 g), loosely covered, on High for 7 minutes or until no longer pink inside.

1-1/4 cups	2% evaporated milk	300 mL
4 tsp	all-purpose flour	20 mL
1/2 tsp	salt	2 mL
1/4 tsp	each pepper and grated nutmeg	1 mL
2	pkg (300 g each) frozen chopped spinach, thawed	2
2 tbsp	butter	25 mL
2	cloves garlic, minced	2
1/4 cup	pine nuts or sunflower seeds	50 mL
1/4 cup	dried cranberries	50 mL
1	egg	1
2 cups	cooked cubed (3/4-inch/2 cm pieces) chicken*	500 mL
4	sheets phyllo pastry	4

1 In small saucepan, whisk milk with flour; bring to simmer over medium-high heat, stirring, until thickened. Stir in salt, pepper and nutmeg, let cool slightly.

2 Drain spinach; press out moisture. In nonstick skillet, melt 1 tbsp (15 mL) of the butter over medium-high heat; cook spinach, garlic, pine nuts and cranberries, stirring, until garlic begins to color, about 5 minutes.

3 Stir egg into milk mixture; stir into spinach mixture along with chicken.

4 Melt remaining 1 tbsp (15 mL) butter. Spray 9-inch (23 cm) pie plate with nonstick spray. Cut phyllo in half crosswise; drape a half sheet across pie plate so one-third overhangs plate. Brush lightly with butter; press into plate. Repeat with each sheet, layering and fanning sheets to overlap slightly and evenly cover pie plate.

5 Spoon filling into pastry; fold edges over filling to form 2-1/2-inch (7 cm) border.

6 Place pie on baking sheet; cover lightly with foil. Bake in 375°F (190°C) oven for 35 to 40 minutes or until pastry is golden. Let stand for 5 minutes before serving.
Makes 6 servings.

Make ahead: Through step 5, cover and refrigerate for up to 3 hours.

Per serving:

calories	308
protein	24 g
total fat	14 g
saturated fat	5 g
cholesterol	92 mg
carbohydrate	24 g
dietary fiber	4 g
sodium	476 mg

R.D.I. Vit A 61%, D 22%, E 14%, C 23%, Folate 40%, Ca 24% (261 mg), Iron 22%, Zinc 26%.

Canada's Food Guide Serving:
½ 🌾 1¾ 🥕 ¼ 🥛 1 🍗

Sesame Herb Chicken

Bake or barbecue these crunchy herb-and-mustard
coated chicken legs or breasts.

1/3 cup	fine dry bread crumbs	75 mL
2 tbsp	toasted sesame seeds	25 mL
3 tbsp	Dijon mustard	50 mL
1 tbsp	vegetable oil	15 mL
2 tsp	dried Italian herb seasoning	10 mL
1/4 tsp	each salt and pepper	1 mL
2 lb	skinless chicken pieces	1 kg

1 In shallow bowl, mix bread crumbs with sesame seeds.

2 In small bowl, mix mustard, oil, Italian seasoning, salt and pepper; spread over chicken. Roll in crumb mixture.

3 Place on greased baking sheet. Bake in 350°F (180°C) oven for 40 to 45 minutes or until breast is no longer pink inside and juices run clear when legs are pierced. Broil for 1 to 2 minutes to brown. Or barbecue, bone side up, on preheated grill over medium heat with lid down for 25 to 35 minutes, turning once or twice. *Makes 4 servings.*

Make ahead: Through step 2, cover and refrigerate for up to 4 hours. Or cook, cover and refrigerate for up to 2 days to serve cold.

Per serving:

calories	282
protein	38 g
total fat	11 g
saturated fat	2 g
cholesterol	111 mg
carbohydrate	6 g
dietary fiber	trace
sodium	373 mg

R.D.I. Vit A 2%, E 10%, Folate 6%,
Ca 4% (47 mg), Iron 15%, Zinc 30%.

Canada's Food Guide Serving:
¼ 🌾 1¾ 🍗

Provençal Saffron Chicken

I've lightened up this recipe, which I learned at Lydie Marshall's cooking school in Nyons, France. It is a splendid entertaining dish, especially in the fall when tomatoes are at their best. Sometimes I omit the saffron and serve this with saffron rice. Otherwise, serve with mashed potatoes and a green salad.

4 lb	skinless chicken parts or legs	2 kg
1 tsp	each paprika and turmeric	5 mL
1/2 tsp	each salt and pepper	2 mL
2 tbsp	olive oil	25 mL
1 tsp	saffron threads	5 mL
6	medium onions, thinly sliced (6 cups/1.5 L)	6
1 tsp	granulated sugar	5 mL
8	large cloves garlic, chopped	8
6	large tomatoes (3-1/2 lb/1.75 kg) peeled and coarsely chopped or 2 cans (19 oz/540 mL each) tomatoes, chopped	6
2 tbsp	chopped gingerroot	25 mL
1 tsp	coarsely grated lemon rind	5 mL
2/3 cup	pitted green olives	150 mL

1 Arrange chicken in large shallow glass baking dish. In small bowl, mix paprika, turmeric, salt and pepper; stir in 1 tbsp (15 mL) of the oil; spread over chicken. Cover and refrigerate for at least 4 hours or for up to 24 hours.

2 In small dish, pour 2 tbsp (25 mL) hot water over saffron; let stand for 20 minutes.

3 In large nonstick skillet, heat remaining oil over medium-high heat; brown chicken; transfer to plate. Add onions, sugar and any remaining marinade to skillet; cook over medium heat, stirring occasionally, until tender, about 10 minutes. Add garlic, tomatoes and ginger; cook for 10 minutes.

4 Return chicken to pan. Stir in lemon rind and saffron with liquid. Cover and simmer for 20 to 25 minutes or until juices run clear when chicken is pierced.

5 Add olives; cook just until warmed. *Makes 8 servings.*

Make ahead: Through step 1 for up to 1 day. Through step 4, cover and refrigerate for up to 1 day. Reheat.

Romaine Salad with Grilled Lemon Chicken

I first had this at a wonderful, lazy summer lunch at Ellen and Dwain Wright's, our cottage neighbors. I also like to add arugula, croutons, sweet onion slices, or freshly grated Parmesan cheese to the greens. Serve with Focaccia (page 246) or bruschetta.

3 tbsp	each balsamic vinegar and lemon juice	50 mL
	Grated rind from 1 small lemon	
2 tsp	Dijon mustard	10 mL
1/2 tsp	each salt, granulated sugar and pepper	2 mL
1	clove garlic, minced	1
3 tbsp	olive oil	50 mL
4	boneless skinless chicken breasts (1 lb/500 g)	4
6 cups	torn romaine leaves	1.5 L
3 cups	sliced mushrooms (8 oz/250 g)	750 mL
2 cups	lightly packed sliced radicchio	500 mL
1/3 cup	chopped fresh dill or parsley	75 mL

1 In small bowl, combine vinegar, lemon juice and rind, 1 tbsp (15 mL) water, mustard, salt, sugar, pepper and garlic; whisk in 1 tbsp (15 mL) of the oil.

2 Place chicken in single layer in shallow glass baking dish. Pour 2 tbsp (25 mL) of the lemon mixture over top; turn to coat. Cover and refrigerate chicken and remaining mixture separately for at least 1 hour or for up to 24 hours.

3 Place chicken on greased grill over medium-high heat or under broiler; close lid and cook for 5 minutes per side or until no longer pink inside. Transfer to platter; tent with foil. Let stand for 5 minutes.

4 Meanwhile, in large bowl, combine romaine, mushrooms, radicchio and dill.

5 Whisk remaining oil into reserved lemon mixture; pour over salad and toss.

6 Divide salad among 4 plates. Slice chicken crosswise into thin strips; arrange over salad. *Makes 4 servings.*

Make ahead: Through step 2, cover and refrigerate for up to 1 day. Through step 4, cover and refrigerate for up to 4 hours.

Grilled Lemon Chicken

For marinade, mix grated rind from 1 small lemon, 1 tbsp (15 mL) each lemon juice, olive oil and balsamic vinegar, 1/2 tsp (2 mL) Dijon mustard, 1 clove minced garlic, and salt and pepper to taste. Marinate and grill 1 lb (500 g) boneless skinless chicken breasts as in salad recipe.

Nutrition Tip

Romaine lettuce is an excellent source of the B vitamin folate and a high source of vitamin A, and a source of zinc and vitamins C and E. About two-thirds of the vitamin E in this salad is from the olive oil.

Per serving:

calories	267
protein	29 g
total fat	12 g
saturated fat	2 g
cholesterol	67 mg
carbohydrate	11 g
dietary fiber	3 g
sodium	393 mg

R.D.I. Vit A 22%, E 23%, C 48%, Folate 65%, Ca 5% (51 mg), Iron 16%, Zinc 17%.

Canada's Food Guide Serving:
2¾ 🥕 1 🍴

173

Roasted Chicken, Fennel and Sweet Potatoes

Pesto Roast Chicken
Instead of the herb mixture, spread a few spoonfuls of Pesto Sauce (page 85) under the skin.

*Substitution Tip
If you have fresh herbs, use 1 tbsp (15 mL) each chopped fresh rosemary, thyme and sage.

Per serving:

calories	323
protein	16 g
total fat	10 g
saturated fat	1 g
cholesterol	37 mg
carbohydrate	44 g
dietary fiber	8 g
sodium	396 mg

R.D.I. Vit A 271%, E 16%, C 72%, Folate 27%, Ca 11% (117 mg), Iron 11%, Zinc 18%.

Canada's Food Guide Serving:

4 🥕 1 🍖

Here's an easy, succulent Sunday dinner. By stuffing a herb mixture under the chicken skin, you seal in the flavors even though you remove the skin when carving. Parsnips, carrots, onions and leeks are also delicious roasted this way.

3/4 tsp	each dried rosemary, thyme, sage and paprika*	4 mL
1/2 tsp	each salt and pepper	2 mL
1	chicken (3 lb/1.5 kg)	1
3	large cloves garlic, chopped	3
2	onions, quartered	2
2	medium fennel bulbs	2
2	sweet potatoes (1-1/2 lb/750 g total)	2

1 Crumble rosemary into small bowl; mix in thyme, sage, paprika and 1/4 tsp (1 mL) each of the salt and pepper. Sprinkle half inside chicken cavity. Starting at neck end and using fingers, gently loosen skin from each breast up to thigh to form pocket; rub remaining herb mixture under skin.

2 Stuff cavity with garlic and onions. Tie legs together with string; tuck wings under back. Place on rack in roasting pan. Roast in 325°F (160°C) oven for 2 hours or until juices run clear when chicken is pierced and meat thermometer registers 185°F (85°C).

3 Meanwhile, trim base, top and any bruised layers from fennel; cut into quarters. Peel and slice potatoes 1/2 inch (1cm) thick. Place potatoes and fennel in shallow baking dish. Remove 3 tbsp (50 mL) chicken pan juices, adding up to 2 tbsp (25 mL) vegetable oil if not enough juice; spoon over vegetables and toss to coat evenly. Sprinkle with remaining salt and pepper. Roast in oven for 1 hour or until tender when pierced with fork.

4 Transfer chicken to platter. Let stand for 10 minutes. Arrange vegetables around chicken. Pour juices into sauceboat, skimming off fat; pass separately. Remove skin before carving. *Makes 4 servings.*

Cornish Hens with Porcini Mushroom and Basil Stuffing

*I love Cornish hens but for years I've avoided cooking them because I thought
you had to serve a whole hen per person, which is too much, or you had to bone them,
which is fiddly. Since I've discovered that cooked Cornish hens are very easy to cut in half,
I now serve them for dinner party fare. I use dried porcini mushrooms because of
their wonderful flavor and availability. You can also use other fresh or dried
mushrooms such as shiitake or portobello.*

Make Your Own Bread Crumbs

Fresh bread crumbs are very easy to make. Use one or two day-old bread slices and process in a food processor or pass over a hand grater to form crumbs. Don't substitute the fine dry bread crumbs that you buy.

1 oz	dried porcini mushrooms	30 g
1 tbsp	olive oil	15 mL
8 oz	fresh mushrooms, coarsely chopped (2-1/2 cups/625 mL)	250 g
1	leek (white part only), thinly sliced (1-1/2 cups/375 mL)	1
1	large clove garlic, minced	1
	Salt and pepper	
2 cups	soft fresh bread crumbs	500 mL
1/3 cup	packed fresh basil, chopped	75 mL
2 tbsp	sherry	25 mL
3	Cornish hens (about 1-1/3 lb/670 g each)	3

Sherry Gravy:

1 cup	chicken stock and mushroom soaking liquid	250 mL
2	green onions, minced	2
1	clove garlic, minced	1
1 tbsp	all-purpose flour	15 mL
2 tbsp	sherry	25 mL

1 Rinse porcini mushrooms under cold water to remove grit. Place in small bowl and pour in 1 cup (250 mL) very hot water; let stand for 30 minutes or until softened. Drain, reserving liquid; chop large mushrooms.

2 In skillet, heat oil over medium heat; cook fresh mushrooms, leek and garlic for 5 minutes, stirring often; sprinkle with salt and pepper to taste.

Per serving:

calories	330
protein	38 g
total fat	12 g
saturated fat	3 g
cholesterol	106 mg
carbohydrate	15 g
dietary fiber	2 g
sodium	504 mg

R.D.I. Vit A 2%, E 8%, C 5%, Folate 13%, Ca 5% (52 mg), Iron 21%, Zinc 36%.

Canada's Food Guide Serving:
½ 🌾 ¾ 🥕 2 🍗

3 In bowl, stir together leek mixture, bread crumbs, 1/4 cup (50 mL) reserved mushroom liquid and porcini mushrooms, basil, sherry, 1/2 tsp (2 mL) salt and 1/4 tsp (1 mL) pepper. Stuff into hen cavities. Use skewers to fasten closed. Tie legs together with string; tuck wings under back.

4 Place on rack in roasting pan. Roast in 375°F (190°C) oven, basting 2 or 3 times, for 50 to 60 minutes or until juices run clear when hens are pierced. Transfer to warmed platter; tent with foil.

5 Sherry Gravy: Pour pan juices into gravy separator or measuring cup; skim off fat. Add reserved mushroom soaking liquid then chicken stock to make 1 cup (250 mL); set aside. In same roasting pan, cook green onions and garlic, stirring, for 2 minutes. Sprinkle with flour; cook, stirring, for 1 minute. Whisk in chicken stock mixture and sherry; simmer, whisking, for 3 to 5 minutes or until thickened slightly.

6 Using kitchen scissors, cut hens along each side of the backbone. Using scissors or large knife, cut rib cage to divide hens in half. Pile stuffing in center of each half. Serve drizzled with gravy. *Makes 6 servings.*

Special Holiday Dinner

Spiced Shrimp (page 29)
Arugula Salad with Grilled Chèvre (page 48)
Sweet Potato and Ginger Soup (page 66)
Cornish Hens with Porcini Mushroom and Basil Stuffing (opposite page)
Carrot and Squash Purée with Citrus (page 150)
Lemon Cheesecake with Raspberry Glaze (page 284) OR
French Lemon Tart (page 282)

Cranberry-Glazed Turkey Breast

*When I first cooked a whole turkey breast for my family, we were all amazed
at how tender and juicy it was. This recipe is now a family favorite.
It's extremely easy and great for Sunday dinners, Thanksgiving or Christmas
when you don't want to cook a whole turkey.*

3 lb	bone-in thick piece of turkey breast	1.5 kg
1-1/2 cups	fresh cranberry sauce or 1 can (14 oz/398 mL) whole cranberry sauce	375 mL
1/4 cup	packed brown sugar	50 mL
1/4 cup	soy sauce	50 mL
2 tbsp	fresh lemon juice	25 mL
1 tbsp	chopped gingerroot or 1 tsp (5 mL) ground ginger	15 mL
1 tbsp	Dijon mustard or 1 tsp (5 mL) dry mustard	15 mL
1	large clove garlic, minced	1

1 Remove skin and fat from turkey; place, meat side up, in baking dish sprayed with nonstick cooking spray or lined with foil.

2 In bowl, combine cranberry sauce, sugar, soy sauce, lemon juice, ginger, mustard and garlic; spread about 1/3 cup (75 mL) over turkey.

3 Roast, uncovered, in 325°F (160°C) oven for 1-1/2 hours or until thermometer inserted in thickest part registers 170°F (77°C), basting every 30 minutes. Cover loosely with foil and let stand for 15 minutes before slicing. Microwave remaining cranberry mixture until hot; pass separately. *Makes 6 servings.*

Cooking Tip

Turkey breasts vary tremendously in size. I have bought a whole one that weighed 2 lb (1 kg) and a quarter of a turkey breast that weighed 3 lb (1.5 kg). You can get breasts boneless and butterflied or bone-in. Boneless and larger breasts are easier to carve. Butterflied boneless are easy to barbecue when flat and are best for stuffing and rolling.

Sodium-Reduced Cooking

For a sodium-reduced diet, omit soy sauce.

Per serving:

calories	363
protein	42 g
total fat	3 g
saturated fat	1 g
cholesterol	94 mg
carbohydrate	41 g
dietary fiber	1 g
sodium	835 mg

R.D.I. Vit E 2%, C 5%, Folate 5%,
Ca 4% (44 mg), Iron 18%, Zinc 32%.

Canada's Food Guide Serving:
½ 🥕 2 🍗

Turkey Potato Patties

*Here's a great way to use up extra mashed potatoes and cooked turkey
or chicken. Serve these with relish, chutney, chili sauce or salsa, and coleslaw and
a green vegetable. Add a few tablespoons of any chopped fresh herbs such as
parsley, basil or dill if desired.*

1-1/2 cups	mashed potatoes	375 mL
1 cup	finely chopped cooked turkey	250 mL
1/3 cup	chopped green onions	75 mL
1	egg, lightly beaten	1
2 tbsp	light mayonnaise	25 mL
1 tsp	Dijon mustard	5 mL
1/2 tsp	each salt and Worcestershire sauce	2 mL
	Pepper	
2 tsp	butter or soft margarine	10 mL

1 In small bowl, combine potatoes, turkey and onions; stir in egg, mayonnaise,
mustard, salt, Worcestershire sauce, and pepper to taste. Shape into four 1/2-inch
(1 cm) thick patties.

2 In nonstick skillet, melt butter over medium heat; cook patties until browned, about
5 minutes on each side, turning carefully with spatula. *Makes 4 servings.*

Make ahead: Through step 1, cover and refrigerate for up to 2 hours.

Nutrition Tip

Skinless turkey breast is very
low in fat, an excellent source
of niacin and protein, and a
source of potassium, thiamin,
riboflavin and iron.

Per serving:

calories	183
protein	14 g
total fat	8 g
saturated fat	3 g
cholesterol	87 mg
carbohydrate	15 g
dietary fiber	2 g
sodium	658 mg

R.D.I. Vit A 6%, D 4%, E 3%, C 10%,
Folate 8%, Ca 4% (44 mg), Iron 8%,
Zinc 17%.

Canada's Food Guide Serving:
½ 🥕 ¾ 🍗

179

Grilled Turkey Scaloppini in Citrus Ginger Sauce

*Orange, lemon, garlic and ginger marinade adds flavor to turkey scaloppini
and is the base for a delicious sauce you can make in a minute. Serve with grilled zucchini
(page 156) and Wild and Basmati Rice with Lemon and Herbs (page 103)*

Cooking Tip

No-fat sour cream does not curdle when added to this hot sauce; however, whisk well to form a smooth sauce.

1 lb	turkey scaloppini	500 g
1/4 cup	chicken stock	50 mL
2 tbsp	no-fat sour cream	25 mL
2 tbsp	finely chopped fresh parsley	25 mL
Marinade:		
2	cloves garlic, minced	2
2	green onions, chopped	2
	Grated rind from 1 orange	
3 tbsp	each fresh orange and lemon juice	50 mL
2 tbsp	soy sauce	25 mL
1 tbsp	each vegetable oil and minced gingerroot	15 mL
2 tsp	each granulated sugar and Dijon mustard	10 mL

1 Marinade: In small bowl, stir together garlic, onions, orange rind, orange juice, lemon juice, soy sauce, oil, ginger, sugar and mustard.

2 Arrange turkey in large shallow dish; pour marinade over top. Cover and refrigerate for at least 2 hours or for up to 4 hours.

3 Reserving marinade, place turkey on grill over medium-high heat. Cook for 1-1/2 minutes per side or until no longer pink inside. Place on platter.

4 Meanwhile, pour marinade into small saucepan; stir in chicken stock. Bring to boil and boil for 1 minute. Remove from heat. Whisk in sour cream and parsley. Pass separately or pour over turkey. *Makes 4 servings.*

Make ahead: Through step 2, cover and refrigerate for up to 4 hours.

Per serving:

calories	204
protein	29 g
total fat	6 g
saturated fat	1 g
cholesterol	68 mg
carbohydrate	9 g
dietary fiber	1 g
sodium	676 mg

R.D.I. Vit A 2%, E 9%, C 33%, Folate 8%, Ca 5% (58 mg), Iron 14%, Zinc 22%.

Canada's Food Guide Serving:

¼ 🥕 1 🍗

Turkey Scaloppini with Tomato and Herbs

Thin slices of turkey scaloppini, which cook in minutes,
are now available at most supermarkets. Serve this dish with asparagus and
new potatoes.

3	cloves garlic, minced	3
1/4 cup	balsamic vinegar	50 mL
2 tbsp	olive oil	25 mL
1 tbsp	each chopped fresh thyme, rosemary and oregano or 1/2 tsp (2 mL) each dried	15 mL
1/2 tsp	each salt and pepper	2 mL
1 lb	turkey scaloppini	500 g
1/2 cup	finely chopped green onion	125 mL
1	large tomato, diced	1

1 In bowl, combine garlic, vinegar, oil, thyme, rosemary, oregano, salt and pepper. Arrange turkey in large shallow dish. Spoon half of the herb mixture over top; sprinkle with half of the green onion. Cover and refrigerate for 15 minutes or for up to 4 hours.

2 Stir remaining onion and tomato into remaining herb mixture; set aside.

3 Place turkey on lightly greased grill over medium-high heat; cook for 2 minutes on each side or until no longer pink inside.

4 To serve, spoon tomato mixture over slices. *Makes 4 servings.*

Make ahead: Through step 1 for up to 4 hours.

Per serving:

calories	202
protein	27 g
total fat	6 g
saturated fat	1 g
cholesterol	68 mg
carbohydrate	8 g
dietary fiber	1 g
sodium	275 mg

R.D.I. Vit A 3%, E 8%, C 18%, Folate 9%, Ca 3% (32 mg), Iron 14%, Zinc 22%.

Canada's Food Guide Serving:
½ 🌿 1 🍗

Ginger Beef and Broccoli Stir-Fry

Marinating sliced beef in a mixture of cornstarch and soy sauce even for
ten minutes tenderizes and flavors the beef considerably in this family favorite dish.
The sherry also adds taste and tenderizes but it can be omitted.
Serve over rice or Chinese noodles.

* Shopping Tip

To save time, buy stir-fry strips of beef, or thinly slice 1 lb (500 g) of sirloin tip or inside round or other lean cut of beef.

Lower-Fat Tip

Trim all fat from meat and poultry and learn to prepare them without adding extra fat. Grill, bake, poach, steam and braise these foods to keep them as lean as possible.

1 tbsp	each cornstarch, soy sauce and sherry	15 mL
1/2 tsp	each hot pepper sauce and sesame oil	2 mL
2 tbsp	minced gingerroot	25 mL
1 lb	stir-fry beef strips*	500 g
2 tsp	vegetable oil	10 mL
1	onion, sliced	1
3	cloves garlic, minced	3
6 cups	broccoli pieces (1-inch/2.5 cm), about 1 lb (500 g)	1.5 L
1/2 cup	water	125 mL
Sauce:		
1/2 cup	water	125 mL
2 tbsp	soy sauce	25 mL
1 tbsp	cornstarch	15 mL

1 In bowl, mix cornstarch, soy sauce, sherry, hot pepper sauce, sesame oil and half of the ginger; stir in beef strips to coat. Let stand for at least 10 minutes.

2 Sauce: In small bowl, mix together water, soy sauce and cornstarch; set aside.

3 In nonstick skillet or wok, heat 1 tsp (5 mL) of the oil over high heat; stir-fry beef, in two batches, until browned. Transfer to side plate.

4 Reduce heat to medium-high. Add remaining oil; stir-fry onion, garlic and remaining ginger for 1 minute. Stir in broccoli and water; cover and steam for 3 minutes.

5 Return beef to pan. Stir sauce and add to pan; bring to boil, stirring to coat beef well. *Makes 4 servings.*

Make ahead: Through step 1, cover and refrigerate for up to 2 hours.

Per serving:

calories	258
protein	30 g
total fat	9 g
saturated fat	2 g
cholesterol	55 mg
carbohydrate	14 g
dietary fiber	3 g
sodium	879 mg

R.D.I. Vit A 14%, E 23%, C 130%, Folate 29%, Ca 6% (66 mg), Iron 25%, Zinc 73%.

Canada's Food Guide Serving:
2½ 🥕 1 🍗

Szechuan Green Beans and Beef with Rice

Instead of regular brown or white rice, fragrant jasmine rice pairs well with this spicy dish. You can easily adjust the hotness by varying the amount of chili paste or red pepper flakes.

1-1/2 cups	long-grain rice	375 mL
8 oz	extra lean or lean ground beef	250 g
2 tsp	vegetable oil	10 mL
1 lb	green beans, cut in 1-inch (2.5 cm) lengths (4 cups/1 L)	500 g
6 to 8	cloves garlic, minced	6 to 8
1 tsp	hot chili paste or 1/2 tsp (2 mL) crushed red pepper flakes	5 mL
4	green onions (including tops), diagonally sliced	4
Sauce:		
3 tbsp	soy sauce	50 mL
2 tbsp	each granulated sugar and cider or rice vinegar	25 mL
4 tsp	cornstarch	20 mL

1 In saucepan, bring 3 cups (750 mL) water to boil. Stir in rice; cover, reduce heat and simmer for 20 minutes (40 minutes if brown) or until liquid is absorbed.

2 Sauce: Meanwhile, in small bowl, stir together soy sauce, sugar, vinegar, cornstarch and 1/2 cup (125 mL) water; set aside.

3 In nonstick skillet, cook beef over medium-high heat, breaking up with spoon, for 5 minutes or until browned. Remove beef to side dish; drain off fat from pan.

4 Add oil to skillet. Add beans and garlic; stir-fry for 1 minute. Stir in chili paste then 3/4 cup (175 mL) water; cover and cook, stirring occasionally, for 2 to 3 minutes or until beans are tender-crisp. Stir in reserved beef. Stir soy sauce mixture and stir into beef mixture; bring to boil. Stir in green onions; cook for 1 minute. Serve over rice. *Makes 4 servings.*

Make ahead: Through step 3, cover and refrigerate for up to 2 hours; reheat rice and beef in microwave.

Vegetarian Szechuan Green Beans with Rice
Omit beef. If desired, stir in 1 cup (250 mL) crumbled firm tofu or 2 cups (500 mL) drained and rinsed chickpeas at the end of step 4.

Per serving:

calories	447
protein	19 g
total fat	7 g
saturated fat	2 g
cholesterol	29 mg
carbohydrate	76 g
dietary fiber	4 g
sodium	821 mg

R.D.I. Vit A 7%, E 6%, C 22%, Folate 25%, Ca 10% (113 mg), Iron 24%, Zinc 39%.

Canada's Food Guide Serving:
2½ 🌾 2 🥕 ¾ 🍗

183

Salsa Meat Loaf

Rare Hamburger Alert
Why is it safe to eat rare steaks but not hamburgers? Meat is susceptible to a harmful bacteria called verotoxigenic E. coli (VTEC). Limited usually to the outside of meat, VTEC is easily destroyed by searing or grilling the surfaces of a steak. When meat is ground, however, the bacteria are distributed throughout, making it necessary to cook ground meat products right through.

This recipe is one of my son Jeff's favorites. We love it made with coriander, but you can leave it out. I sometimes add a chopped sweet green pepper, stalk of celery and peeled carrot; other times I add some kernel corn. Use any kind of salsa depending on the hotness you prefer. Any leftovers are always delicious hot or cold or in sandwiches.

1 lb	extra lean ground beef	500 g
1	large onion, finely chopped	1
2	cloves garlic, minced	2
3	slices whole wheat bread, crumbled	3
1-1/2 tsp	each crushed dried thyme and oregano	7 mL
1 cup	tomato salsa	250 mL
1	egg, lightly beaten	1
1/4 cup	chopped fresh coriander (cilantro) and/or parsley	50 mL
1/2 tsp	each salt and pepper	2 mL

1 In bowl, combine beef, onion, garlic, bread, thyme, oregano, half of the salsa, the egg, coriander and/or parsley, salt and pepper, mixing just until combined. Spoon into 9- x 5-inch (2 L) loaf pan, smoothing top.

2 Spread remaining salsa evenly over top.

3 Bake in 350°F (180°C) oven for 55 minutes or until firm to the touch and meat thermometer registers 170°F (75°C). Pour off fat. *Makes 4 servings.*

Make ahead: Through step 2, cover and refrigerate for up to 3 hours.

Per serving:

calories	282
protein	27 g
total fat	12 g
saturated fat	5 g
cholesterol	114 mg
carbohydrate	17 g
dietary fiber	4 g
sodium	641 mg

R.D.I. Vit A 8%, D 4%, E 6%, C 27%, Folate 15%, Ca 7% (81 mg), Iron 30%, Zinc 61%.

Canada's Food Guide Serving:
1¼ 🌾 ¼ 🥕 1 🍖

Picadillo

Picadillo is a Spanish or Mexican ground meat hash with vegetables and usually capers and green olives. Serve it over rice or use it as a filling for sweet peppers, tortillas, taco shells or pita, or spoon over toasted buns.

1 lb	lean ground beef	500 g
2	onions, chopped	2
4	cloves garlic, minced	4
2	small sweet green peppers, chopped	2
1	can (5-1/2 oz/156 mL) tomato paste*	1
1 cup	water	250 mL
1/2 cup	raisins	125 mL
1/4 cup	chopped pitted green olives	50 mL
2 tbsp	capers, drained	25 mL
2 tbsp	each Worcestershire sauce** and red wine vinegar	25 mL
1/4 tsp	each salt and pepper	1 mL

1 In large nonstick skillet, cook beef over medium heat, breaking up with spoon, until browned; drain off any fat.

2 Add onions; cook, stirring often, for 5 minutes or until nearly tender. Add garlic and green peppers; cook, stirring often, for 2 to 3 minutes or until onions are softened.

3 Mix tomato paste with water; stir into beef mixture along with raisins, olives, capers and Worcestershire sauce. Simmer for 5 minutes to blend flavors. Stir in vinegar, salt and pepper. *Makes 5 servings.*

Substitution Tips

*You can substitute 1 can (14 oz/398 mL) tomato sauce for the tomato paste and water but it will be much higher in sodium.

**For a flavor variation, substitute 1-1/2 tsp (7 mL) ground cumin for the Worcestershire sauce and add with the garlic.

Per serving:

calories	264
protein	20 g
total fat	10 g
saturated fat	3 g
cholesterol	45 mg
carbohydrate	27 g
dietary fiber	4 g
sodium	464 mg

R.D.I. Vit A 10%, E 18%, C 67%, Folate 10%, Ca 4% (47 mg), Iron 26%, Zinc 47%.

Canada's Food Guide Serving:
3 🌾 1 🥕

Beef Fajitas

Flavored with Mexican spices and wrapped in tortillas, this popular restaurant dish makes a quick and easy supper at home. It's just as delicious with chicken.

Dairy-Free Beef Fajitas

Omit yogurt. Mash 1 ripe peeled avocado with 2 tbsp (25 mL) fresh lime or lemon juice and the jalapeño pepper. Spread over tortillas; top with beef mixture and sprinkle with remaining coriander.

Hamburger Fajitas

Substitute lean ground beef, chicken or turkey for the beef strips.

Spicy Chicken Fajitas

Substitute boneless skinless chicken breasts for the beef.

8 oz	boneless inside round steak or sirloin, sliced in thin strips	250 g
1/2 cup	chopped fresh coriander (cilantro)	125 mL
1 tbsp	fresh lime or lemon juice	15 mL
1 tsp	each chili powder and ground cumin	5 mL
1/2 tsp	pepper	2 mL
1 tsp	vegetable oil	5 mL
1	onion, sliced	1
2	cloves garlic, minced	2
1	each sweet red and green pepper, thinly sliced	1
1 cup	corn kernels	250 mL
4	10-inch (25 cm) flour tortillas	4
1/2 cup	2% plain yogurt or light (5%) sour cream	125 mL
1 tsp	minced fresh jalapeño pepper or 1/4 tsp (1 mL) hot pepper sauce	5 mL

1 In bowl, toss together beef, 2 tbsp (25 mL) of the coriander, lime juice, chili powder, cumin and half of the pepper; let stand for 10 minutes.

2 In heavy nonstick skillet, heat oil over medium-high heat; stir-fry beef for 3 minutes or until browned. Transfer to plate.

3 Add onion and garlic to skillet; stir-fry for 2 minutes, adding 1 tbsp (15 mL) water if necessary to prevent scorching. Add red and green peppers, 2 tbsp (25 mL) of the remaining coriander and remaining pepper; sprinkle with salt to taste. Stir-fry for 3 to 5 minutes or until tender. Stir in beef and corn until heated through.

4 Meanwhile, wrap tortillas in foil; warm in 350°F (180°C) oven for 5 minutes.

5 Mix yogurt, remaining coriander and jalapeño pepper; spread evenly over tortillas. Spoon beef mixture evenly down center of each; roll up to enclose. *Makes 4 servings.*

Per serving:

calories	345
protein	22 g
total fat	7 g
saturated fat	1 g
cholesterol	26 mg
carbohydrate	49 g
dietary fiber	4 g
sodium	337 mg

R.D.I. Vit A 17%, E 4%, C 127%, Folate 18%, Ca 9% (104 mg), Iron 29%, Zinc 35%.

Canada's Food Guide Serving:

2¼   2   ½

Mexican Food Toppers to Compare

Item	Calories	Grams of fat
Regular corn tortilla chips (1 oz/28 g)	144	6 to 7
Homemade baked corn tortilla chips (1 oz/28 g)	110	0.8
Sour cream, 14% B.F. (2 tbsp/25 mL)	44	4
Sour cream, 1% B.F. (2 tbsp/25 mL)	31	0.4
Guacamole (2 tbsp/25 mL)	43	4
Cheddar cheese, grated (2 tbsp/25 mL)	57	5
Light-style Cheddar cheese, grated (2 tbsp/25 mL)	42	3
Salsa (2 tbsp/25 mL)	9	trace
Green chili peppers, diced (2 tbsp/25 mL)	5	trace
Tomatoes, chopped (2 tbsp/25 mL)	5	trace

Red Meat and Health

Many people have stopped eating red meat out of concern for its fat content. However, although red meat isn't essential for good health, it is the best source of iron, bar none. And we know that women who eat red meat have superior iron stores and are less likely to suffer from iron depletion and iron deficiency anemia. (See page 194.)

HEALTHY EATING TIPS: Red Meat

- Eat less red meat by reducing portions; a 3 to 4 oz (90 to 125 g) serving is plenty.
- Buy the leanest cuts and varieties most of the time.
- Choose lean or extra lean ground meat. When possible, precook ground meat and drain off the fat.
- Always trim visible fat from meat before cooking it.
- Cook in low-fat ways: broil, bake or roast, braise or sauté in a nonstick pan.

The Leanest Red Meats

- Beef: eye of round cuts, all round cuts, ribeye, flank steak, sirloin and strip loin steak, rump roast, stewing beef, tenderloin, extra-lean and lean ground beef.
- Pork: center cut loin roast, leg butt portion, tenderloin, picnic shoulder roast (cottage rolls)
- Lamb: loin chop, leg roast
- Processed red meat: ham, pastrami, back bacon (pea meal)

Mexican Pork Loin Roast

The flavors of toasted sesame seeds and mild green chilies spike up this pork roast. Serve with salsa or fruit chutney.

Hoisin Fast-Fry Pork Chops

For a very quick and easy dish, spread pork chops with hoisin sauce to coat; grill over medium-high heat until just barely pink in center, 2 to 3 minutes on each side for 1/4-inch (5 mm) thick chops, 5 to 7 minutes per side for 1/2-inch (1 cm) thick chops. Sprinkle with chopped fresh coriander (cilantro).

2 tbsp	sesame seeds	25 mL
2 tbsp	chopped canned or fresh green chilies	25 mL
2 tbsp	cider vinegar	25 mL
3	cloves garlic, minced	3
1/4 tsp	each pepper, crushed red pepper flakes and cinnamon	1 mL
Pinch	ground cloves	Pinch
2 lb	boneless pork loin roast	1 kg

1 In small skillet, toast sesame seeds over medium-high heat, stirring, until golden, 3 to 4 minutes. In small bowl, combine sesame seeds, chilies, vinegar, garlic, pepper, red pepper flakes, cinnamon and cloves; set aside.

2 Trim any fat from pork; place in roasting pan. Cut slits in top of pork; spread with sesame seed mixture.

3 Pour hot water into pan, about 1/4 inch (5 mm) deep. Roast in 325°F (160°C) oven for about 90 minutes or until meat thermometer inserted in center registers 160°F (70°C). Transfer to cutting board; tent with foil and let stand for 10 minutes before carving. *Makes 6 servings.*

Make ahead: Through step 2, cover and refrigerate for up to 6 hours.

Per serving:

calories	210
protein	30 g
total fat	9 g
saturated fat	3 g
cholesterol	81 mg
carbohydrate	1 g
sodium	69 mg

R.D.I. Vit A 3%, E 1%, C 10%, Folate 3%, Ca 3% (34 mg), Iron 10%, Zinc 28%.

Canada's Food Guide Serving:
1¼ 〉

Sunday Dinner

Mexican Pork Loin Roast (this page)
Two-Potato Scallop (page 148)
Broccoli Carrot Stir-Fry (page 149)
Black Forest Frozen Yogurt Cake (page 287)

Chinese Barbecued Pork Tenderloin

Five-spice powder, which lends an extra depth of flavor to this savory pork, is
available in many supermarkets. Serve this dish with a green vegetable
and mashed potatoes, or with Chinese noodles seasoned with hoisin sauce, coriander and
green onions. Garnish the meat with slivers of green onions or chopped fresh
coriander and accompany it with a fruit relish, chutney or Mango Salsa (page 11).

Oven-Roasted Chinese Barbecued Pork Tenderloin

Roast marinated tenderloins in roasting pan in 350°F (180°C) oven for 25 to 35 minutes or until just a hint of pink remains in center and juices run clear when pork is pierced.

1/4 cup	hoisin sauce	50 mL
1 tbsp	sake, scotch or sherry	15 mL
1 tbsp	grated gingerroot	15 mL
1/2 tsp	five-spice powder	2 mL
1/2 tsp	hot chili paste or hot pepper sauce	2 mL
2	pork tenderloins (about 12 oz/375 g each)	2

1 In small bowl, combine hoisin sauce, sake, ginger, five-spice powder and hot chili paste, mixing well. Spread evenly over pork; cover and refrigerate for at least 1 hour.

2 Place on greased grill over medium-high heat; cook for 3 minutes on each side or until browned all over. Reduce heat to low; close lid and cook, brushing occasionally with any remaining marinade, for 15 to 20 minutes or until just a hint of pink remains in center. Transfer to cutting board; tent with foil and let stand for 5 minutes. Slice diagonally into 1/4-inch (5 mm) thick slices. *Makes 6 servings.*

Make ahead: Through step 1, cover and refrigerate for up to 1 day.

Easy Asian Dinner

Teriyaki Chicken Bites (page 33)
OR Spicy Thai Chicken Noodle Soup (page 70)
Chinese Barbecued Pork Tenderloin (this page) with Mango Salsa page 11)
Broccoli Carrot Stir-Fry (page 149)
Coconut Rice (page 125)
Lemon Cake (page 260) with Raspberry Sauce (page 261)

Per serving:

calories	171
protein	28 g
total fat	4 g
saturated fat	1 g
cholesterol	61 mg
carbohydrate	5 g
dietary fiber	trace
sodium	226 mg

R.D.I. Vit E 2%, Folate 4%, Ca 1% (11 mg), Iron 11%, Zinc 27%.

Canada's Food Guide Serving:

Thai Pork and Vegetable Curry with Fresh Basil

The influence of Indian cuisine on Thai cooking is evident in this fresh-flavored mild curry, one of my favorite dishes. Serve over steaming mounds of rice.

1 tbsp	vegetable oil	15 mL
5 tsp	red curry paste* (or 1-1/2 tsp/7 mL curry powder)	25 mL
1 lb	lean boneless pork, cut in thin slices	500 g
1	onion, cut in wedges	1
1 cup	cut green beans (1-1/2 inch/4 cm long)	250 mL
2 tbsp	fish sauce	25 mL
1-1/2 cups	corn kernels (frozen or canned) or baby corn cobs	375 mL
1 cup	thickly sliced mushrooms (regular or Chinese)	250 mL
1	sweet red pepper, thinly sliced	1
1/3 cup	chopped fresh basil	75 mL
1 tsp	granulated sugar	5 mL

1 In nonstick wok or skillet, heat oil over high heat; stir-fry red curry paste for 1 minute. Add pork; stir-fry for 3 minutes.

2 Add onion, green beans and fish sauce; stir-fry for 5 minutes (cover for 2 minutes instead of stir-frying if needed to cook beans).

3 Add corn, mushrooms and red pepper; stir-fry until tender, about 2 minutes. Sprinkle with basil and sugar; stir-fry for 1 minute. *Makes 4 servings.*

Thai Chicken and Vegetable Curry with Fresh Basil

Substitute 1 lb (500 g) boneless skinless chicken breast for the pork.

*Curry Paste

Curry paste is available in many supermarkets. It keeps its fresh flavor better than curry powder, which loses intensity over time. Pastes bought in a jar keep well for months in the refrigerator.

Thai Dinner

Thai Coconut, Ginger and Chicken Soup (page 72)
Thai Pork and Vegetable Curry with Fresh Basil (this page)
Jasmine Rice (page 116)
Ginger Citrus Fruit Salad (page 274)

Per serving:

calories	281
protein	27 g
total fat	11 g
saturated fat	3 g
cholesterol	63 mg
carbohydrate	21 g
dietary fiber	3 g
sodium	458 mg

R.D.I. Vit A 14%, E 11%, C 93%, Folate 23%, Ca 6% (66 mg), Iron 15%, Zinc 43%.

Canada's Food Guide Serving:
2½ 🥕 1 🍖

Rack of Lamb with Wine Sauce and Cucumber Mint Raita

Tender and fast to cook, racks of lamb are perfect for entertaining and are available in the freezer section of most supermarkets. To serve eight people, use the same amount of marinade and four racks of lamb. Serve with a chutney or Mango Salsa (page 11) or this refreshing East Indian raita and sauce made from the marinade.

* **Substitution Tip**

White wine can be used instead of red wine, or substitute 2 tbsp (25 mL) each lemon juice and water.

2	cloves garlic, minced	2
2	green onions, chopped	2
1/4 cup	each soy sauce and red wine*	50 mL
1 tbsp	each Dijon mustard and granulated sugar	15 mL
	Juice and grated rind of 1 medium orange	
1 tsp	curry powder	5 mL
1/2 tsp	each dried thyme and pepper	2 mL
2	racks of lamb (about 1 lb/500 g each),** trimmed of fat	2
	Cucumber Mint Raita (opposite page)	

1 In small bowl, combine garlic, onions, soy sauce, wine, mustard, sugar, orange rind and juice, curry powder, thyme and pepper; mix well.

2 Place lamb in shallow dish; pour marinade over top and turn to coat. Cover and refrigerate for at least 4 hours or for up to 24 hours.

3 Remove from refrigerator 30 minutes before cooking. Reserving marinade, place lamb on grill over medium-high heat, or in roasting pan; cook on grill, with lid closed, or roast in 425°F (220°C) oven, basting occasionally, for 15 to 20 minutes for medium-rare or until pinkish-red in center. Transfer to cutting board; tent with foil and let stand for 5 to 10 minutes before cutting racks in half between bones.

4 Meanwhile, pour marinade into small saucepan; bring to boil and cook for 1 minute. Serve in small pitcher along with lamb and Cucumber Mint Raita. *Makes 4 servings.*

Make ahead: Through step 2, cover and refrigerate for up to 1 day.

**If racks of lamb are smaller than 1 lb (500 g) each, cook 3 racks for 4 people.

Per serving (with raita):

calories	224
protein	22 g
total fat	9 g
saturated fat	4 mg
cholesterol	73 mg
carbohydrate	14 g
dietary fiber	2 g
sodium	857 mg

R.D.I. Vit A 4%, E 1%, C 38%, Folate 9%, Ca 10% (109 mg), Iron 21%, Zinc 35%.

Canada's Food Guide Serving:
½ 🥕 1½ 🍖

Cucumber Mint Raita

This cool, refreshing condiment goes well with curries or lamb.
You can prepare it about six hours in advance if you sprinkle the cucumber
with the salt, let it drain for an hour, then
mix all the ingredients together.

1/2 cup	1% to 2% plain yogurt (regular or extra-thick)	125 mL
2 tbsp	each chopped fresh parsley and mint leaves	25 mL
1-1/2 tsp	finely chopped onion	7 mL
1/4 tsp	each salt and ground cumin	1 mL
1 cup	finely chopped seeded peeled cucumber	250 mL

1 In bowl, combine yogurt, parsley, mint, onion, salt and cumin.

2 Stir in cucumber. *Makes 1 cup (250 mL).*

Make ahead: Through step 1, cover and refrigerate for up to 2 hours. Through step 2, cover and refrigerate for up to 1 hour.

Special Dinner Party

Marinated Shrimp and Mango Salad (page 46)
Rack of Lamb with Wine Sauce and Cucumber Mint Raita (opposite page)
Tomatoes Provençal (page 142)
Mashed Potatoes
Make-Ahead Cumin-Spiced Broccoli (page 137)
Strawberries with Lemon Cream in Phyllo Pastry Cups (page 281)
or Orange Mousse Meringue Pie (page 288)

Per 1/4 cup (50 mL):

calories	23
protein	2 g
total fat	trace
cholesterol	1 mg
carbohydrate	3 g
dietary fiber	trace
sodium	167 mg

R.D.I. Vit A 3%, C 8%, Folate 5%, Ca 6% (64 mg), Iron 3%, Zinc 4%.

Canada's Food Guide Serving:
½ 🥕

Iron-Clad Advice

Iron Supplements

If you take iron supplements, keep these guidelines in mind:

- Supplements contain non-heme iron and are best absorbed when taken with meat, poultry, fish and/or a source of vitamin C such as orange juice.

- Large doses of iron may cause nausea, constipation or diarrhea and complicate gastrointestinal problems such as ulcerative colitis.

- Take extra care to keep iron supplements out of reach of children since iron supplements are an all-too-common source of accidental poisoning in the home.

- Since long-term use of 30 mg or more of elemental iron will reduce the absorption of copper and zinc, don't take this dosage of iron supplement for long periods without checking with your doctor.

- If you suffer from low iron and take calcium supplements, take the calcium between meals since calcium can reduce the absorption of iron up to 50%.

Getting enough iron each day is more of an issue for women and children than for men because women and children eat less iron-rich food. If a person fails to get enough iron, iron stores gradually deplete, eventually resulting in iron-deficiency anemia. People with low iron stores generally look pale, feel weak and tired, and are short of breath. In young children, a lack of iron has been linked to a reduction in learning ability.

There are two types of iron, heme and non-heme. Heme iron, which is the best absorbed, is found only in meat, poultry and fish. All other sources of iron, including the iron in supplements, are non-heme iron, which isn't always absorbed well, although there are ways to improve its absorption.

HEALTHY EATING TIPS: Improving Your Iron Intake

Here's how to maximize absorption of iron from food:

- Unless you are vegetarian, include red meat in your diet several times a week. Lake trout, clams and oysters are also rich in iron.

- Combine small bits of meat, poultry and fish with iron-enriched pasta and rice. Meat, poultry and fish contain a substance dubbed the "meat factor," which improves the absorption of iron from other foods in the same meal.

- Enriched pasta can be a significant source of iron.

- Include a source of vitamin C at each meal (see page 214).

- Avoid drinking coffee and tea within 2 hours of a meal. Coffee reduces iron absorption by 35 to 39%, whereas tea cuts it by some 60%.

- Don't eat natural wheat bran if you suffer from chronically low iron because it significantly reduces iron absorption.

What Popeye Didn't Know

Dark green spinach, Swiss chard, beet greens and other dark green vegetables are nutritious foods but are not good sources of iron. The oxalate in these vegetables binds the iron, making it largely unavailable. The iron in legumes (dried beans, peas and lentils), nuts, seeds and whole grains faces a similar fate except it is phytate in these foods that binds the iron. The effects of phytate can be reduced by the presence of vitamin C in the same meal, making these foods a source of iron.

Greek Marinated Leg of Lamb

Cookbook author and great cook Rose Murray prepared this easy-to-make recipe as part of a Greek dinner at our cottage in the Gatineau hills of Quebec. Everyone loved it. Serve with tzatziki or Herbed Yogurt-Cheese (page 22).

2	boneless legs of lamb (2 lb/1 kg each) or 1 large	2
2	large cloves garlic, minced	2
1 tbsp	dried leaf oregano	15 mL
	Grated rind of 1 medium lemon	
1/3 cup	fresh lemon juice	75 mL
2 tbsp	extra-virgin olive oil	25 mL
1 tsp	pepper	5 mL

1 Remove all fat from lamb; if not butterflied, cut horizontally and open like a book to lie flat. Place in shallow container just large enough to hold lamb in single layer.

2 Sprinkle with garlic, oregano, lemon rind and juice, oil and pepper; cover and refrigerate for 6 hours or for up to 24 hours.

3 Remove from refrigerator 30 minutes before cooking. Remove lamb from marinade. Place on lightly greased grill over high heat or under broiler; cook, brushing occasionally with marinade, for 10 minutes on each side for medium-rare. Let stand for 5 to 10 minutes before carving. *Makes 10 servings.*

Make ahead: Through step 2 for up to 1 day.

Greek Dinner

Spicy Hummus (page 12) with Crudités or Pita Bread
**Greek Marinated Leg of Lamb (this page) with tzatziki
or Herbed Yogurt-Cheese (page 22)**
Herb-Roasted Potatoes and Onions (page 146)
Grilled Sweet Peppers, Zucchini and Baby Eggplant (page 156)
Greek Salad (page 43)
Fresh Fruit Salad and Greek Pastries

Top Foods for Iron

- red meat
- poultry
- fish: lake trout, clams, oysters
- ready-to-eat breakfast cereals
- enriched pasta (not all products are enriched)
- legumes (dried beans, peas and lentils), nuts, seeds and whole grains.

Per serving:

calories	216
protein	31 g
total fat	9 g
saturated fat	4 g
cholesterol	112 mg
carbohydrate	1 g
sodium	51 mg

R.D.I. Vit E 4%, C 2%, Ca 1% (11 mg), Iron 19%, Zinc 51%.

Canada's Food Guide Serving:
1½

Fish

Hoisin-Glazed Sea Bass

Red Snapper with Lime Coriander Marinade

Monkfish with Sun-Dried Tomatoes, Capers and Basil

Oven-Fried Fish Fillets

Grilled Teriyaki Tuna

Fish Fillets, Tomato and Mushroom Packets

Baked Whole Salmon with Lime Ginger Mayonnaise

Phyllo-Wrapped Salmon Fillets with Coconut Rice

Salmon in Black Bean Sauce

Tomatoes, Mussels and Rice

Cioppino

Shrimp and Scallops in Coconut Milk

Shrimp and Scallop Skewers

Shrimp Provençal Casserole

Pan-Seared Sea Bass with Red Onion and Lemon

Nutrition Notes

Blood Pressure: "Keeping a Check on High Blood Pressure"

Arthritis: "Arthritis? What You Eat Might Help"

Hoisin-Glazed Sea Bass

All my tasters loved this dish, whether it was made with swordfish, tuna,
halibut or salmon; in the oven, on the grill or in the microwave.
Strips of green onion or chives add a fresh colorful garnish to the plate.

Hoisin-Glazed Salmon Steaks

My favorite way to barbecue salmon is to simply spread it with hoisin sauce. Grill over medium-high heat, with lid down, for 3 to 5 minutes per side or until fish flakes when tested with fork.

Cooking Tip

For very tender, moist results, microwave the Hoisin-Glazed Sea Bass at High for 5 minutes instead of grilling or baking.

2 tbsp	hoisin sauce	25 mL
1 tsp	minced gingerroot	5 mL
1 tsp	sesame oil	5 mL
1/4 tsp	chili paste (optional)	1 mL
4	sea bass fillets, 1-inch (2.5 cm) thick (4 oz/125 g each)	4

1 In small bowl, mix together hoisin sauce, ginger, oil, and chili paste (if using).

2 Spread over each side of fish. Place on greased grill or on broiler pan or on baking sheet. Grill over medium heat with lid down, basting occasionally with any remaining hoisin mixture, for 5 minutes. Turn and grill for another 5 minutes or until fish flakes easily when tested with fork. (Or bake in 425°F/220°C oven for 10 minutes.)
Makes 4 servings.

Per serving:

calories	135
protein	21 g
total fat	3 g
saturated fat	1 g
cholesterol	47 mg
carbohydrate	4 g
dietary fiber	trace
sodium	207 mg

R.D.I. Vit A 6%, Folate 3%, Ca 1% (14 mg), Iron 3%, Zinc 5%.

Canada's Food Guide Serving:
1 ❯

Red Snapper with Lime Coriander Marinade

These moist, flavorful fillets are easy to prepare and quick to cook.
You can also substitute sea bass, rainbow trout, grouper or swordfish fillets.
Serve with wedges of lime and garnish plate with sprigs of coriander.

1-1/2 lb	red snapper fillets	750 g
1/4 cup	chopped fresh coriander (cilantro)	50 mL
	grated lime rind from 1 medium lime	
1/4 cup	fresh lime juice	50 mL
2 tbsp	olive oil	25 mL
2	cloves garlic, minced	2
1 tsp	minced canned or fresh green chilies (optional)	5 mL
1/4 tsp	each salt and pepper	1 mL

1 Place fillets in 8-inch (2 L) square baking dish. Whisk together coriander, lime rind and juice, oil, garlic, chilies, salt and pepper; pour over fillets. Cover and marinate for 30 minutes.

2 Bake in 425°F (220°C) oven for 15 minutes or until fish flakes easily when tested with fork. *Makes 4 servings.*

Grilled Fillets with Lime Coriander Marinade

Prepare through step 1. Grease and preheat barbecue to medium heat; grill fillets for 3 to 5 minutes on each side (time will vary depending on thickness of fish and temperature of barbecue and weather if outside) or until fish is opaque and flakes easily when tested with fork.

Per serving:

calories	204
protein	35 g
total fat	6 g
saturated fat	1 g
cholesterol	62 mg
carbohydrate	1 g
sodium	145 mg

R.D.I. Vit A 5%, E 4%, C 7%, Folate 4%, Ca 5% (56 mg), Iron 3%, Zinc 7%.

Canada's Food Guide Serving:
1¾

Per serving:

calories	178
protein	27 g
total fat	6 g
saturated fat	1 g
cholesterol	45 mg
carbohydrate	5 g
dietary fiber	1 g
sodium	349 mg

R.D.I. Vit A 7%, E 6%, C 17%, Folate 11%, Ca 4% (49 mg), Iron 11%, Zinc 11%.

Canada's Food Guide Serving:
½ 🥕 2 🍖

Monkfish with Sun-Dried Tomatoes, Capers and Basil

Monkfish is a deliciously moist fish that is wonderful in this easy Provençal-type recipe. If unavailable, use fresh cod, sea bass or halibut fillets. (I tried it with frozen cod fillets and prefer the fresh.)

1/3 cup	dry-packed sun-dried tomatoes	75 mL
2	cloves garlic	2
1/2 cup	lightly packed fresh Italian parsley	125 mL
1/4 cup	lightly packed fresh basil leaves	50 mL
1 tbsp	capers, drained	15 mL
6	black olives, pitted and chopped	6
3	anchovies, chopped	3
1-1/2 tsp	olive oil	7 mL
1-1/2 lb	monkfish fillets, skinless	750 g

1 Cover tomatoes with hot water; soak for 15 minutes or until softened. Drain.

2 In food processor, combine tomatoes, garlic, parsley, basil, capers, olives, anchovies and oil; chop coarsely.

3 Place fish on lightly greased baking sheet; evenly spread tomato mixture over fish.

4 Bake in 375°F (190°C) oven for 10 to 15 minutes or until opaque throughout. (Time will vary depending on thickness of fish.) *Makes 4 servings.*

Make ahead: Through step 3, cover and refrigerate for up to 4 hours.

Mediterranean Spring Dinner

Monkfish with Sun-Dried Tomatoes, Capers and Basil (this page)
Leek and Rice Pilaf (page 116)
Asparagus with Shaved Parmesan (page 137)
French Lemon Tart (page 282)

Oven-Fried Fish Fillets

Serve this pleasing family supper with Sesame-Spiced Oven-Fried
Potatoes (page 144). You can use almost any white fish fillets.
If using frozen, be sure to thaw them before cooking.

1/2 cup	fine dry bread crumbs	125 mL
1-1/2 tsp	dried Italian herb seasoning (or basil and oregano)	7 mL
1 tsp	grated lemon rind	5 mL
1/2 tsp	each salt and pepper	2 mL
1	egg or 2 egg whites	1
1 tsp	water	5 mL
1 lb	fish fillets (halibut or cod)	500 g
1 tsp	vegetable oil	5 mL

1 In shallow dish, stir together bread crumbs, herb seasoning, lemon rind, salt and pepper.

2 In small bowl, beat egg or whites with water.

3 Dip fillets into egg; dip into bread crumb mixture to coat both sides.

4 Spread oil on baking sheet; place in 450°F (230°C) oven for 30 seconds. Place fish in single layer on hot baking sheet. Bake in top half of oven for 4 minutes; turn and bake for another 4 minutes for 1/2-inch (1 cm) thick fillets, another 6 minutes for 1-inch (2.5 cm) thick fillets. *Makes 4 servings.*

Cooking Tip

Oven-frying reduces the fat but keeps the coating and flavor of fried fish. In place of the hot oil in a frying pan, use a teaspoon (5 mL) of oil on a baking sheet.

Toaster Oven Method

This dish cooks fine in a toaster oven. Be sure to pre-heat oven. Cook two pieces of fish at a time for 10 minutes or until fish flakes when tested with a fork.

Per serving:

calories	198
protein	27 g
total fat	5 g
cholesterol	36 mg
carbohydrate	10 g
dietary fiber	1 g
sodium	492 mg

R.D.I. Vit A 5%, E 12%, C 2%, Folate 7%, Ca 8% (92 mg), Iron 14%, Zinc 7%.

Canada's Food Guide Serving:

½ 🌾 1¼ 🍗

Grilled Teriyaki Tuna

Tuna is the only fish I prefer to eat slightly undercooked. When it is overcooked, its texture changes dramatically from being so delicate and tender that it melts in your mouth to dry and flaky. It is therefore best to watch the fish closely during the entire cooking time, which, luckily, is brief. Serve each fillet on a bed of greens mixed with some chopped fresh coriander and tossed with a light vinaigrette, such as Herb and Ginger Vinaigrette (page 57).

Cooking Tips

For easy grilling of delicate fish and vegetables, use a fish or vegetable grilling basket sprayed with nonstick cooking spray. The basket allows you to turn the fish without breaking and to keep small vegetables from falling onto the coals. Cooking time will vary depending on thickness and temperature of fish, outdoor temperature (if barbecuing) and distance from heat.

2 tbsp	each soy sauce and water	25 mL
2 tbsp	rice wine or sherry	25 mL
1 tbsp	finely chopped gingerroot	15 mL
1 tsp	each sesame oil and granulated sugar	5 mL
1	clove garlic, minced	1
4	tuna fillets, 3/4- to 1-inch (2 to 2.5 cm) thick (4 oz/125 g each)	4

1 Combine soy sauce, water, rice wine, ginger, sesame oil, sugar and garlic. Arrange fillets in single layer in shallow dish; pour sauce over top. Cover and marinate for 15 minutes or refrigerate for up to 2 hours.

2 Place fish on greased grill over high heat; cook, basting with marinade once, for about 3 minutes or until brown to depth of 1/8 inch (3 mm). Turn and cook, basting with marinade once, for another 3 minutes or until brown to depth of 1/8 inch (3 mm) yet still red in centre. Remove from heat; cover and let stand until centre is reddish-pink. (It continues to cook upon standing.) *Makes 4 servings.*

Make ahead: Through step 1 for up to 2 hours.

Grilled Teriyaki Swordfish: Substitute swordfish steaks for the tuna. Grill over medium heat for 3 to 4 minutes on each side (or 5 minutes on first side and 2 to 3 on second side) or until white outside yet pinkish white in center.

Per serving:

calories	180
protein	27 g
total fat	6 g
saturated fat	2 g
cholesterol	43 mg
carbohydrate	2 g
sodium	352 mg

R.D.I. Vit A 67%, Folate 1%, Ca 1% (11 mg), Iron 9%, Zinc 8%.

Canada's Food Guide Serving:

Fish Fillets, Tomato and Mushroom Packets

This no-mess dinner in a packet is easy to make for one or two.
You can use any vegetable that cooks in less than 10 minutes, such as sweet peppers,
canned artichokes, spinach, thinly sliced celery or thawed vegetables.
Vegetables that take longer to cook can also be used but sauté them first.
Be sure to preheat the oven completely before cooking.
Serve with cooked rice, couscous, barley or mashed potatoes.

2	fish fillets (6 oz/175 g each)	2
1	medium tomato, coarsely chopped	1
1/2 cup	sliced mushrooms	125 mL
2 tbsp	packed chopped fresh basil or dill or 1/4 tsp (1 mL) dried basil, herbes de Provence or oregano	25 mL
1 tsp	each fresh lemon juice and olive oil	5 mL
1	clove garlic, minced	1
1	green onion, diagonally sliced	1

1 Place each fish fillet on 12-inch (30 cm) square of foil.

2 In bowl, toss together tomato, mushrooms, basil, lemon juice, oil, garlic, green onion, and salt and pepper to taste; spoon evenly over fish. Fold foil loosely over top, sealing tightly. Place on baking sheet. Bake in 450°F (230°C) oven for about 10 minutes or until fish flakes easily when tested with fork. *Makes 2 servings.*

FISH RICH IN OMEGA-3 FAT

Two key omega-3 fats, eicosapentenoic acid (EPA) and docosahexanoic acid (DHA), are found mainly in fattier fish such as salmon, swordfish, trout, cod, herring, mackerel and bluefish. Both EPA and DHA have been linked to wide-ranging health benefits such as lower blood triglyceride levels, lower blood pressure, relief from symptoms associated with rheumatoid arthritis and premenstrual syndrome. The amount of omega-3 fat in omega-3-enriched eggs is small compared to what you get in fish, and the heart benefits of these eggs are not yet established.

Nutrition Tip

Don't worry about the amount of fat in some fish such as salmon. Fish oils contain omega-3 fatty acids, of which we need to get more.

Per serving:

calories	189
protein	33 g
total fat	4 g
saturated fat	1 g
cholesterol	97 mg
carbohydrate	5 g
dietary fiber	1 g
sodium	123 mg

R.D.I. Vit A 9%, E 3%, C 18%, Folate 10%, Ca 7% (74 mg), Iron 17%, Zinc 10%.

Canada's Food Guide Serving:
¾ 🥕   1¾ 🍖

203

Baked Whole Salmon
with Lime Ginger Mayonnaise

*This fish dish is my favorite for buffet parties. For a large crowd, I cook it ahead of time,
completely wrapped in foil, and serve it cold. When I plan to serve hot salmon,
I place it on a foil-lined baking sheet because I like the flavor of it roasted uncovered.
For easier serving, I have the fish store remove the bones.*

Pesto Salmon Fillets

Spread thick salmon fillets
with Pesto Sauce (page 85).
Bake in 425°F (220°C) oven
or grill on greased grill over
medium heat with lid down
for 10 minutes.

1	whole salmon, cleaned and head removed (6 lb/2.7 kg)	1
1	bunch fresh dill	1
2	lemons	2
	Lime Ginger Mayonnaise (opposite page)	
	Garnish: lettuce, cherry tomatoes, lemon slices, cucumber, fresh dill	

I Rinse salmon under cold water; paper-towel dry. Let stand at room temperature for
30 minutes. Cut piece of foil large enough to completely wrap salmon; place foil on
baking sheet. Place one-third of the dill on foil; place salmon on top of dill.

2 Cut 1 of the lemons into thin slices. Place half the slices and half the remaining dill
in salmon cavity; sprinkle with salt and pepper to taste. Arrange remaining lemon
slices and dill on top of salmon.

3 Squeeze juice from remaining lemon; drizzle over salmon. Wrap in foil, folding
edges to seal. Bake in 425°F (220°C) oven for about 40 minutes or until just barely
opaque and flakes easily when tested with fork. (Test by making a small slit in
thickest part of salmon.)

4 To serve hot: Either place whole salmon on large serving platter; remove cooked
lemon and dill. Garnish platter, then cut and serve at the table. Or cut lengthwise
along backbone; remove skin and discard. Cut lengthwise again along midline.
Cut cross-wise into single-serving portions. Using spatula, transfer salmon pieces to
warm serving platter. Lift off bone (if not removed before baking). Repeat with
underside, easing salmon away from skin. Pass Lime Ginger Mayonnaise separately.

5 To serve cold: Remove foil from top of salmon; let salmon cool for at least 1 hour.
Gently pull off skin from top of salmon. Using sharp knife, scrape off darkish brown

**Per 3 oz (90 g) serving of
salmon without sauce:**

calories	155
protein	22 g
total fat	7 g
saturated fat	I g
cholesterol	60 mg
carbohydrate	0 mg
sodium	48 mg

R.D.I. Vit A 1%, D 174%, E 21%,
Folate 11%, Ca 1% (13 mg), Iron 6%,
Zinc 8%.

Canada's Food Guide Serving:

I 🐟

fatty flesh; discard. Discard juices, cooked dill and lemon slices. Cut salmon into serving-size pieces as in step 4. Or, for whole salmon, transfer salmon to serving platter by inverting platter over salmon and flipping salmon and platter over so skin side is up. Remove remaining foil, skin and dark fatty flesh Garnish platter. Pass Lime Ginger Mayonnaise separately. *Makes 14 to 16 servings.*

Make ahead: Through step 3, cool and refrigerate for up to 1 day.

Lime Ginger Mayonnaise

Serve this with any fish or seafood

1/2 cup	light mayonnaise	125 mL
1/2 cup	2% plain yogurt	125 mL
	Grated rind of 1 lime	
2 tsp	fresh lime juice	10 mL
2 tsp	finely minced gingerroot	10 mL
1	clove garlic, minced	1

l In small bowl, stir together mayonnaise, yogurt, lime rind and juice, ginger and garlic. Cover and refrigerate for 1 hour or for up to 24 hours. *Makes 1 cup (250 mL).*

Spring / Summer Cold Buffet

Hoisin Smoked-Turkey Spirals (page 30)
Mango Salsa in Mini Phyllo Tarts (page 11)
Whole Baked Salmon with Lime Ginger Mayonnaise (page 204)
Cold Spanish-Style Asparagus (page 136) or
Garlic Green Beans with Flavored Oil (page 40)
Curried Lentil, Wild Rice and Orzo Salad (page 50)
Cantaloupe and Blueberries with Fresh Strawberry Sauce (page 269)
and Lemon Cake (page 260)

l tbsp:	
calories	28
protein	trace
total fat	2 g
saturated fat	trace
cholesterol	0 mg
carbohydrate	lg
sodium	55 mg

R.D.I. Ca 1% (15 mg), Zinc 1%.

Phyllo-Wrapped Salmon Fillets
and Coconut Rice

This intriguing dish can be made early in the day and served later to guests.
Accompany it with Carrot and Squash Purée with Citrus (page 150)
or steamed spinach and a green salad.

Cooking Tip

Salmon fillets should be about 1-inch (2.5 cm) thick; either buy them cut or buy a thick, skinless salmon fillet about 1 to 1-1/4 lb (500 to 625 g) and cut crosswise into 4 strips.

1	recipe Salmon in Black Bean Sauce (opposite page)	1
1	recipe Coconut Rice (page 125)	1
4	sheets phyllo pastry	4
1/2 cup	coarsely chopped fresh coriander (cilantro)	125 mL
4 tsp	butter, melted	20 mL

1 Prepare Salmon in Black Bean Sauce through step 1. Cook Coconut Rice; let cool.

2 Lay one sheet of phyllo on counter (keep others covered with damp cloth). About 2 inches (5 cm) from long side of pastry, spoon one-quarter of the rice lengthwise into 3- to 4-inch (8 to 10 cm) strip about size of salmon fillet, leaving 4-inch (10 cm) border on each side; sprinkle with 1 tbsp (15 mL) coriander.

3 Lay salmon over rice; sprinkle with 1 tbsp (15 mL) coriander, and salt and pepper to taste. Brush pastry with 1/2 tsp (2 mL) butter. Fold 2-inch (5 cm) border over filling; fold each side over and roll up. Place seam side down on greased baking sheet. Brush with butter. Repeat to form 4 packages.

4 Bake in 425°F (220°C) oven for 15 minutes or until golden brown. Let stand for 5 minutes. *Makes 4 servings.*

Make ahead: Through step 3, cover and refrigerate for up to 4 hours. Remove from refrigerator 30 minutes before baking or add 3 to 5 minutes to baking time.

Per serving:

calories	552
protein	35 g
total fat	18 g
saturated fat	7 g
cholesterol	88 mg
carbohydrate	59 g
dietary fiber	2 g
sodium	772 mg

R.D.I. Vit A 6%, D 227%, E 31%, C 3%, Folate 20%, Ca 4% (49 mg), Iron 18%, Zinc 19%.

Canada's Food Guide Serving:

 2 ▨ 1½ ◗

Hot Buffet

Baked Whole Salmon with Lime Ginger Mayonnaise (page 204)
Coconut Rice (page 125) or Two-Potato Scallop (page 148)
Carrots Provençal (page 147) or Braised Fennel with Parmesan (page 151)
Spinach Salad with Walnut Vinaigrette (page 38)
Deep-Dish Apple Apricot Phyllo Pie (page 277)

Salmon in Black Bean Sauce

Chinese black bean sauce adds a salty and distinct flavor to salmon or any other fish.
However, use it in small amounts as it has a strong taste.
I like to sprinkle chopped fresh coriander over the salmon and serve it with
Jasmine rice or Coconut Rice (page 125).

2 tbsp	Chinese black bean sauce	25 mL
1 tbsp	soy sauce	15 mL
2 tsp	minced gingerroot	10 mL
1-1/2 tsp	sherry	7 mL
1 tsp	liquid honey	5 mL
1 tsp	rice vinegar	5 mL
4	salmon fillets (5 oz/150 g each)	4

1 Combine black bean sauce, soy sauce, ginger, sherry, honey and vinegar. Arrange fillets in single layer in baking dish; pour sauce mixture over top. Cover and marinate for 30 minutes or refrigerate for up to 24 hours.

2 Bake in 400°F (200°C) oven for 14 minutes or just until opaque and fish flakes easily when tested with fork. *Makes 4 servings.*

Make ahead: Through step 1, cover and refrigerate for up to 1 day.

Cooking Tips

To microwave two salmon fillets, cover loosely with waxed paper and microwave on High for about 4 minutes. It's very important not to overcook fish. Fish is cooked when it flakes easily when tested with a fork and just turns opaque. Keep in mind that the fish continues to cook slightly after it has been removed from the heat source.

Per serving:

calories	**231**
protein	**29 g**
total fat	**9 g**
saturated fat	**1 g**
cholesterol	**78 mg**
carbohydrate	**6 g**
dietary fiber	trace
sodium	**446 mg**

R.D.I. Vit A 1%, D 227%, E 27%, Folate 15%, Ca 2% (18 mg), Iron 9%, Zinc 10%.

Canada's Food Guide Serving:
1½ 🍖

Make-Ahead Dinner Party

Porcini Mushroom Bisque (page 73)
Phyllo-Wrapped Salmon Fillets and Coconut Rice (page 206)
Tossed Greens with Herb and Ginger Vinaigrette (page 57)
Lemon Cake with Raspberry Sauce (page 260)

Keeping a Check on High Blood Pressure

Blood Pressure: What's Healthy?

Blood pressure is measured by two numbers: the larger, top number is the systolic, and the smaller, bottom number is the diastolic.

- A target blood pressure is 120/80 mmHg or lower.
- A high blood pressure is 140/90 mmHg
- Pressures in between, such as 130/85 mmHg, should be treated as a wake-up call to make some lifestyle changes since they, too, are associated with an increased risk of disease.

High blood pressure, or hypertension, is a common medical problem and one of the key risk factors for heart disease, stroke and kidney disease.

HEALTHY EATING TIPS: High Blood Pressure

If you've been diagnosed with high blood pressure, these dietary strategies may help you.

- Lose weight if needed. Even small weight losses can make a difference.
- Restrict sodium intake to 2000 mg or less per day. (See below.)
- Avoid alcohol.
- Increase your intake of potassium by eating some of these potassium-rich vegetables and fruit every day: cantaloupe, broccoli, oranges, bananas, carrots, squash.
- Get 2 to 4 servings of milk products daily for calcium, and eat fish rich in omega-3 fat (see page 203) two or more times a week. The links between lower blood pressure and dietary calcium and omega-3 fat aren't fully understood yet, but preliminary findings identify these nutrients as potentially useful.

Salt Under Pressure

Although there is controversy about whether healthy people need to cut back on salt, people with high blood pressure should take salt restriction seriously.

HEALTHY EATING TIPS: Reducing Salt and Sodium

- Reduce salt used to prepare foods. The recipes in this book show you how to use herbs and spices to flavor foods without a lot of salt. One teaspoonful (5 mL) of salt contains approximately 2400 mg sodium.
- Use as few commercially prepared foods as possible. Approximately 75% of the salt we eat comes from these foods. Foods generally high in salt include cheese, particularly processed cheese; luncheon and deli meats; canned soups and vegetables; bouillon; crackers; cookies; packaged casserole mixes; snack foods; frozen foods and fast foods.
- When possible, choose packaged foods such as crackers that contain less sodium. Remember, though, that claims such as "50% less sodium" don't mean low sodium. Check the label since these products can still be high in sodium.

Tomatoes, Mussels and Rice

When the mussels open, their liquid adds a delicate seafood flavor to the rice in this paella-type dish.

1 tbsp	olive oil	15 mL
3/4 cup	long-grain converted rice	175 mL
2	cloves garlic, minced	2
1/4 tsp	turmeric	1 mL
Pinch	hot pepper flakes	Pinch
1	bay leaf	1
1 tsp	saffron threads (optional)	5 mL
1-1/2 cups	chopped tomatoes*	375 mL
2/3 cup	bottled clam juice or chicken stock	150 mL
1/2 cup	dry white wine	125 mL
2 lb	mussels	1 kg
1/4 cup	chopped fresh parsley	50 mL

1 In large skillet, heat oil over medium heat; cook rice, garlic, turmeric, hot pepper flakes, bay leaf, and saffron (if using), stirring often, for 2 minutes. Stir in tomatoes, clam juice and wine; bring to boil. Reduce heat to medium-low; cover and simmer for 15 minutes.

2 Meanwhile, wash mussels and remove any beards. Discard any mussels that have broken or open shells that do not close when tapped. Nestle mussels into rice mixture; cover and cook until mussels open and rice is tender, 5 to 8 minutes. Discard any mussels that do not open. Discard bay leaf. Sprinkle with parsley. *Makes 3 servings.*

Cooking Tip

Don't refrigerate mussels wrapped in plastic; instead remove from plastic bag and place in bowl, cover with ice and refrigerate.

* **Substitution Tip**

You can substitute 1 can (19 oz/540 mL) tomatoes, drained and chopped, for the fresh.

Nutrition Tip

Mussels are low in fat, high in iron, folate, zinc and are a good source of protein.

Per serving:

calories	317
protein	15 g
total fat	7 g
saturated fat	1 g
cholesterol	26 mg
carbohydrate	45 g
dietary fiber	2 g
sodium	380 mg

R.D.I. Vit A 17%, E 11%, C 43%, Folate 24%, Ca 6% (65 mg), Iron 35%, Zinc 25%.

Canada's Food Guide Serving:

1¼ 🌾 ¾ 🥕 1 🍖

Cioppino

Here's an excellent dish for a dinner party. The shellfish make it look and taste special, yet it is easy to prepare and has a nice light broth.

* Substitution Tip

*Substitution Tip

If crab isn't available, add small clams or 8 oz (250 g) scallops along with the fish, or increase mussels to 2 lb (1 kg).

Cooking Tip

Crab can be left in the shell or removed. If leaving shell on, crack the legs so it is easy to remove the meat.

Serving Tip

Serve Cioppino in bowls with toasted cheese bread or with grilled slices of Italian bread, rubbed with a cut clove of garlic and drizzled with olive oil, and a green salad.

Per serving:

calories	221
protein	29 g
total fat	5 g
saturated fat	1 g
cholesterol	117 mg
carbohydrate	12 g
dietary fiber	2 g
sodium	512 mg

R.D.I. Vit A 22%, E 12%, C 88%, Folate 18%, Ca 8% (90 mg), Iron 28%, Zinc 21%.

Canada's Food Guide Serving:
1¾ 🍴 2 🥩

1 tbsp	olive oil	15 mL
1	onion, chopped	1
4	cloves garlic, minced	4
1	sweet red pepper, chopped	1
1	can (28 oz/796 mL) tomatoes (undrained)	1
1 cup	dry red or white wine	250 mL
1	bottle (8 oz/240 mL) clam juice	1
1/3 cup	chopped fresh parsley	75 mL
1/2 tsp	each dried basil, oregano and fennel seeds	2 mL
1/4 tsp	hot pepper sauce or red pepper flakes	1 mL
1 lb	white fish fillets (monkfish, cod or halibut)	500 g
1 lb	mussels (in shells)	500 g
1 lb	crab legs (in shells), cut in 3-inch (8 cm) pieces*	500 g
1 lb	large shrimp, peeled and deveined	500 g
1/4 cup	chopped fresh basil	50 mL

1 In large saucepan, heat oil over medium heat; cook onion, garlic and red pepper, stirring often, until onion is tender, 5 to 8 minutes. Stir in tomatoes, breaking up with knife. Add wine, clam juice, parsley, dried basil, oregano, fennel seeds and hot pepper sauce; bring to boil. Reduce heat and simmer, uncovered, for 20 minutes, stirring occasionally.

2 Cut fish fillets into 2-inch (5 cm) pieces. Scrub mussels and remove beards; discard any that don't close when tapped.

3 Add fillets, mussels, and crab if uncooked; cover and simmer for 2 minutes. Stir in shrimp and fresh basil (and crab if cooked); simmer for 3 to 5 minutes or until shrimp turn pink and mussel shells open. Discard any that don't open. Season with salt and pepper to taste. *Makes 6 servings.*

Make ahead: Through step 2. Cover and refrigerate for up to 6 hours; reheat.

SHRIMP FACTS

Buying

- Look for tightly sealed packages of solidly frozen shrimp without ice crystals or frost.
- Shrimp is packaged according to the number of shrimp per pound (500 grams): In a package containing 21 to 30 per pound (500 grams), the shrimp are larger than in a package with 36 to 45. In most recipes, you can substitute one size for another. However, small salad shrimp are more often used in salads, sandwiches and dips, and larger shrimp in casseroles, pastas and other main-course dishes.

Thawing

- Most shrimp are frozen, or have likely already been frozen and thawed.
- Do not refreeze thawed shrimp; once thawed, use immediately.
  - *In microwave:* Defrost until partially thawed.
  - *In refrigerator:* Place in sealed container overnight.
  - *In cold water:* Place sealed package in cold water for 30 to 60 minutes (time depends on size, frozenness).

Peeling and Deveining

- Use kitchen shears to cut through soft undershell. Peel off shell, leaving tail if desired.
- It is not necessary to devein small and medium shrimp. It is, however, a good idea to devein large shrimp since the vein may contain grit. Cut through rounded side of shrimp; use tip of knife to pull away black vein.

Cooking

- Most frozen shrimp are sold cooked and need only to be thawed and reheated. Overcooking toughens them.
- For unpeeled cooked shrimp: Rinse and drain. Place in saucepan of hot water; cover and bring to boil. Remove shrimp as soon as water comes to boil. Peel off shell, and tail if desired.
- For peeled cooked shrimp. Thaw and drain; use as is or add to recipe near end of cooking time.
- Raw shrimp: Whether peeled or unpeeled, thawed raw shrimp can be cooked in simmering water for 3 to 8 minutes, depending on size. Shrimp are cooked when they curl into circles and turn bright red or pink.

Shrimp and Scallops in Coconut Milk

This popular dish for entertaining contains some of my favorite flavors: ginger, garlic, lemon and coriander. It's easy to make and looks very attractive, too. Canned coconut milk is available in many supermarkets and Asian food stores. It adds a creamy texture and delightful taste yet is rather high in fat, so I use a moderate amount of the light variety. Serve over rice with Garlic Green Beans with Flavored Oil (page 40).

1	medium lemon	1
1 tbsp	vegetable oil	15 mL
1/2 cup	chopped onion	125 mL
6	cloves garlic, minced	6
1/4 cup	finely chopped gingerroot	50 mL
1 tbsp	all-purpose flour	15 mL
3/4 cup	light coconut milk	175 mL
1/4 cup	white wine	50 mL
1/4 tsp	crushed red pepper flakes	1 mL
1-1/2 lb	extra-large shrimp (raw or cooked), peeled and deveined	750 g
8 oz	large scallops	250 g
1/3 cup	each chopped fresh parsley and coriander (cilantro)	75 mL
3	green onions, finely chopped	3

1 Grate rind and squeeze juice from lemon; set aside. In large nonstick saucepan, heat oil over medium heat; cook onion, garlic and ginger, stirring, until tender, about 5 minutes.

2 Sprinkle with flour and stir to mix. Stir in coconut milk, wine, lemon rind and juice and red pepper flakes; bring to simmer, stirring constantly.

3 Stir in shrimp and scallops; cover and cook, stirring occasionally, for 5 to 10 minutes or until shrimp are pink and scallops are opaque. Stir in parsley and coriander; sprinkle with green onions. *Makes 6 servings.*

Make ahead: Through step 2, cover and set aside for up to 2 hours.

Do you have food allergies or asthma?

Valuable information, allergy-related products and support about any allergy, asthma or anaphylaxis is available from the Allergy/Asthma Information Association (AAIA). The AAIA publishes a medically approved quarterly magazine covering the latest finding and practical tips about living with a variety of allergic conditions. Write to Allergy/Asthma Information Association, 30 Eglinton Avenue West, Suite 750 Mississauga, Ontario L5R 3E7 Local calls: (905) 712-2242 Long-distance calls: 1-800-611-7011 Fax: (905) 712-2245

Per serving:

calories	223
protein	30 g
total fat	6 g
saturated fat	2 g
cholesterol	185 mg
carbohydrate	9 g
dietary fiber	1 g
sodium	245 mg

R.D.I. Vit A 8%, E 6%, C 20%, Folate 10%, Ca 5% (57 mg), Iron 19%, Zinc 18%.

Canada's Food Guide Serving:
¼ 🥕 1¼ 🍗

Arthritis? What You Eat Might Help

Vitamin C:
Top Food Sources
- citrus: oranges, grapefruits*
- papaya
- cantaloupe
- kiwi
- strawberries
- broccoli
- brussels sprouts
- peppers
- potato
- all juices

Vitamin E:
Top Food Sources
- vegetable oils
- margarine
- wheat germ
- nuts and seeds
- spinach, Swiss chard

Beta Carotene:
Top Food Sources
- carrots
- Swiss chard, spinach
- cooked pumpkin
- squash
- sweet potatoes
- cantaloupe
- mango
- papaya

Probably no disease is more plagued with unproved cures than arthritis. Special diets, foods and supplements top the list, but few are backed up by solid science. The main treatment for arthritis continues to center on anti-inflammatory drugs. However, healthy eating plays an important part in coping with the disease, which can leave one weak, tired and lacking an appetite. And more recent findings offer some hope that certain foods and dietary changes may give additional support to traditional arthritis treatments.

HEALTHY EATING TIPS: Arthritis

- Weight loss is key to improving osteoarthritis in feet, knees, hips and fingers, particularly if it's in the weight-bearing joints. What's more, some research indicates that higher intakes of vitamin C, beta carotene and vitamin E may slow the progression of the disease and reduce the pain.

- If you suffer from the symptoms of rheumatoid arthritis — tender and swollen joints, morning stiffness, loss of grip strength and fatigue, you might be helped by an increased intake of two omega-3 fatty acids: eicosapentaenoic acid (EPA) and docosahexaenoic acid (DHA). To increase your intake of omega-3 fat, eat more fish (see page 203). You may also want to consult with your doctor about an omega-3 fatty acid supplement. Do not self-medicate with fish oil supplements as they are not suitable for everyone. People with bleeding disorders, those on anticoagulant medications and those with uncontrolled high blood pressure shouldn't take fish oil supplements at all.

- For those with gout, the days of eliminating high-purine foods such as liver, mussels and sardines to reduce levels of uric acid are pretty much over. In addition to medication, you may find some relief if you lose weight, avoid alcohol altogether and drink 6 to 8 glasses of water a day to help eliminate the uric acid that crystallizes in joints and causes the pain. If you need to lose weight, approach it sensibly. Severe calorie restriction can bring on an attack of gout in susceptible people.

*Grapefruit and grapefruit juice should not be taken if on cyclosporine medication.

Shrimp and Scallop Skewers

Each year I have a new barbecue favorite that I make over and over again; last year it was these. They are absolutely delicious made with any combination of salmon, shark, scallops and shrimp. The shrimp can be raw or cooked. My husband's favorite combination is scallops, sweet peppers and onion. Serve over rice or couscous.

1 lb	medium to large scallops	500 g
1	sweet green pepper, cut into 1-inch (2.5 cm) pieces	1
Half	red onion, quartered and separated into wedges	Half
8 oz	peeled large shrimp (raw or cooked)	250 g
Marinade:		
1/4 cup	hoisin sauce	50 mL
2 tbsp	chopped fresh coriander (cilantro)	25 mL
2 tbsp	each soy sauce and rice vinegar	25 mL
2 tbsp	granulated sugar or liquid honey	25 mL
1 tbsp	chopped gingerroot	15 mL
1 tbsp	chopped garlic	15 mL
1/4 tsp	hot pepper sauce or chili paste	1 mL

1 **Marinade:** In small bowl, combine hoisin sauce, coriander, soy sauce, vinegar, sugar, ginger, garlic, and hot pepper sauce.

2 Thread scallops, green pepper, onion and shrimp onto soaked wooden skewers. Place on plate; brush marinade all over. Cover and refrigerate for up to 4 hours.

3 Place on greased grill over medium heat, brush with marinade in dish. Close cover and grill for 10 to 12 minutes or until scallops are opaque and shrimp bright pink, turning once or twice. *Makes 4 servings.*

Make ahead: Add seafood to marinade; cover and refrigerate for up to 1 day. Or prepare through step 2, cover and refrigerate for up to 4 hours.

Marinated Salmon on Skewers

Prepare as directed using 1 lb (500 g) skinless salmon fillet, 3/4- to 1-inch (2 to 2.5 cm) thick; cut salmon into cubes.

Summer Barbecue

Shrimp and Scallop Skewers (this page)
Basmati Rice
Sliced Tomatoes with Herb and Ginger Vinaigrette (page 57)
Garlic Green Beans with Flavored Oil (page 40)
Peach Blueberry Pie (page 279)

Per serving:

calories	240
protein	32 g
total fat	3 g
saturated fat	trace
cholesterol	124 mg
carbohydrate	21 g
dietary fiber	2 g
sodium	789 mg

R.D.I. Vit A 6%, E 1%, C 42%, Folate 12%, Ca 5% (60 mg), Iron 13%, Zinc 20%.

Canada's Food Guide Serving:
1 🍴 1½ 🥄

215

Shrimp Provençal Casserole

The Provençal flavorings of garlic, parsley and fresh basil make this a well-liked
make-ahead dish. Extra large or large shrimp work best.
Serve with Spinach Salad with Walnut Vinaigrette (page 38) and crusty bread.

Cholesterol-Lowering Tip

Yes, shrimp do contain some cholesterol, but because they are also so low in calories and fat, they can be eaten in moderation on a cholesterol-lowering diet.

1 tbsp	olive oil	15 mL
1-1/4 cups	long-grain converted rice	300 mL
3/4 cup	chopped fresh parsley	175 mL
1/3 cup	chopped fresh basil or 2 tsp (10 mL) dried	75 mL
1	large onion, chopped	1
1	sweet green pepper, chopped	1
6	large cloves garlic, minced	6
6 cups	halved mushrooms (1 lb/500 g)	1.5 L
1	can (28 oz/796 mL) tomatoes, chopped	1
1/4 tsp	crushed red pepper flakes	1 mL
1-1/2 lb	large peeled shrimp (raw or cooked)	750 g
3/4 cup	freshly grated Parmesan cheese	175 mL

Per serving:

calories	400
protein	34 g
total fat	9 g
saturated fat	3 g
cholesterol	182 mg
carbohydrate	45 g
dietary fiber	4 g
sodium	626 mg

R.D.I. Vit A 18%, E 10%, C 58%, Folate 18%, Ca 25% (277 mg), Iron 32%, Zinc 29%.

Canada's Food Guide Serving:
1¼ ☙ 2¾ 🥕 ¼ 🥛 1 🍖

1 In saucepan, heat 1/2 tsp (2 mL) of the oil over medium heat; cook rice, stirring, for 1 minute. Add 2-1/2 cups (625 mL) boiling water; cover, reduce heat and simmer for 15 to 20 minutes or until water is absorbed and rice is still slightly firm. Sprinkle with 1/4 cup (50 mL) of the parsley, half of the basil, and salt and pepper to taste. Spread in greased 13- x 9-inch (3 L) baking dish.

2 In large nonstick skillet, heat remaining oil over medium heat; cook onion and green pepper, stirring occasionally, for 5 minutes. Add two-thirds of the garlic and the mushrooms; increase heat to high and cook, stirring often, for 5 minutes or until vegetables are tender.

3 Add tomatoes and red pepper flakes; bring to boil. Reduce heat to medium; simmer, uncovered and stirring occasionally, for 10 to 15 minutes or until sauce-like consistency. Stir in shrimp, half of the remaining parsley, half of the cheese and remaining basil. Spoon over rice.

4 Combine remaining cheese, chopped garlic and parsley; sprinkle over tomato mixture. Bake, uncovered, in 325°F (160°C) oven for 30 to 40 minutes or until bubbling. *Makes 6 servings.*

Make ahead: Through step 3, but reduce cooking time to 8 minutes; cover and refrigerate for up to 1 day. Increase baking time by 10 to 15 minutes.

Pan-Seared Sea Bass with Red Onion and Lemon

I love sea bass; it's very juicy and rich-tasting. Like most fish, it is best when prepared simply.

4	sea bass fillets, 4 to 5 oz (125 to 150 g) each, skin on	4
	Salt and pepper	
4 tsp	olive oil	20 mL
1/2 cup	thinly sliced red onion	125 mL
2 tbsp	fresh lemon juice	25 mL
3/4 tsp	fennel seeds, crushed	4 mL

1 Sprinkle fillets with salt and pepper to taste. In nonstick skillet, heat 1 tsp (5 mL) of the oil over medium-high heat; cook fillets, skin side down, for 2 minutes. Turn and cook for 2 minutes.

2 Reduce heat to medium. Add onion; cover and cook for 4 minutes or until opaque. Remove fish to warmed plates.

3 Add remaining oil, lemon juice and fennel seeds to skillet; bring to simmer and cook, stirring, for 1 minute or until onion is tender. Season with salt and pepper to taste. Drizzle over fish and top with onion. *Makes 4 servings.*

Per serving:

calories	151
protein	19 g
total fat	7 g
saturated fat	1 g
cholesterol	42 mg
carbohydrate	3 g
dietary fiber	trace
sodium	71 mg

R.D.I. Vit A 5%, E 6%, C 5%, Folate 4%, Ca 2% (19 mg), Iron 3%, Zinc 5%.

Canada's Food Guide Serving:
¼ 🥕 1 🐟

Brunch

Salmon and Spinach Strata

Potato and Onion Tortilla Espanola

Asparagus and Mushroom Gratin

Fresh Fruit, Granola and Yogurt Trifle

Roasted Red Pepper Smoked Mackerel Focaccia Sandwich

Avocado Cheese Focaccia Sandwich

Seafood Salad

Roasted Red Pepper, Onion and Hummus Pita Wrap

Tuna and Veggie Pita Wrap

Spinach and Mushroom Calzones

Scrambled Eggs and Smoked Salmon on Focaccia

Nutrition Notes

Caffeine: "Caffeine, Coffee and Tea Talk"

Butter or Margarine: "Will it Be Butter or Margarine?"

Fiber: "Boost Your Fiber Intake"

Teenagers: "Raising Healthy Teenagers"

Herbal Teas

So many herbs are used in herbal teas that it is difficult to give advice about their use. Many herbal teas offer a refreshing, caffeine-free alternative to regular tea or coffee. But some herbs such as hemlock, common russian or prickly comfrey are not safe to use, and others like dong quai are definitely not recommended during pregnancy. Some herbs may also bring about unwanted effects, such as a rapid heart rate, excessive urination or diarrhea.

Use your common sense. Drink herbal teas in moderation as you would regular tea and stop if unpleasant symptoms arise.

Caffeine Content of Coffee, Tea and Cola

Coffee: 6 oz (200 mL)	
filter drip	**108 to 180 mg**
instant regular	**60 to 90 mg**
Espresso coffee:	
common serving 2 oz	**90 to 110 mg**
(60 mL) specialty coffees made with 1 serving espresso	**90 to 110 mg**
Tea: 6 oz (200 mL)	
weak brew	**18 to 24 mg**
strong brew (5 minutes)	**78 to 108 mg**
Colas: 12 oz (355 mL) can	**28 to 64 mg**

Caffeine, Coffee and Tea Talk

To talk about caffeine is to talk about coffee and tea since these two beverages provide 90% of caffeine consumed. Over the years the health effects of caffeine — and coffee, in particular — have been called into question. However, we now know that although large doses of caffeine (1000 mg daily) are not healthy, moderate intakes of caffeine (400 to 450 mg per day) or coffee (3 to 4 cups of percolated or filtered* coffee) are not linked to any serious health problems.

Tea, too, provides caffeine but it hasn't suffered from the nagging doubts people have over coffee. In fact, some recent studies propose that natural compounds in tea called polyphenols, or tannins, may be beneficial to health. Whether these early findings prove true remains to be seen. In the meantime, tea drinkers can rest assured that a moderate intake of tea, like coffee, poses no major health risk.

HEALTHY DRINKING TIPS: Coffee and Tea

- If you drink more than 3 to 4 cups daily of regular coffee or strong brew tea, cut back.
- Drink less coffee and tea if you start to suffer from the shakes, irritability, an uptight feeling, headaches, a racing heartbeat, or have trouble sleeping.
- Avoid both regular and decaffeinated coffee if you suffer from stomach ulcers, hiatus hernia or heartburn.
- Avoid coffee or tea for at least an hour after eating. They can interfere with iron absorption.
- For some extra calcium, combine your coffee with milk in a café au lait or caffé latte.

*Unfiltered, European-style coffee (Turkish-Greek coffee or coffee made in a carafe with a plunger) contains substances identified as diterpenes that do boost blood cholesterol slightly.

Salmon and Spinach Strata

Fresh dill is lovely in this ideal brunch dish. It can be prepared a day in advance then baked just before serving. (See Brunch Menu, page 269.)

1	pkg (10 oz/284 g) fresh spinach, trimmed	1
8	slices whole wheat bread	8
1 cup	grated light Swiss-style cheese	250 mL
1/2 cup	chopped green onion	125 mL
2	cans (each 7-1/2 oz/213 g) salmon*	2
3	eggs plus 3 egg whites	3
2-1/2 cups	1% milk	625 mL
2 tsp	dried dillweed or 1/3 cup (75 mL) chopped fresh dill	10 mL
1 tsp	each dry mustard and dried basil	5 mL
1/4 tsp	each salt and pepper	1 mL
2 tbsp	freshly grated Parmesan cheese	25 mL

1 Rinse spinach; shake off excess water. In large saucepan, cover and cook spinach, with just the water clinging to leaves, over medium-high heat until wilted, about 5 minutes; drain, pressing out moisture. Chop and set aside.

2 Trim crusts and cut bread into cubes; spread in greased 13- x 9-inch (3 L) baking dish. Top with half of the Swiss cheese, then onions and chopped spinach. Drain salmon and discard skin; flake salmon and crush bones. Sprinkle over spinach. Sprinkle with remaining Swiss cheese.

3 In bowl, beat eggs with whites. Add milk, dillweed, mustard, basil, salt and pepper; pour over bread mixture, smoothing top. Cover and refrigerate for at least 4 hours.

4 Sprinkle with Parmesan cheese. Bake in 350°F (180°C) oven for 1 hour or until golden. Let stand for 10 minutes before serving. *Makes 8 servings.*

Make ahead: Through step 3, cover and refrigerate for up to 12 hours.

* Substitution Tip

Instead of canned salmon, use 1 lb (500 g) cooked fresh salmon, about 2 cups (500 mL) flaked; increase salt to 1/2 tsp (2 mL).

Per serving:

calories	236
protein	23 g
total fat	9 g
saturated fat	2 g
cholesterol	96 mg
carbohydrate	17 g
dietary fiber	3 g
sodium	520 mg

R.D.I. Vit A 34%, D 117%, E 11%, C 7%, Folate 34%, Ca 39% (431 mg), Iron 20%, Zinc 17%.

Canada's Food Guide Serving:
¾ 🌾 ½ 🥕 ½ 🥛 1 🐟

Potato and Onion Tortilla Espanola

This comforting dish is a lightened-up version of a Spanish tortilla or Italian frittata.

Lower-Fat Cooking Tips

Cooking onion and garlic in chicken stock instead of butter or oil saves at least 15 grams of fat; using 2 egg whites instead of 1 egg saves 5 grams of fat; using light-style cheese saves 8 grams of fat. These add up to a saving of 28 grams of fat or 14 grams per person.

Cooking Tip

If your skillet has a wooden handle, wrap it in foil before placing in the oven.

1	potato, peeled and diced (1-1/2 cups/375 mL)	1
1	onion, thinly sliced	1
2	cloves garlic, minced	2
1/2 cup	chicken or vegetable stock	125 mL
2	eggs	2
2	egg whites	2
1/4 cup	1% to 2% milk	50 mL
2 tbsp	chopped fresh parsley	25 mL
1/2 tsp	Dijon mustard	2 mL
1/4 tsp	each salt and pepper	1 mL
1 tsp	olive oil	5 mL
1/2 cup	grated light old Cheddar-style cheese	125 mL

1 In nonstick ovenproof skillet, cover and cook potato, onion, garlic and chicken stock over medium heat, stirring occasionally, for about 20 minutes or until potato is tender and stock is absorbed.

2 In bowl, whisk eggs, egg whites, milk, parsley, mustard, salt and pepper; add potato mixture and stir gently to combine.

3 Wipe out skillet. Add oil and heat over medium heat; pour in egg mixture and cook for 2 minutes or until bottom is set. Sprinkle cheese over top.

4 Bake in 350°F (180°C) oven until slightly puffed and set, about 10 minutes. Broil for 2 minutes. Run knife around edge. Cut into wedges and serve. Or invert plate onto skillet; turn upside down and shake gently to loosen. *Makes 2 servings.*

Smoked Salmon, Potato and Onion Tortilla Espanola: Add 2 oz (60 g) smoked salmon, coarsely chopped; substitute chopped fresh dill (if available) for the parsley.

Per serving:

calories	334
protein	23 g
total fat	14 g
saturated fat	6 g
cholesterol	234 mg
carbohydrate	30 g
dietary fiber	2 g
sodium	853 mg

R.D.I. Vit A 13%, D 23%, E 9%, C 23%, Folate 19%, Ca 29% (317 mg), Iron 14%, Zinc 13%.

Canada's Food Guide Serving:
1½ 🥕 ½ ▮ 1 ▷

Will It Be Butter or Margarine?

One of the most frequently asked nutrition questions is: "Which is better for me, margarine or butter?" The answer is that a high-quality soft margarine is the healthier choice for everyday use. Why? Because the fat in a high-quality soft margarine is mostly unsaturated whereas butter's fat is mostly saturated. Given that Canada's top health problem — heart disease — is linked to diets high in saturated fat, any dietary choice that reduces saturated fat intake is a good one. But even though soft margarine is a better choice than butter, it should still be used sparingly.

HEALTHY EATING TIPS: Choosing a Margarine

- Look for a margarine packaged in a tub container, not in stick or brick form.
- Read the list of ingredients. Avoid margarines made with hydrogenated or partially hydrogenated vegetable oil.
- Next, look for nutrition information on the label. No nutrition information given? Don't buy the product.
- One serving (2 tsp/10 g) of a full-fat margarine should contain:
  - 6 grams or more of polyunsaturated fat (PUFA) plus monounsaturated fat (MUFA) and;
  - 1.4 grams or less saturated fat (SF)
- A serving of light, calorie-reduced margarine should contain:
  - 3 grams or more of PUFA + MUFA;
  - 0.7 or less of SF
- Don't be put off by the presence of some saturated fat such as palm or palm kernel oil in the list of ingredients. Small quantities of these hard fats must be used to make a solid, spreadable product from oil. The presence of such fats is reflected in the SF content of the product. If the SF values fall within these guidelines, the margarine is as good as it gets!

Nutrition Label for a Quality Margarine

NUTRITION INFORMATION
2 tsp (10 g) serving

Energy	73 cal/310 kJ
Protein	0 g
Fat	8 g
Polyunsaturates	3.3 g
Monounsaturates	3.3 g
Saturates	1.1 g
Cholesterol	0 mg
Carbohydrates	0.1 g

Asparagus and Mushroom Gratin

This brunch casserole is just as enjoyable as a quiche yet is much lower in fat.
Serve with Carrot Slaw with Radicchio (page 39) or Thai Vegetarian Salad (page 44) and
Fig and Cottage Cheese Quick Bread (page 245) and Fresh Fruit, Granola
and Yogurt Trifle (opposite page)

1 lb	asparagus	500 g
2 tsp	butter	10 mL
2	onions, chopped	2
6 cups	thickly sliced mushrooms (about 1 lb/500 g)	1.5 L
1/3 cup	all-purpose flour	75 mL
3	eggs	3
1-1/2 cups	1% or 2% milk	375 mL
1 tsp	Dijon mustard	5 mL
1/2 tsp	salt	2 mL
Pinch	each cayenne pepper and grated nutmeg	Pinch
1 cup	grated light Swiss-style cheese or Danbo	250 mL

1 Snap ends off asparagus; cut stalks into 1-inch (2.5 cm) pieces. In saucepan of boiling water, cook asparagus until tender-crisp, about 3 minutes. Drain and cool in cold water; dry and set aside.

2 In nonstick skillet, melt butter over medium-high heat; cook onions, stirring occasionally, for 5 minutes. Add mushrooms; cook, stirring often, until browned, about 8 minutes. Sprinkle with flour; cook, stirring, for 1 minute. Remove from heat.

3 In large bowl, beat eggs lightly; whisk in milk, mustard, salt, cayenne and nutmeg. Add onion mixture, asparagus and half of the cheese. Pour into greased 11- x 7-inch (2 L) baking dish, smoothing top. Sprinkle with remaining cheese. Bake in 350°F (180°C) oven for 45 to 55 minutes or until set. Broil for 2 minutes. *Makes 8 servings.*

Make ahead: Through step 1, wrap in paper towels and refrigerate for up to 1 day.

Per serving:

calories	144
protein	11 g
total fat	6 g
saturated fat	2 g
cholesterol	85 mg
carbohydrate	13 g
dietary fiber	2 g
sodium	247 mg

R.D.I. Vit A 9%, D 15%, E 5%, C 12%, Folate 35%, Ca 19% (212 mg), Iron 11%, Zinc 11%.

Canada's Food Guide Serving:
¼ 🌾 1¾ 🥕 ¼ 🍶 ¼ 🧀

Fresh Fruit, Granola and Yogurt Trifle

Daphna Rabinovitch, associate food director at Canadian Living *magazine, developed this perfect brunch or special breakfast dish. She uses mango, fresh pineapple, kiwifruit, grapes and strawberries, which are wonderful together. Use fresh fruit in season and serve as part of a buffet or as the main dish or to end the meal.*

1	orange	1
2 cups	low-fat granola	500 mL
3 cups	2% plain yogurt	750 mL
1/3 cup	granulated sugar	75 mL
1/3 cup	dried cherries (optional)	75 mL
4 cups	fresh fruit*	1 L

1 Grate rind or zest from orange. Cut off all white membranes; cut orange into segments and set aside.

2 Spoon granola into 8-cup (2 L) glass serving bowl. Combine yogurt, sugar and grated orange rind; reserve 1/2 cup (125 mL). Spoon remaining yogurt mixture over granola. Sprinkle with dried cherries (if using). Cover and refrigerate for 1 hour.

3 Just before serving, spoon fresh fruit over top. Drizzle with reserved yogurt mixture. *Makes 8 servings.*

Make ahead: Cover and refrigerate prepared fruit for up to 1 day. Through step 2, cover and refrigerate for up to 4 hours.

* Use 1/2 cup (125 mL) sliced peeled mango, 1 cup (250 mL) cubed peeled fresh pineapple, 2 kiwifruit, peeled, halved and sliced, 1 cup (250 mL) halved seedless grapes, 3/4 cup (175 mL) sliced strawberries, 1 orange, in segments.

Easy Granola

In large bowl, combine 5 cups (1.25 L) quick-cooking rolled oats, 1 cup (250 mL) wheat bran, 1/2 cup (125 mL) toasted wheat germ, 1/4 cup (50 mL) each chopped almonds, sesame seeds and sunflower seeds. Stir in 3/4 cup (175 mL) liquid honey. Spread on 2 lightly greased baking sheets; squeeze together to form small clumps. Bake in 300°F (150°C) oven for 20 minutes or until golden brown, stirring often so granola will brown evenly. Stir in 1-1/2 cups (375 mL) raisins. Let cool completely. Store in airtight containers. *Makes 9 cups (2.25 L).*

Per serving:

calories	237
protein	8 g
total fat	3 g
saturated fat	1 g
cholesterol	4 mg
carbohydrate	45 g
dietary fiber	4 g
sodium	111 mg

R.D.I. Vit A 6%, E 6%, C 73%, Folate 10%, Ca 19% (211 mg), Iron 8%, Zinc 9%.

Canada's Food Guide Serving:
¾ 1 ½

Boost Your Fiber Intake

A Healthy Fiber Intake
Try to get 25 to 35 grams of fiber daily from brans, whole grain breads and cereals, legumes (dried beans, peas and lentils), fruits and vegetables.

Of all the food components that affect your health the most, fiber is a close runner-up to fat. But whereas fat has a negative effect, fiber offers a host of benefits. Foods high in fiber include legumes (dried beans, peas and lentils), whole grains, vegetables and fruits.

Five Good Reasons to Up Your Fiber Intake
- Fiber prevents constipation but also firms up diarrhea.
- Fiber is a key part of the management for diverticulosis, irritable bowel syndrome and hemorrhoids.
- Fiber reduces blood cholesterol.
- Fiber improves blood-sugar control in people with diabetes by slowing the absorption of glucose and reducing the requirement for insulin.
- Fiber may reduce risk of colon cancer.

Key Food Sources of Insoluble Fiber
- wheat bran
- whole grain breads, bagels, pitas and tortillas
- whole grain cereals, rice and pasta
- fruit and vegetables
- legumes (dried beans, peas and lentils)
- psyllium-containing cereal

Different Fibers . . . Different Effects
There are two types of dietary fiber: insoluble and soluble. Most fiber-containing foods have some of each kind, but some foods stand out as being particularly rich in one type or the other. In certain circumstances you may want to put more emphasis on one type of fiber. For instance, if you have diabetes or high blood cholesterol, you will benefit more from soluble fiber, whereas gastrointestinal discomforts such as constipation, hemorrhoids and diverticulosis are relieved with insoluble fiber.

Key Food Sources of Soluble Fiber
- oat bran and oatmeal
- barley
- all legumes: beans, peas, lentils
- psyllium-containing cereal
- fruit and vegetables

HEALTHY EATING TIPS: Handling Fiber
- As you eat more fiber, also drink more fluids. Fluids make the insoluble fiber more effective.
- Gas and bloating are common when you first increase your fiber intake. To minimize this reaction, add fiber gradually. If intestinal gas becomes an ongoing problem, see the tips on page 128.

Fiber Boosters

Cereals	grams fiber
1 cup (250 mL) cooked	
• oat bran	4.9
• oatmeal	3.0
1 serving ready-to-eat	
• oat bran, 3/4 cup (175 mL)	4.0
• bran flakes, 3/4 cup (175 mL)	5.0
• All-Bran, 1/2 cup (125 mL)	11.8
Natural wheat bran, 2 tbsp (25 mL)	3.3

Bread	grams fiber
1 slice whole wheat	2.0
Pasta and rice: 1 cup (250 mL) cooked	
• whole wheat pasta	4.8
• whole grain (brown) rice	3.5

Legumes: 1/2 cup (125 mL) cooked	grams fiber
• baked beans, 1/2 cup (125 mL) cooked	10.3
• lentils, 1/2 cup (125 mL) cooked	4.4

Vegetables/Fruit	grams fiber
1 piece or 1/2 cup (125 mL)	
• Most vegetables/fruits average	2.0
• Some higher fiber exceptions:	
peas	4.7
canned corn	2.3
raisins	3.2
apple (with skin)	2.6
orange	2.4
pear	5.1
strawberries (8)	2.6

Roasted Red Pepper
Smoked Mackerel Focaccia Sandwich

I like to serve these for a weekend entertaining lunch or for an easy supper.
You can buy focaccia and cut it into single-serving portions or make your own.
Smoked mackerel is available in the refrigerated section of many
supermarkets, however smoked trout, salmon or sardines are also delicious.

Per serving:

calories	333
protein	15 g
total fat	10 g
saturated fat	2 g
cholesterol	28 mg
carbohydrate	45 g
dietary fiber	4 g
sodium	763 mg

R.D.I. Vit A 8%, D 45%, E 14%, C 97%, Folate 21%, Ca 9% (101 mg), Iron 23%, Zinc 14%.

Canada's Food Guide Serving:
2½ ▮ ¾ ▼ ½ ▶

	Baked Focaccia (page 246) or 12 slices whole wheat bread	
1/3 cup	Herbed Yogurt-Cheese (page 22) or tzatziki or light cream cheese, softened	75 mL
6	large leaves lettuce	6
6	large leaves radicchio	6
1	each grilled sweet red pepper and onion (page 156)	1
6 oz	smoked mackerel, flaked	175 g

1 Cut focaccia into 6 portions; cut each in half horizontally. Spread each half evenly with Herbed Yogurt-Cheese.

2 Arrange lettuce leaf and radicchio leaf on each bottom. Cut red pepper into strips; separate onion slices into rings. Arrange over lettuce. Divide mackerel evenly over top. Sandwich with focaccia tops. *Makes 6 servings.*

Vegetarian Focaccia: Spread focaccia with Pesto Sauce (page 85); substitute grilled eggplant for the mackerel.

Avocado Cheese Focaccia Sandwich

Offer a choice of focaccia sandwiches for a pool lunch, shore picnic, after-golf snack or pre-theater party. Make your own focaccia or use the store-bought variety. Other sandwich toppings to include are salad shrimp, sliced cucumbers, roasted eggplant or zucchini.

Substitution Tip

Instead of cheese or avocado, you can use grilled portobello mushrooms (page 124) or grilled eggplant or zucchini (page 156).

	Baked Focaccia (page 246) or 12 slices whole wheat bread	
2 tbsp	each 1% sour cream and light mayonnaise	25 mL
6	large leaves Boston lettuce	6
2	small avocados (each 6 oz/175 g), peeled and thinly sliced	2
6	thin slices light (9%) Danbo, provolone or Jarlsberg cheese (175 g)	6
1	large tomato, sliced, or grilled onion (page 156)	1

1 Cut focaccia into 6 portions; cut each in half horizontally. Mix sour cream with mayonnaise; spread evenly over each half focaccia.

2 Arrange lettuce leaf on each bottom. Top with avocado, then cheese, then tomato. Sandwich with focaccia tops. *Makes 6 servings.*

LIGHTEN UP THE BRUNCH BUFFET

Per sandwich:

calories	410
protein	17 g
total fat	18 g
saturated fat	4 g
cholesterol	9 mg
carbohydrate	47 g
dietary fiber	4 g
sodium	803 mg

R.D.I. Vit A 9%, E 14%, C 72%, Folate 29%, Ca 24% (263 mg), Iron 23%, Zinc 22%.

Canada's Food Guide Serving:

2½ 🌾 ¾ 🥕 ½ 🍞

Choose:	Instead of:
Bagel (3-1/2 in/9 cm in diameter) 200 calories, 2 g fat	**Croissant** 235 calories, 12 g fat
Asparagus and Mushroom Gratin (page 224) 160 calories, 8 g fat	**Quiche Lorraine** (1/8 of 8-in/20 cm diameter pie) 600 calories, 8 g fat
Mushroom Bruschetta (page 23) 60 calories, 3 g fat	**Brie cheese** (1 oz/30 g) 95 calories, 8 g fat
Salmon and Spinach Strata (page 221) 235 calories, 9 g fat	**Eggs Benedict** 495 calories, 40 g fat
Yogurt-based dip (2 tbsp/25 mL) 20 calories, 2 g fat	**Mayonnaise-based dip** (2 tbsp/25 mL) 162 calories, 18 g fat

Seafood Salad

Spread this on bagels or Focaccia (page 246), spoon into pita halves or tortilla wraps or use as a sandwich filling. For an hors d'oeuvre, spoon into Mini Phyllo Tart Shells (page 10). For a special luncheon, spoon onto a bed of tender mixed greens and garnish with avocado wedges and mango slices.

8 oz	scallops (small Bay or large)	250 g
3/4 cup	crab meat (200 g), chopped	175 mL
1 cup	cooked salad shrimp (6 oz/175 g), coarsely chopped	250 mL
2/3 cup	Yogurt Parsley Dressing (page 56)	150 mL
1/2 cup	finely chopped celery	125 mL
1/4 cup	chopped fresh dill	50 mL
3 tbsp	chopped green onions	50 mL
2 tbsp	capers, drained	25 mL

1 Chop scallops if large; place in microwaveable bowl. Microwave, uncovered, on High for 2 minutes, then for 1-1/2 minutes on Medium, stirring after each minute. Drain, reserving liquid. Squeeze any liquid from crab.

2 In bowl, lightly stir together scallops, crab, shrimp, yogurt dressing, celery, dill, onions and capers. Add reserved scallop liquid if necessary to moisten.
Makes 6 servings, about 2/3 cup (150 mL) each.

Make ahead: Cover and refrigerate for up to 1 day.

Nutrition Tip

Bagels, like bread, are low in fat and equal to bread nutritionally. But the average 4-inch (10 cm) bagel weighs around 4 oz (125 g), about equal to 4 slices of bread.

Per serving:

calories	152
protein	23 g
total fat	4 g
cholesterol	96 mg
carbohydrate	4 g
sodium	629 mg

R.D.I. Vit A 6%, E 1%, C 13%, Folate 13%, Ca 6% (68 mg), Iron 15%, Zinc 23%.

Canada's Food Guide Serving:
¼ 🥕 1 🍖

Raising Healthy Teenagers

When children become teenagers, parents' influence over their eating habits diminishes. Like many other adolescent attitudes, beliefs and behavior, eating is now much more influenced by the child's peer group.

Faced with their child's changing and sometimes bizarre eating patterns, many parents wonder how to distinguish between behavior that is simply characteristic of a growing independence and habits that may indicate a more serious eating disorder.

For all we know about food and eating these days, some people, adults and children alike, have lost sight of what is a normal, natural way of eating. Many of the typical adolescent eating habits—snacking, skipping breakfast and indulging a well-developed taste for snack food—are no cause for concern on their own.

Healthy Eating Habits Include:

- enjoying food and eating—sometimes with great gusto—without feeling guilty
- eating regularly
- being willing to try new foods, but also being comfortable turning them down
- eating when hungry and stopping when they are full
- generally—if not always—following the basic principles of healthy eating

Warning Signs of Eating Disorders

Eating disorders such as emotional overeating, anorexia and bulimia are distortions in eating accompanied by an underlying emotional difficulty. If you think your child is developing an eating disorder, seek professional medical help.

Be concerned about teenagers who exhibit these warning signs:

- a preoccupation with weight
- a feeling of being "fat" when clearly not overweight
- a preoccupation with food, calories, eating, ritualistic eating patterns
- hiding food
- an obsession with exercise
- periods of starvation followed by binges on high-calorie foods
- denying hunger
- self-induced vomiting (watch for trips to the bathroom after eating)
- evidence that laxatives, diuretics, or diet pills are used
- feelings of guilt or shame about eating
- low self-esteem, feelings of stupidity in a competent, contentious teen
- chronic fatigue, irritability, depression
- complaints about being cold, bloated

Roasted Red Pepper, Onion and Hummus Pita Wrap

This combination is particularly tasty and colorful. Grilled eggplant and zucchini (page 156) would make interesting additions. You can substitute tortillas for the pitas.

3	9-inch (23 cm) pitas	3
3 cups	Spicy Hummus (page 12)	750 mL
1-1/2 cups	thinly sliced red onion	375 mL
6	leaves lettuce, shredded	6
6	leaves raddichio, shredded	6
2	roasted sweet red peppers (page 32), thinly sliced	2
12	black olives, pitted and sliced	12
1/2 cup	whole fresh coriander (cilantro) leaves	125 mL
2 tbsp	chopped pickled hot banana peppers (optional)	25 mL

Lower-Fat Tip

Choose plain breads and rolls for sandwiches. A croissant can contain as much as 15 grams of fat.

1 Cut each pita in half to form rounds; evenly spread entire surface of each with hummus.

2 In rows down center, evenly arrange onion, lettuce, raddichio, red peppers, olives, coriander, and hot peppers (if using). Roll up tightly; cut in half on the diagonal.
Makes 6 servings, 2 pieces each.

Make ahead: Through step 2, wrap in plastic wrap and refrigerate for up to 3 hours.

Per serving:

calories	306
protein	12 g
total fat	7 g
saturated fat	1 g
cholesterol	0 mg
carbohydrate	51 g
dietary fiber	5 g
sodium	501 mg

R.D.I. Vit A 12%, E 7%, C 93%, Folate 40%, Ca 9% (95 mg), Iron 24%, Zinc 15%.

Canada's Food Guide Serving:
1¼ 🌾 1½ 🥕 1¼ 🫓

233

Tuna and Veggie Pita Wrap

Colorful and crunchy, these are great for a lunch, picnic or children's party.
You can set out the fillings and let each child fill and roll their own.
Large soft flour tortillas can also be used for the wrap. Cook a few extra vegetables
at night and save them to use in a pita or tortilla wrap. Vary the fillings to
suit your tastes and what you have on hand. Don't worry if you don't have snow peas;
substitute asparagus or green beans or just leave them out.

Tortilla Wraps

Soft flour tortilla wraps make a fast and easy lunch or supper. One of my favorite summer fillings is chunks of tomato, feta cheese and chopped fresh basil. Another filling I love is roasted red peppers, chèvre and arugula. Experiment with the foods you like best and any leftovers in your refrigerator.

4 oz	snow peas (1 cup/250 mL)	125 g
3	9-inch (23 cm) pitas	3
3/4 cup	tzatziki or Herbed Yogurt-Cheese (page 22)	175 mL
6	leaves leaf or Boston lettuce, shredded	6
1	large sweet red or yellow pepper (fresh or roasted), thinly sliced	1
Half	small bulb fennel, very thinly sliced or 3 stalks celery, halved and cut in strips	Half
1	medium beet or 2 carrots, peeled and grated	1
1/2 cup	thinly sliced red onion	125 mL
1 tbsp	capers, drained (optional)	15 mL
1/3 cup	packed chopped fresh basil	75 mL
1	can (198 g) water-packed tuna, drained	1

1 Trim tops and remove strings from snow peas; cook in saucepan of boiling water or in microwave with 2 tbsp (25 mL) water, covered, for 2 minutes on High. Drain and let cool; thinly slice lengthwise.

2 Cut each pita in half to form rounds; spread entire surface of each with tzatziki. In rows down center of each pita, evenly arrange lettuce, red pepper, fennel, beet, snow peas, onion, capers (if using), basil and tuna. Roll up tightly; cut in half on the diagonal. *Makes 6 servings, 2 pieces each.*

Make ahead: Through step 2, wrap in plastic wrap and refrigerate for up to 3 hours.

Per serving:

calories	200
protein	15 g
total fat	1 g
saturated fat	trace
cholesterol	10 mg
carbohydrate	32 g
dietary fiber	3 g
sodium	417 mg

R.D.I. Vit A 19%, E 4%, C 115%, Folate 26%, Ca 15% (169 mg), Iron 17%, Zinc 14%.

Canada's Food Guide Serving:
1¼ 1½ ¼ ½

Spinach and Mushroom Calzones

*The combination of mushrooms, spinach and cheese
is delicious in this pizza turnover. It's not difficult to make, and you can save
time by using frozen pizza dough.*

2 tsp	vegetable oil	10 mL
3 cups	thickly sliced mushrooms (8 oz/250 g)	750 mL
3	cloves garlic, minced	3
1	egg	1
1	pkg (10 oz/300 g) frozen chopped spinach, thawed	1
1 cup	ricotta or creamed cottage cheese	250 mL
1/2 tsp	salt	2 mL
1/4 tsp	each dried thyme, marjoram and pepper	1 mL
1 lb	pizza dough (thawed if frozen)	500 g
1/2 cup	grated part-skim mozzarella cheese	125 mL

I In nonstick skillet, heat oil over medium-high heat; cook mushrooms, stirring, for 3 minutes. Add garlic; cook until mushrooms are browned and tender. Let cool slightly.

2 In bowl, beat egg. Squeeze out moisture from spinach; add spinach to bowl along with ricotta, salt, thyme, marjoram, pepper and mushrooms. Mix well.

3 Divide pizza dough in half. On lightly floured surface, roll out one half into 15-inch (38 cm) circle; transfer to lightly greased baking sheet. Spread with half of the mushroom mixture, leaving 1/2-inch (1 cm) border around edge. Sprinkle with half of the cheese. Moisten edge of dough with water; fold over filling and press edges together to seal tightly. Repeat with remaining dough.

4 Bake in lower half of 450°F (230°C) oven for 10 minutes. Reduce heat to 350°F (180°C); bake for 10 to 15 minutes longer or until golden brown and crisp. Let stand for 5 minutes. To serve, cut into wedges. *Makes 2 calzone, 4 servings each.*

Make ahead: Through step 3, cover and refrigerate for up to 3 hours.

Per serving:

calories	**258**
protein	**12 g**
total fat	**10 g**
saturated fat	**4 g**
cholesterol	**49 mg**
carbohydrate	**31 g**
dietary fiber	**2 g**
sodium	**509 mg**

R.D.I. Vit A 25%, D 2%, E 11%, C 7%, Folate 24%, Ca 16% (179 mg), Iron 17%, Zinc 11%.

Canada's Food Guide Serving:
1¾ 🌾   ¾ 🥕   ¼ 🍞

Scrambled Eggs and Smoked Salmon on Focaccia

My friend Suzanne Kopas served this great brunch or breakfast dish to us one weekend at her cottage on Georgian Bay, Ontario. Make your own focaccia (page 246) or buy one about 3/4 inch (2 cm) thick and 10 to 12 inches (25 to 30 cm) in diameter.

1 cup	no-fat sour cream	250 mL
1/3 cup	finely chopped green onions	75 mL
2 tsp	Dijon mustard	10 mL
	Focaccia (page 246) or 12-inch (30 cm) round focaccia	
8	eggs	8
4	egg whites	4
1/3 cup	1% to 2% milk	75 mL
1 tsp	salt	5 mL
1/2 tsp	pepper	2 mL
2 tsp	butter	10 mL
4 oz	thinly sliced smoked salmon, coarsely chopped (or tidbits)	125 g
2 tbsp	chopped fresh parsley and/or dill	25 mL

1 In small bowl, mix together sour cream, green onions and mustard; set aside.

2 Heat focaccia in 350°F (180°C) oven for 10 minutes.

3 In bowl, whisk together eggs, egg whites, milk, salt and pepper.

4 In large nonstick skillet, heat butter over medium-high heat; add eggs and cook, stirring, until scrambled.

5 Spread sour cream mixture over hot focaccia; spoon scrambled eggs over top. Top with smoked salmon; sprinkle with parsley and/or dill. Serve warm or at room temperature cut into wedges. *Makes 8 servings.*

Make ahead: Through step 3 up to 1 hour.

For more breakfast and brunch recipes, see Baking (page 239).

Weekend Breakfast or Brunch

Cranberry Juice Spritzer*
Fresh Fruit Platter
Scrambled Eggs and
Smoked Salmon on Focaccia
(this page)

* Mix equal parts of soda water and cranberry juice; garnish with slice of orange.

Per serving:

calories	316
protein	18 g
total fat	11 g
saturated fat	3 g
cholesterol	222 mg
carbohydrate	36 g
dietary fiber	2 g
sodium	925 mg

R.D.I. Vit A 12%, D 19%, E 12%, C 45%, Folate 18%, Ca 11% (126 mg), Iron 20%, Zinc 14%.

Canada's Food Guide Serving:
1¾ 🌾 1 🍖

Baking

Pumpkin Orange Streusel Muffins

Blueberry Oat Bran Muffins

Lemon Zucchini Muffins

Strawberry-Glazed Banana Pineapple Muffins

Cranberry Orange Bran Muffins

Fig and Cottage Cheese Quick Bread

Focaccia

Festive Fruit Soda Bread

Apple Raisin Spice Loaf

Double-Chocolate Cookies

Oatmeal and Rice Crisp Squares

Cranberry Pecan Squares

New-Fangled Hermits

Chocolate Banana Cupcakes

Lemon Blueberry Coffee Cake

Chocolate Chip Coffee Cake

Nutrition Notes

Nutrition for Children: "Helping Kids to a Healthy Weight"

Pumpkin Orange Streusel Muffins

*A treat for breakfast or snack on the run, these also freeze well and
reheat in seconds in the microwave for a just-baked taste.*

1-1/3 cups	whole wheat flour	325 mL
3/4 cup	wheat bran	175 mL
2 tsp	each baking powder and cinnamon	10 mL
1/2 tsp	each baking soda, nutmeg, ground ginger and salt	2 mL
1 cup	raisins	250 mL
1	egg plus 1 egg white	1
1 cup	mashed or canned cooked pumpkin	250 mL
1/2 cup	corn syrup	125 mL
	Grated rind of 1 medium orange	
1/2 cup	fresh orange juice	125 mL
1/4 cup	vegetable oil	50 mL
Streusel:		
1/4 cup	granulated sugar	50 mL
1 tsp	cinnamon	5 mL
4 tsp	fresh orange juice	20 mL

Per muffin:

calories	**220**
protein	**4 g**
total fat	**6 g**
saturated fat	**1 g**
cholesterol	**18 mg**
carbohydrate	**43 g**
dietary fiber	**5 g**
sodium	**211 mg**

R.D.I. Vit A 46%, D 1%, E 16%, C 15%,
Folate 6%, Ca 5% (56 mg), Iron 14%,
Zinc 9%.

Canada's Food Guide Serving:

1 Lightly grease or spray nonstick muffin pans with nonstick cooking spray. In large bowl, stir together flour, bran, baking powder, cinnamon, baking soda, nutmeg, ginger, salt and raisins.

2 In separate bowl, lightly beat egg with egg white; whisk in pumpkin, corn syrup, orange rind and juice and oil. Pour over flour mixture and stir just enough to moisten, being careful not to overmix. Spoon into prepared pans.

3 Streusel: In small bowl, mix sugar with cinnamon; stir in orange juice until smooth. Drizzle over muffins. Bake in 400°F (200°C) oven for 20 minutes or until tops are firm to the touch. *Makes 12 muffins.*

Make ahead: Store in airtight container for up to 2 days or freeze for up to 1 month.

Blueberry Oat Bran Muffins

These great-tasting muffins are packed with nutrients. Wheat germ is one of the best sources of vitamin E. Here we have two kinds of fiber: the oats provide soluble fiber, which helps to reduce blood cholesterol levels, and the wheat contains insoluble fiber, which may help to reduce colon cancer and keeps us regular.

1 cup	each oat bran and whole wheat flour	250 mL
3/4 cup	wheat germ	175 mL
1/2 cup	packed brown sugar	125 mL
2 tsp	baking powder	10 mL
1 tsp	baking soda	5 mL
1/4 tsp	salt	1 mL
1-1/2 cups	blueberries	375 mL
	Grated rind of 1 medium lemon	
2	eggs	2
1-1/2 cups	buttermilk or soured milk*	375 mL
3 tbsp	vegetable oil	50 mL

1 Lightly grease or spray nonstick muffin pans with nonstick cooking spray.

2 In large bowl, stir together oat bran, whole wheat flour, wheat germ, brown sugar, baking powder, baking soda, salt, blueberries and lemon rind.

3 In separate bowl, lightly beat eggs; stir in buttermilk and oil. Pour over dry ingredients; stir just until combined.

4 Spoon into prepared pans. Bake in 400°F (200°C) oven for 20 minutes or until tops are firm to the touch. *Makes 12 muffins.*

Make ahead: Store in airtight container for up to 2 days or freeze for up to 1 month.

*Substitution Tip

If you don't have buttermilk, you can substitute soured milk. Place 1 tbsp (15 mL) lemon juice or vinegar into measuring cup. Add milk to the 1-1/2 cup (375 mL) level; let stand for 10 minutes, then stir.

Cooking Tip

To reheat frozen muffins, wrap in paper towel and microwave at High for 30 to 40 seconds.

Nutrition Tip

Whole wheat flour, oat bran, wheat germ and blueberries all contribute fiber to these muffins. Wheat germ is also one of the best sources of vitamin E.

Per muffin:

calories	180
protein	7 g
total fat	6 g
saturated fat	1 g
cholesterol	37 mg
carbohydrate	29 g
dietary fiber	4 g
sodium	237 mg

R.D.I. Vit A 2%, D 3%, E 22%, C 3%, Folate 11%, Ca 7% (79 mg), Iron 12%, Zinc 19%.

Canada's Food Guide Serving:

1 🌾 ¼ 🥕

Lemon Zucchini Muffins

Grated zucchini adds moistness and texture
to these lemon-spiked muffins.

Lower-Fat Baking Tip

Add grated fruits such as apple, or vegetables such as zucchini or carrots, to muffins or quick-breads to keep them from drying out.

2 cups	all-purpose flour	500 mL
1 cup	shredded (unpeeled) zucchini	250 mL
1/2 cup	granulated sugar	125 mL
	Coarsely grated rind from 1 large lemon	
1 tsp	each baking powder and baking soda	5 mL
1/2 tsp	salt	2 mL
1	egg	1
3/4 cup	buttermilk or soured milk*	175 mL
1/4 cup	vegetable oil	50 mL
1/4 cup	fresh lemon juice	50 mL

1 Lightly grease or spray nonstick muffin pans with nonstick cooking spray.

2 In large bowl, stir together flour, zucchini, sugar, lemon rind, baking powder, baking soda and salt.

3 In separate bowl, lightly beat egg; whisk in buttermilk, oil and lemon juice. Pour over flour mixture and stir just enough to moisten, being careful not to overmix.

4 Spoon into prepared pans. Bake in 375°F (190°C) oven for 25 to 30 minutes or until tops are golden and firm to the touch. *Makes 12 muffins.*

Make ahead: Store in airtight container for up to 2 days or freeze for up to 2 months.

Per muffin:

calories	164
protein	3 g
total fat	5 g
saturated fat	1 g
cholesterol	18 mg
carbohydrate	26 g
dietary fiber	1 g
sodium	237 mg

R.D.I. Vit A 1%, D 1%, E 10%, C 5%, Folate 4%, Ca 3% (35 mg), Iron 7%, Zinc 3%.

Canada's Food Guide Serving:
1 🌾

* To sour milk, measure 2 tsp (10 mL) lemon juice or vinegar into measuring cup. Add milk to 3/4 cup (175 mL) level; let stand for 5 minutes, then stir.

Strawberry-Glazed Banana Pineapple Muffins

*A spoonful of strawberry jam bakes into
the top of these intriguing and nutritious muffins.*

2 cups	whole wheat flour	500 mL
1/2 cup	granulated sugar	125 mL
1 tsp	each baking powder and baking soda	5 mL
1/4 tsp	salt	1 mL
1	egg	1
1 cup	mashed bananas	250 mL
1/2 cup	drained crushed unsweetened pineapple	125 mL
1/4 cup	each vegetable oil and milk	50 mL
1 tsp	grated lemon or orange rind	5 mL
1/4 cup	strawberry jam	50 mL

1 Lightly grease or spray nonstick muffin pans with nonstick cooking spray.

2 In large bowl, stir together flour, sugar, baking powder, baking soda and salt.

3 In separate bowl, lightly beat egg; stir in bananas, pineapple, oil, milk and lemon rind. Pour over flour mixture and stir just enough to moisten, being careful not to overmix.

4 Spoon into prepared pans. Top each with dollop of jam. Bake in 400°F (200°C) oven for 20 to 25 minutes or until tops are firm to the touch. *Makes 12 muffins.*

Make ahead: Store in airtight container for up to 2 days or freeze for up to 2 months.

Baking Tip

Lower-fat muffins tend to stick to paper liners. For best results, use a nonstick pan lightly greased or sprayed with a nonstick coating instead.

Fiber-Booster

Whole grain foods add fiber to your diet. Use whole wheat bread, bagels, brown rice and whole wheat pasta. Use more whole grain flour in your baking, too.

Per muffin:

calories	188
protein	4 g
total fat	5 g
saturated fat	1 g
cholesterol	18 mg
carbohydrate	34 g
dietary fiber	3 g
sodium	179 mg

R.D.I. Vit A 1%, D 2%, E 13%, C 5%, Folate 5%, Ca 3% (29 mg), Iron 7%, Zinc 8%.

Canada's Food Guide Serving:

1 🌾 ¼ 🥕

Cranberry Orange Bran Muffins

I often make these at Christmas when I have cranberries in the refrigerator or freezer.

Lower-Fat Tip

Buttermilk is wonderful in lower-fat baking because it helps to make muffins, biscuits and breads tender. And, contrary to its name, it is low in fat.

Fiber-Booster

One of the best opportunities to get at least one-third of your day's fiber is at breakfast. Take advantage of the many high-fiber cereals available. To ensure your cereal is high in fiber, check the nutrition information panel on the side of your cereal box. Include some fruit too: raisins, prunes, a banana or an orange.

1 cup	wheat bran	250 mL
3/4 cup	each whole wheat flour and all-purpose flour	175 mL
1/3 cup	packed brown sugar	75 mL
	Grated rind from 1 medium orange	
1-1/2 tsp	baking powder	7 mL
1/2 tsp	baking soda	2 mL
1-1/4 cups	cranberries (fresh or frozen)	300 mL
1	egg	1
1 cup	buttermilk or soured milk*	250 mL
1/4 cup	each vegetable oil and molasses	50 mL

1 Lightly grease or spray nonstick muffin pans with nonstick cooking spray.

2 In large bowl, stir together bran, whole wheat flour, all-purpose flour, sugar, orange rind, baking powder, baking soda and cranberries.

3 In separate bowl, lightly beat egg; stir in buttermilk, oil and molasses. Pour over dry ingredients; stir just until moistened.

4 Spoon into prepared pans. Bake in 375°F (190°C) oven for 20 to 25 minutes or until tops are firm to the touch. *Makes 12 muffins.*

Make ahead: Store in airtight container for up to 3 days or freeze for up to 1 month.

Per muffin:

calories	168
protein	4 g
total fat	6 g
saturated fat	1 g
cholesterol	19 mg
carbohydrate	28 g
dietary fiber	4 g
sodium	102 mg

R.D.I. Vit A 2%, D 5%, E 12%, C 7%, Folate 4%, Ca 6% (70 mg), Iron 12%, Zinc 9%.

Canada's Food Guide Serving:
1 🌾

*To sour milk, measure 1 tbsp (15 mL) lemon juice or vinegar into measuring cup. Add milk to 1 cup (250 mL) level; let stand for 5 minutes, then stir.

Fig and Cottage Cheese Quick Bread

I first tasted the delightful combination of fig and anise in bread from Tarro Bakery in Vancouver. This easy-to-make breakfast or tea bread is especially good toasted and spread with preserves or marmalade. Instead of figs, you can use chopped dates, prunes or apricots.

2 cups	all-purpose flour	500 mL
2 tbsp	granulated sugar	25 mL
1 tbsp	baking powder	15 mL
1/2 tsp	salt	2 mL
1/2 tsp	aniseed (optional)	2 mL
1 cup	chopped dried figs	250 mL
3/4 cup	2% cottage cheese	175 mL
2 tbsp	vegetable oil	25 mL
1	egg	1
1	egg white	1
2 tsp	milk	10 mL

Lower-Fat Tip

Use puréed cottage cheese or yogurt or buttermilk instead of some of the butter or oil in a quick-bread.

Nutrition Tip

Spread toast with marmalade or another preserve and you won't miss the butter or margarine.

1 In bowl, stir together flour, sugar, baking powder, salt, and aniseed (if using); stir in figs.

2 In food processor, purée cottage cheese; mix in oil, egg and egg white. Pour over flour mixture; stir just until shaggy dough forms. Gather into ball.

3 Transfer to lightly floured surface (dough may be sticky); knead 2 or 3 times or just until dough holds together. Place on greased baking sheet; flatten into 8-inch (20 cm) round. Brush top with milk. Bake in 350°F (180°C) oven for 35 minutes or until cake tester inserted in center comes out clean. Let stand for 20 minutes.
Makes 16 slices.

Make ahead: Wrap and store at room temperature for up to 1 day.

Per slice:

calories	122
protein	4 g
total fat	3 g
saturated fat	trace
cholesterol	14 mg
carbohydrate	21 g
dietary fiber	2 g
sodium	172 mg

R.D.I. Vit A 1%, D 1%, E 4%, C 2%, Folate 2%, Ca 4% (49 mg), Iron 7%, Zinc 3%.

Canada's Food Guide Serving:

1 🌾 ¾ 🥕

Focaccia

Warm from the oven, salt-and-herb-topped focaccia bread is wonderful.
I like to use a little whole wheat flour for texture and color, even though focaccia
is usually made just with all-purpose flour.

Food Processor Focaccia

Pulse dough ingredients together in food processor until mixed, then process on High for 2 minutes or until in ball and smooth and elastic. Continue with rising as in recipe.

Cooking Tip

Check the "best before" date on the yeast you use. There are a number of kinds of yeast. This recipe was developed using quick-rising yeast which you add to the flour (other kinds you add to warm water). Be sure the water is hot.

2 cups	all-purpose flour	500 mL
1/2 cup	whole wheat flour	125 mL
1	pkg (8 g) quick-rising yeast (or 1 tbsp/15 mL)	1
2 tsp	crumbled dried rosemary	10 mL
1 tsp	salt	5 mL
1 cup	hot water or hot milk (120 to 130°F/50 to 55°C)	250 mL
2 tbsp	extra-virgin olive oil	25 mL
1 tsp	granulated sugar	5 mL
Topping:		
1 tsp	extra-virgin olive oil	5 mL
1 tsp	each dried Italian herb seasoning and dried rosemary	5 mL
1/2 tsp	coarse salt	2 mL
1/4 tsp	coarsely ground pepper	1 mL

1 In large bowl, combine all-purpose flour, whole wheat flour, yeast, rosemary and salt. Combine water, oil and sugar; pour over flour mixture. Using wooden spoon, stir until dough begins to come together and rough ball forms.

2 Turn out dough onto lightly floured surface; knead for about 10 minutes or until smooth and elastic. Place in lightly greased bowl, turning to grease all over. Cover with plastic wrap; let rest in warm place for 1 hour.

3 Turn out dough onto lightly floured surface; pat and stretch into 11- x 10-inch (28 x 25 cm) rectangle, about 1 inch (2.5 cm) thick. Transfer to lightly floured baking sheet; press back of spoon into dough to create "dimples".

4 Topping: Spread oil over dough. Cover lightly with plastic wrap; let stand at room temperature for 30 minutes.

5 Sprinkle dough with Italian herbs, rosemary, salt and pepper. Bake in 400°F (200°C) oven for 15 to 20 minutes or until golden brown and bread sounds hollow when tapped. Let cool slightly on pan on rack before cutting. *Makes 12 pieces.*

Per piece:
calories	121
protein	3 g
total fat	3 g
saturated fat	trace
cholesterol	trace
carbohydrate	20 g
dietary fiber	1 g
sodium	251 mg

R.D.I. Vit E 4%, Folate 5%,
Ca 1% (11 mg), Iron 8%, Zinc 5%.

Canada's Food Guide Serving:
1¼

Festive Fruit Soda Bread

I never seem to have enough time to make a Christmas or Easter yeast bread,
but I like this bread just as much — and I can prepare it in only 5 minutes.

Lower-Fat Tip

Any combination of dried
fruits works well in this
recipe. If raisins or currants
are hard, pour boiling water
over them and let them
stand for 10 minutes to
plump, then drain thoroughly.
Hard dried fruits will draw
moisture from the bread
instead of adding juiciness.

4 cups	all-purpose flour	1 L
3 tbsp	granulated sugar	50 mL
1 tbsp	baking powder	15 mL
1 tsp	baking soda	5 mL
1/2 tsp	salt	2 mL
1/3 cup	each raisins, currants, mixed candied fruit and chopped figs	75 mL
1	egg	1
1-3/4 cups	buttermilk	425 mL
3 tbsp	vegetable oil	50 mL
	Grated rind from 1 medium orange	
Glaze:		
1/2 cup	icing sugar	125 mL
1 tbsp	fresh orange juice	15 mL

1 In bowl, stir together flour, sugar, baking powder, baking soda and salt; stir in raisins, currants, mixed candied fruit and figs.

2 In separate bowl, lightly beat egg; whisk in buttermilk, oil and orange rind. Pour over flour mixture and stir just until combined.

3 Transfer to lightly floured surface; knead 10 times or just until dough holds together. Place on greased baking sheet; flatten into 9-inch (23 cm) circle. Bake in 350°F (180°C) oven for 45 to 50 minutes or until toothpick inserted in center comes out clean; let cool on rack for 5 minutes.

4 Glaze: Mix icing sugar with orange juice until smooth; spread over warm bread. Cut into wedges or slices. *Makes 20 slices.*

Make ahead: Wrap and store at room temperature for up to 1 day or wrap again with foil and freeze for up to 1 month.

Per slice:

calories	174
protein	4 g
total fat	3 g
saturated fat	trace
cholesterol	11 mg
carbohydrate	34 g
dietary fiber	2 g
sodium	185 mg

R.D.I. Vit A 1%, D 1%, E 5%, C 5%,
Folate 3%, Ca 5% (57 mg), Iron 9%,
Zinc 4%.

Canada's Food Guide Serving:

1¼ 🌾 ½ 🥕

Apple Raisin Spice Loaf

This moist tea loaf is a good choice for an evening snack or at brunch for dessert along with fruit. It also makes a nice treat in a packed lunch.

2 cups	all-purpose flour	500 mL
2 tsp	each cinnamon and baking powder	10 mL
1 tsp	baking soda	5 mL
1/2 tsp	each ground ginger, nutmeg, allspice and salt	2 mL
1 cup	raisins	250 mL
1/4 cup	butter, softened	50 mL
3/4 cup	granulated sugar	175 mL
1	egg	1
1	egg white	1
2/3 cup	unsweetened applesauce	150 mL
1/2 cup	1% or 2% plain yogurt	125 mL
2 tsp	pure vanilla	10 mL

1 Spray 9- x 5-inch (2 L) loaf pan with nonstick cooking spray.

2 In large bowl, stir together flour, cinnamon, baking powder, baking soda, ginger, nutmeg, allspice, salt and raisins.

3 In separate bowl, using electric mixer, beat butter with sugar until combined; beat in egg and egg white until fluffy. Stir in applesauce, yogurt and vanilla. Pour over flour mixture and stir just until combined. Spoon into pan.

4 Bake in 350°F (180°C) oven for 50 to 60 minutes or until cake tester inserted in center comes out clean. Let cool in pan on rack for 10 minutes. Remove from pan and let cool completely on rack. *Makes 1 loaf, about 18 slices.*

Make ahead: Wrap and store at room temperature for up to 3 days or freeze for up to 1 month.

Fiber-Booster

Add 1/4 cup (50 mL) All-Bran or other high-fiber cereal (one with more than 4 grams of fiber per serving) to your favorite cereal. Sprinkle cereal or yogurt with raisins or other dried fruits or with sunflower seeds.

Per slice:

calories	149
protein	3 g
total fat	3 g
saturated fat	2 g
cholesterol	19 mg
carbohydrate	28 g
dietary fiber	1 g
sodium	197 mg

R.D.I. Vit A 3%, D 1%, E 2%, C 2%, Folate 2%, Ca 3% (38 mg), Iron 7%, Zinc 3%.

Canada's Food Guide Serving:

1 🌾 ½ 🥕

249

Helping Kids to a Healthy Weight

For the most part, Canadian children are a healthy lot, but a disturbing weight-gaining trend has some health experts worried. Overweight children, like overweight adults, are more likely to suffer more physical problems like high blood pressure, respiratory illnesses, diabetes and orthopedic problems. And just like adults, they face the social, emotional and psychological challenges of being fat in a society that reveres thinness. At this point, we can only speculate about why children are getting fatter. Eating habits most certainly play a part. However, if the American experience has any application to Canada, then lack of physical activity is at the top of the list. It is estimated that children today are 40% less active than their parents were.

What can be done about this unhealthy trend? The answer clearly lies in establishing healthy eating and activity patterns early in childhood.

HEALTHY EATING TIPS: Helping the Overweight Child

- Calorie-restricted diets are not recommended; healthy eating is. Establish a healthy eating pattern and encourage more activity for the whole family.
- Make a variety of nutritious food available and allow your child to decide how much he or she wants to eat. Restricting food and denying favorite desserts, treats and snacks can lead to an unhealthy preoccupation with food.
- Encourage your child to participate in activities he or she enjoys. And participate yourself as well. Find activities you and your child enjoy — walking, exploring, skating, tobogganing, swimming, building a snowman, biking. Don't force a child into an activity he or she hates.
- Be sensitive to your child's feelings about weight and the social and emotional burdens. Overweight children often suffer terribly at the hands of other people, and their self-esteem is often low.
- Work with your child to build self-esteem and self-worth through activities and accomplishments unrelated to size, shape and physical performance. Don't send the message that your love and acceptance depend on weight loss.
- Finally, be prepared to accept the fact that not all children will achieve a healthy weight. Nevertheless, these children still need to maintain a pattern of healthy eating and regular physical activity.

Preventive Strategies

If your children aren't overweight, it is easier to overlook the importance of healthy eating and being active. But the habits developed in childhood are critical to maintaining a healthy weight as adults. All children, fat or thin, need to learn to choose a healthy diet, to eat appropriate quantities of food, to enjoy sweet and snack foods in moderation and to be physically active every day.

Double-Chocolate Cookies

Rich in chocolate flavor, these cookies have less than half the fat of crisp chocolate chip cookies. Cocoa powder contributes a deep chocolate flavor without adding fat. Adding coffee heightens the chocolate flavor.

1 tbsp	each instant coffee granules and pure vanilla	15 mL
1	egg	1
2	egg whites	2
3/4 cup	each granulated sugar and packed brown sugar	175 mL
1/4 cup	butter or margarine, melted	50 mL
3 tbsp	golden corn syrup	50 mL
2 cups	all-purpose flour	500 mL
1/2 cup	unsweetened cocoa powder, sifted	125 mL
1 tbsp	baking powder	15 mL
1/4 tsp	salt	1 mL
1 cup	chocolate chips	250 mL

1 Dissolve coffee granules in vanilla; set aside.

2 In large bowl, using electric mixer, beat egg, egg whites and granulated and brown sugars until light and foamy; beat in butter, corn syrup and coffee mixture.

3 Combine flour, cocoa, baking powder and salt; gradually beat into egg mixture, 1/2 cup (125 mL) at a time, until well mixed. Stir in chocolate chips (mixture will be thick).

4 Drop by tablespoonfuls (15 mL), about 2 inches (5 cm) apart, on nonstick or sprayed baking sheets. Flatten tops with back of spoon. Bake in 350°F (180°C) oven for 8 to 10 minutes or until firm. Let stand on sheets on racks for 2 minutes; transfer to racks to let cool completely. *Makes 60 cookies.*

Make ahead: Store in airtight container for up to 5 days or freeze for up to 3 weeks.

Double-Chocolate Mint Cookies

Substitute 3/4 tsp (4 mL) mint extract for coffee granules; add to batter with vanilla.

Double-Chocolate Orange Cookies

Substitute grated orange rind from 1 orange for coffee granules; add to batter with vanilla.

Per cookie:

calories	63
protein	1 g
total fat	2 g
saturated fat	1 g
cholesterol	6 mg
carbohydrate	12 g
dietary fiber	1 g
sodium	36 mg

R.D.I. Vit A 1%, Ca 1% (12 mg), Iron 3%, Zinc 2%.

Oatmeal and Rice Crisp Squares

With less butter than traditional rice crisp cereal squares and with oatmeal and raisins added for fiber and iron, these busy-day snacks are nutritious as well as delicious. Let your kids help by measuring the ingredients.

Sugar Alert

If you think sugar is to blame for wild behavior in children, you're not alone. However, the evidence—and there's plenty of it—shows that, if anything, sugar has a calming effect. Hyperactive behavior in children has many causes, but it's unlikely that sugar is one of them. However, other ingredients, such as caffeine in candy and pop, might bother a particular child. And hunger and fatigue can make almost any kid cranky and disruptive.

1 cup	quick-cooking rolled oats	250 mL
1/4 cup	butter	50 mL
1	pkg (250 g) marshmallows (40 regular size)	1
1 tsp	pure vanilla	5 mL
5 cups	rice crisp cereal	1.25 L
1 cup	raisins	250 mL

1 Spread rolled oats on baking sheet; bake in 300°F (150°C) oven for about 10 minutes or until toasted. Lightly grease 13- x 9-inch (3 L) baking dish or spray with nonstick cooking spray; set aside.

2 In large saucepan, melt butter over low heat; add marshmallows and cook, stirring often, until smooth. Remove from heat; stir in vanilla. Working quickly, stir in cereal, toasted oats and raisins until combined. Press into prepared dish. Let cool completely. Cut into squares. *Makes 24 squares.*

Make ahead: Store in airtight container for up to 3 days.

Per square:

calories	107
protein	1 g
total fat	2 g
saturated fat	1 g
cholesterol	5 mg
carbohydrate	21 g
dietary fiber	1 g
sodium	87 mg

R.D.I. Vit A 2%, E 1%, Folate 2%, Ca 1% (7 mg), Iron 8%, Zinc 2%.

Canada's Food Guide Serving:
¼ 🌾 ¼ 🥕

Cranberry Pecan Squares

Dried cranberries add tartness and color to these tasty, easy-to-make squares.
They are available in supermarkets.

3/4 cup	firmly packed dried cranberries	175 mL
1/4 cup	cold butter	50 mL
1 cup	all-purpose flour	250 mL
3/4 cup	granulated sugar	175 mL
2 tbsp	1% plain yogurt	25 mL
2	eggs	2
Pinch	salt	Pinch
1/2 cup	coarsely chopped pecans	125 mL

1 In small saucepan, combine cranberries with enough water to cover. Cover and bring to boil; remove from heat and let stand for 1 minute (or microwave*). Drain and let cool. Set aside.

2 In bowl, cut butter into flour until mixture resembles fine crumbs. Stir in 1/4 cup (50 mL) of the sugar and yogurt, mixing well. Press evenly into lightly greased or sprayed 8-inch (2 L) square cake pan. Bake in 350°F (180°C) oven for 15 minutes.

3 Meanwhile, in bowl, beat eggs with remaining 1/2 cup (125 mL) sugar and salt until light; stir in cranberries. Pour over base. Sprinkle pecans evenly over top. Bake in 350°F (180°C) oven for 30 minutes or until set and golden. Let cool slightly in pan; cut into squares. *Makes 18 squares.*

Make ahead: Store in airtight container for up to 5 days or freeze for up to 1 month.

*Cooking Tip

Cranberries are plumped in hot water to make them juicy and tender. This can also be done in the microwave; place in microwaveable dish and add water to cover; microwave on High for 1 minute.

Per square:

calories	125
protein	2 g
total fat	5 g
saturated fat	2 g
cholesterol	31 mg
carbohydrate	18 g
dietary fiber	1 g
sodium	35 mg

R.D.I. Vit A 4%, D 2%, E 2%, C 2%, Folate 2%, Ca 1% (9 mg), Iron 3%, Zinc 4%.

Canada's Food Guide Serving:
¼ 🌾 ¼ 🥕

New-Fangled Hermits

These terrific cookies are a new favorite at our house.
Use any combination of dried fruits (cranberry, cherry, blueberry).

Fiber-Booster

For added fiber in the Hermits, use half whole wheat flour and half all-purpose flour instead of the whole amount of all-purpose flour.

Cooking Tip

If raisins are hard and very dry, plump by pouring boiling water over them and let stand for 10 minutes, then drain well.

2/3 cup	packed brown sugar	150 mL
1/3 cup	butter, softened	75 mL
1	egg	1
1/3 cup	corn syrup	75 mL
1 tsp	each grated orange rind and pure vanilla	5 mL
2 tbsp	fresh orange juice	25 mL
1-3/4 cups	all-purpose flour	425 mL
1/2 tsp	each baking soda and baking powder	2 mL
1/2 tsp	each cinnamon, allspice and nutmeg	2 mL
1/2 cup	each dried blueberries, cranberries, cherries and raisins	125 mL

1 In large bowl, using electric mixer, beat brown sugar with butter until mixed; beat in egg, corn syrup, orange rind, vanilla and orange juice until light and fluffy.

2 In separate bowl, combine flour, baking soda, baking powder, cinnamon, allspice and nutmeg; stir in blueberries, cranberries, cherries and raisins. Stir into butter mixture, mixing well.

3 Drop by rounded tablespoonfuls (15 mL), about 2 inches (5 cm) apart, onto lightly greased baking sheets; flatten tops with back of spoon. Bake in 350°F (180°C) oven for 8 to 10 minutes or until golden. Let stand on baking sheets for 2 to 3 minutes; transfer to racks and let cool completely. *Makes 30 cookies.*

Make ahead: Store in airtight container for up to 1 week or freeze for up to 1 month.

Per cookie:

calories	106
protein	1 g
total fat	2 g
saturated fat	1 g
cholesterol	13 mg
carbohydrate	21 g
dietary fiber	1 g
sodium	52 mg

R.D.I. Vit A 2%, D 1%, E 1%, C 2%, Folate 1%, Ca 1% (13 mg), Iron 4%, Zinc 1%.

Canada's Food Guide Serving:
¼ 🌾 ½ 🥕

Chocolate Banana Cupcakes

Just perfect for a family celebration, these attractive cupcakes make good use of chocolate chips because a few go a long way when studding the tops.

3/4 cup	mashed ripe bananas (2 small)	175 mL
3/4 cup	buttermilk	175 mL
3/4 cup	packed brown sugar	175 mL
1/4 cup	corn syrup	50 mL
3 tbsp	vegetable oil	50 mL
2 tsp	pure vanilla	10 mL
1-3/4 cups	all-purpose flour	425 mL
1/4 cup	unsweetened cocoa powder, sifted	50 mL
1 tsp	baking soda	5 mL
1/2 tsp	salt	2 mL
1/2 cup	chocolate chips	125 mL
1 tbsp	icing sugar	15 mL

1 In bowl, mix bananas, buttermilk, brown sugar, corn syrup, oil and vanilla.

2 Mix together flour, cocoa, baking soda and salt; sprinkle over banana mixture and stir just until moistened.

3 Spray muffin pans with nonstick cooking spray; spoon in batter, filling two-thirds full. Sprinkle chocolate chips over top. Bake in 400°F (200°C) oven for 15 to 20 minutes or until toothpick inserted in center comes out clean. Let cool in pans on rack. Sift icing sugar over top. *Makes 12 cupcakes.*

Make ahead: Store in airtight container for up to 2 days.

To Sift or Not To Sift

- When a recipe calls for sifting, use a sifter specially designed for baking or a fine-mesh sieve.
- All-purpose flour does not require sifting.
- Sift cocoa powder and icing sugar to eliminate any lumps.
- If "sifted" is written before the ingredient, you sift before you measure; if "sifted" is written after the ingredient (i.e, 1/4 cup/ 50 mL cocoa powder, sifted), you measure then sift.

Per cupcake:

calories	232
protein	3 g
total fat	6 g
saturated fat	2 g
cholesterol	1 mg
carbohydrate	43 g
dietary fiber	2 g
sodium	221 mg

R.D.I. Vit E 8%, C 2%, Folate 3%, Ca 4% (39 mg), Iron 12%, Zinc 5%.

Canada's Food Guide Serving:
¾ ▦

Lemon Blueberry Coffee Cake

Serve this terrific cake anytime — for breakfast, brunch, dessert, with coffee or just as a snack.

3 cups	all-purpose flour	750 mL
1 cup	granulated sugar	250 mL
1 tbsp	baking powder	15 mL
1 tsp	baking soda	5 mL
1/2 tsp	salt	2 mL
	Grated rind from 2 medium lemons	
1	can (385 mL) 2% evaporated milk	1
2 tbsp	vegetable oil	25 mL
2	eggs, lightly beaten	2
Half	pkg (300 g pkg) frozen blueberries or 1-1/4 cups (300 mL) other small berries	Half
Topping:		
1/3 cup	granulated sugar	75 mL
1-1/2 tsp	cinnamon	7 mL
2 tbsp	fresh lemon juice	25 mL

1 Line 13- x 9-inch (3 L) baking dish with foil; spray with nonstick cooking spray.

2 In large bowl, stir together flour, sugar, baking powder, baking soda, salt and lemon rind. Add evaporated milk, oil and eggs; stir just until moistened. Spread half in pan. Sprinkle with blueberries. Gently spread remaining batter over top.

3 Topping: In small bowl, mix sugar with cinnamon; stir in lemon juice. Drizzle over batter. Bake in 350°F (180°C) oven for 45 minutes or until cake tester inserted in center comes out clean. Let cool in pan on rack for 10 minutes. Remove from pan and let cool on rack. *Makes 16 servings.*

Make ahead: Wrap and refrigerate for up to 2 days or freeze for up to 1 month.

Chocolate Chip Coffee Cake

*Chocolate chips and toasted pecans add a richness and crunch
to this easy-to-make cake.*

1/4 cup	coarsely chopped pecans	50 mL
1 cup	chocolate chips (6 oz/175 g)	250 mL
1/4 cup	packed brown sugar	50 mL
2 tsp	cinnamon	10 mL
Cake:		
1	egg	1
1 cup	2% evaporated milk	250 mL
2 tbsp	vegetable oil	25 mL
2 tsp	pure vanilla	10 mL
2 cups	all-purpose flour	500 mL
3/4 cup	granulated sugar	175 mL
1 tbsp	baking powder	15 mL
1 tsp	baking soda	5 mL
1/4 tsp	salt	1 mL

Cooking Tip

Make the most of the fat you use. Here, a minimum of oil is used; the fat in the nuts and chocolate chips adds flavor and texture as well as richness. Evaporated milk adds creaminess with much less fat than cream.

1 Toast pecans on baking sheet in 350°F (180°C) oven for 5 minutes or until golden; let cool. In bowl, mix chocolate chips, pecans, brown sugar and cinnamon.

2 Cake: In large bowl, beat egg; stir in milk, oil and vanilla. In sieve on top of milk mixture, combine flour, sugar, baking powder, baking soda and salt, stirring to sift into bowl; stir just until dry ingredients are moistened.

3 Lightly grease or spray 10-inch (3 L) Bundt pan with nonstick cooking spray. Spoon in half of the batter; sprinkle with half of the nut mixture. Spread with remaining batter; sprinkle with remaining nut mixture, lightly pressing into batter.

4 Bake in 350°F (180°C) oven for 45 to 60 minutes or until cake tester inserted in center comes out clean. Let cool in pan on rack. Turn out onto serving plate, chocolate and nuts facing up. *Makes 12 servings.*

Make ahead: Cover and store for up to 1 day.

Per serving:

calories	276
protein	5 g
total fat	9 g
saturated fat	3 g
cholesterol	19 mg
carbohydrate	45 g
dietary fiber	2 g
sodium	242 mg

R.D.I. Vit A 2%, D 9%, E 6%, C 3%, Folate 4%, Ca 10% (106 mg), Iron 12%, Zinc 8%.

Canada's Food Guide Serving:

1 🌾

Dessert

Lemon Cake with Lemon Cream or Raspberry Sauce

Apple Cranberry Streusel Cake

Easy Chocolate Cake with Chocolate Buttermilk Icing

Cantaloupe and Blueberries with Fresh Strawberry Sauce

Citrus Frozen Yogurt with Mango

Apple Berry Crisp

Strawberry Apple Cobbler

Apricot Raspberry Parfait

Ginger Citrus Fruit Salad

Orange Mousse

Deep-Dish Apple Apricot Phyllo Pie

Easy, No-Roll Food Processor Pastry

Peach Blueberry Pie

Lemon Chocolate Tart

Strawberries with Lemon Cream in Phyllo Pastry Cups

French Lemon Tart

Lemon Cheesecake with Raspberry Glaze

Cranberry Yogurt Flan

Black Forest Frozen Yogurt Cake or Pie

Orange Mousse Meringue Pie

Nutrition Notes

Lactose Intolerance: "Can't Tolerate Milk?"

Diabetes: "An Update on Diabetes"

Irritable Bowels: "Dietary Help for Irritable Bowels"

Lemon Cake with Lemon Cream or Raspberry Sauce

*The recipe for this great-tasting cake comes from my friend
and recipe tester Shannon Graham. Serve it with Lemon Cream (opposite page)
or Raspberry Sauce (opposite page) or with ice cream or fresh fruit.*

Whey

The whey or drained liquid
from yogurt contains
B vitamins and minerals and
is low in fat. Refrigerate it
and use it in soups.

Kitchen Tip

To measure the size of a cake
pan or Bundt pan, measure
across the top.

1/2 cup	butter or soft margarine	125 mL
2 cups	granulated sugar	500 mL
2	eggs	2
1/4 cup	1% or 2% plain yogurt	50 mL
	Grated rind of 2 medium lemons	
3 cups	all-purpose flour	750 mL
2 tsp	baking powder	10 mL
1 cup	1% milk	250 mL
Glaze:		
1/2 cup	fresh lemon juice	125 mL
1/2 cup	granulated sugar	125 mL

1 In large bowl, using electric mixer, beat butter with sugar until light and fluffy; beat in eggs, yogurt and lemon rind. Mix flour with baking powder; beat into egg mixture alternately with milk, making three additions of flour mixture and two of milk.

2 Spoon into greased and floured 10-inch (3 L) Bundt pan. Bake in 350°F (180°C) oven for 50 minutes or until cake tester inserted in center comes out clean. Let stand in pan on rack for 5 minutes.

3 Glaze: Stir lemon juice with sugar until sugar is dissolved. Invert cake onto rimmed plate; using toothpick, poke 1-inch (2.5 cm) deep holes in top of cake. Brush glaze over cake. Let cool. *Makes 16 servings.*

Make ahead: Cover and store for up to 2 days.

Per serving (no sauce):

calories	278
protein	4 g
total fat	7 g
saturated fat	4 g
cholesterol	43 mg
carbohydrate	51 g
dietary fiber	1 g
sodium	110 mg

R.D.I. Vit A 7%, D 5%, E 2%, C 8%,
Folate 4%, Ca 5% (50 mg), Iron 8%,
Zinc 4%.

Canada's Food Guide Serving:
1 🌾

Lemon Cream

This creamy sauce is perfect with cake, fresh fruit or pie.

1 cup	extra-thick (Greek-style) or drained plain yogurt*	250 mL
1/3 cup	granulated sugar	75 mL
	Grated rind of 1 medium lemon	
1 tbsp	fresh lemon juice	15 mL

▮ In small bowl, combine yogurt, sugar, lemon rind and juice, stirring well. Cover and refrigerate for 30 minutes or for up to 3 days. *Makes about 1-1/4 cups (300 mL).*

Make ahead: Cover and refrigerate for up to 3 days or to "best before" date on yogurt container.

*For information on draining yogurt, see page 22.

Per 2 tbsp:	
calories	**49**
protein	**2 g**
total fat	**trace**
saturated fat	**trace**
cholesterol	**2 mg**
carbohydrate	**9 g**
sodium	**21 mg**

R.D.I. Vit C 3%, Folate 2%, Ca 7% (76 mg), Zinc 4%.

Raspberry Sauce

Serve with Lemon Cake (page 260), Easy Chocolate Cake (page 264), frozen yogurt or fresh fruit.

2	pkg (300 g each) frozen unsweetened raspberries	2
1/4 cup	granulated sugar	50 mL

▮ Thaw raspberries; drain and reserve 1/2 cup (125 mL) juice. Press berries through sieve over bowl to remove seeds. Stir in enough of the reserved juice to make sauce consistency. Stir in sugar. *Makes about 2 cups (500 mL).*

Make ahead: Cover and refrigerate for up to 5 days.

Per 1/4 cup (50 mL):	
calories	**44**
protein	**1 g**
total fat	**0 g**
cholesterol	**0 mg**
carbohydrate	**10 g**
sodium	**0 mg**

R.D.I. Vit A 1%, E 3%, C 25%, Folate 7%, Ca 1% (13 mg), Iron 2%, Zinc 3%.

Canada's Food Guide Serving:
1 🥕

Can't Tolerate Milk?

Don't pass on a recipe just because it has milk in it! You'd be missing out on both taste and nutrition.

If you are one of those people who can't handle milk and milk products without suffering from stomach cramps, bloating, gas and diarrhea, you may have a shortage of lactase enzymes necessary to digest the lactose sugar. Left undigested, lactose sugar ferments in the gastrointestinal tract and causes the unpleasant symptoms. The degree of lactose intolerance varies from person to person, from mild to severe. Sometimes it is only a temporary condition that develops after a bout of severe diarrhea.

Research shows that even people with severe lactose intolerance can tolerate up to 1 cup (250 mL) of milk with a meal. So try using small amounts of milk throughout the day.

HEALTHY EATING TIPS: Lactose Intolerance

- Try lactose-reduced milk (found in the milk section of most grocery stores). It's 99% lactose free. Or use liquid lactase drops (found in drugstores) to make lactose-reduced milk at home.
- Take lactase enzyme tablets (also found in drugstores) at meals containing regular milk or milk products. These tablets take the worry out of dining away from home.
- Try small servings of aged cheeses such as Cheddar, Swiss, brick, camembert, limburger and Parmesan. These cheeses contain very little lactose.
- Eat yogurt. The bacteria in yogurt produce lactase enzyme, which continues to digest lactose even after the yogurt is eaten.
- If you are severely intolerant, drink a plant-based beverage such as a soy or rice beverage in place of milk. Look for a product that is enriched with vitamins A, D, B12, riboflavin, calcium and zinc.

Apple Cranberry Streusel Cake

Serve this golden apple-topped cake with coffee for brunch or dessert.
If you are using frozen cranberries, don't thaw them first.

1/3 cup	butter or margarine, softened	75 mL
3/4 cup	granulated sugar	175 mL
2	eggs	2
1-1/2 cups	all-purpose flour	375 mL
1 tsp	baking powder	5 mL
1/2 tsp	baking soda	2 mL
	Grated rind from 1 medium lemon	
2/3 cup	2% plain yogurt	150 mL
1 cup	cranberries (fresh, frozen or dried)	250 mL
2	apples, peeled and thinly sliced	2
Streusel:		
1/2 cup	packed brown sugar	125 mL
1-1/2 tsp	cinnamon	7 mL

1 In large bowl, using electric mixer, beat butter with sugar until light and fluffy; beat in eggs, one at a time, beating well after each addition.

2 Mix flour, baking powder, baking soda and lemon rind; beat into egg mixture alternately with yogurt, making three additions of flour mixture and two of yogurt.

3 Spread half of the batter into greased and floured 10-inch (3 L) springform pan. Arrange cranberries over top.

4 Streusel: Combine brown sugar with cinnamon; sprinkle half over cranberries. Spread remaining batter over top; arrange apple slices in slightly overlapping circles over top. Sprinkle with remaining sugar mixture.

5 Bake in 350°F (180°C) oven for 50 to 60 minutes or until golden and toothpick inserted in center comes out clean. Let cool on rack for 20 minutes before removing side of pan. *Makes 12 servings.*

Make ahead: Cover and refrigerate for up to 1 day.

Lower-Fat Tip

Choose a soft-tub non-hydrogenated margarine instead of butter most of the time because margarine is lower in saturated fat. However, both butter and margarine contain the same amount of fat and the same number of calories.

Per serving:	
calories	222
protein	3 g
total fat	6 g
saturated fat	4 g
cholesterol	50 mg
carbohydrate	39 g
dietary fiber	1 g
sodium	147 mg

R.D.I. Vit A 7%, D 3%, E 2%, C 3%, Folate 3%, Ca 5% (55 mg), Iron 8%, Zinc 4%.

Canada's Food Guide Serving:
¾ 🌾 ¼ 🥕

Easy Chocolate Cake with Chocolate Buttermilk Icing

This dense, rich chocolate cake has all the taste and about half the fat of a regular chocolate cake. For the most intense chocolate flavor, use Dutch process unsweetened cocoa powder. Domestic brands are available in supermarkets.

Cooking Tip

Adding coffee to chocolate dishes enhances the chocolate flavor.

2 tbsp	espresso powder or instant coffee granules	25 mL
1/2 cup	boiling water	125 mL
2-1/4 cups	all-purpose flour	550 mL
2 cups	granulated sugar	500 mL
3/4 cup	unsweetened cocoa powder, sifted	175 mL
1-1/2 tsp	each baking powder and baking soda	7 mL
1 tsp	salt	5 mL
1-3/4 cups	buttermilk	425 mL
2	eggs, beaten	2
1/4 cup	vegetable oil	50 mL
2 tsp	vanilla	10 mL
	Chocolate Buttermilk Icing (page 266)	

1 Dissolve espresso powder in boiling water; let cool. Grease or spray 13- x 9-inch (3 L) baking dish with nonstick cooking spray; line bottom with waxed paper.

2 In large bowl, mix flour, sugar, cocoa, baking powder, baking soda and salt. Beat in buttermilk, eggs, oil, vanilla and espresso mixture; beat at medium speed for 2 minutes.

3 Pour into prepared pan. Bake in 350°F (180°C) oven for 40 to 45 minutes or until top springs back when lightly touched. Let cool in pan on rack for 20 minutes. Remove from pan; let cool completely on rack. Spread with chocolate icing. *Makes 16 servings.*

Make ahead: Cover and store for up to 2 days.

Per serving (with icing):

calories	258
protein	5 g
total fat	5 g
saturated fat	1 g
cholesterol	28 mg
carbohydrate	51 g
dietary fiber	3 g
sodium	324 mg

R.D.I. Vit A 1%, D 2%, E 8%, Folate 4%, Ca 6% (66 mg), Iron 14%, Zinc 9%.

Canada's Food Guide Serving: ¾

Chocolate Buttermilk Icing

Cooking Tip

For a thicker icing, stir in enough sifted icing sugar to reach desired thickness.

1/2 cup	granulated sugar	125 mL
1/2 cup	unsweetened cocoa powder, sifted	125 mL
1/2 cup	buttermilk	125 mL
1/2 tsp	vanilla	2 mL

I   In small heavy saucepan, mix sugar with cocoa; whisk in buttermilk until smooth. Stirring constantly, cook over medium heat until simmering; cook, stirring constantly, for 2 minutes. Remove from heat; stir in vanilla. Let cool for 2 hours. (Icing will thicken upon cooling.) *Makes 1 cup (250 mL).*

Make ahead: Place plastic wrap directly on surface; store for up to 5 days.

Per 4 tsp (20 mL):

calories	**45**
protein	**1 g**
total fat	**1 g**
saturated fat	**trace**
cholesterol	**0 mg**
carbohydrate	**11 g**
dietary fiber	**1 g**
sodium	**11 mg**

R.D.I. Folate 1%, Ca 1% (16 mg), Iron 4%, Zinc 3%.

KITCHEN TIPS

Measuring Ingredients

- Use a measuring cup with a spout for measuring liquids. Place on a level surface and check at eye level.
- Use metal or plastic measuring cups for measuring dry ingredients. Spoon dry ingredients such as flour into cup, then level off with the flat side of a knife. Avoid shaking or tapping measure to level.
- Pack butter or margarine firmly.
- Use the correct pan size. To check the pan size for traditional cake pans and pie plates (or dishes), turn pan over and measure across the bottom.
- To determine the volume measure of your dish, fill it with water then measure the water. For example, if your cake pan holds approximately 8 cups/2000 mL (2000 mL = 2 L), it will be suitable for a recipe calling for a 2 L cake pan.

Lining and Greasing Pans

- Spray pans with a nonstick cooking spray or brush lightly with vegetable oil.
- When a recipe calls for lining the bottom of a pan, use parchment or waxed paper. Lining the sides of a pan isn't usually necessary unless called for in the recipe to keep the edges of a cake from drying out or to protect the ingredients from discoloration.

Beating Egg Whites

- Start with eggs at room temperature. If you don't have time to let them stand, cover them with warm water for a few minutes.
- Use a glass or metal (not plastic) mixing bowl and clean beaters.
- Make sure there is no yolk in the whites.
- To beat egg whites, beat with electric mixer or whisk until stiff and glossy. Do not overbeat because the egg whites will get lumpy and begin to lose volume.

An Update on Diabetes

People who worry about what to serve a guest who has diabetes may be operating under some outdated views. The diet for diabetes has done a complete turnabout in the last decade or so. What's appropriate for people with diabetes is simply the same healthy eating pattern as outlined on page 1.

A Diabetes Review

People with diabetes lack or are resistant to the hormone insulin and therefore can't properly utilize glucose, the main energy source for every cell in the body. The primary goal in the treatment of diabetes is to control the fluctuations in blood sugar levels so as to improve the person's feelings of well-being and to reduce the longer-term health risks.

HEALTHY EATING TIPS: Feeding a Guest with Diabetes

- People with diabetes can eat according to the same healthy eating pattern (see page 1) as everyone else. No special foods are required.
- Meal regularity and timing are important, especially for those who take insulin. Ask your guest what time is best to serve meals.
- If for some reason a meal can't be served at the required time, make sure a snack — such as low-fat cheese and crackers — is available.
- Keep meals low in fat. Offer lower-fat choices — milk for coffee instead of cream, light salad dressings, vegetables with a lemon wedge not butter.
- Meals should contain complex carbohydrates or starchy foods — pasta, rice, couscous, bread or any legume dish.
- Sugar is allowed when it's part of a total meal. Try the Ginger Citrus Fruit Salad (page 274) or the Apricot Raspberry Parfait (page 273).
- Offer lots of vegetables with dinner.
- Use salt moderately.
- Have a non-alcoholic beverage choice available such as soda or mineral water or a sugar-free soft drink.
- At breakfast, offer whole grain cereal, 1% milk, low-fat yogurt, low-fat whole grain muffins, peanut butter, a poached egg, and fruit such as an orange or grapefruit.

Two Types of Diabetes

- Type 2, the most common type, is associated with being over-weight and physically inactive. Type 2 is treated mainly through healthy diet and exercise, although an oral medication may also be taken to stimulate the pancreas to produce more insulin.
- Type 1 is a disease of the pancreas and less common than Type 2. Healthy eating, exercise and daily injections of insulin are important aspects of treatment.

Cantaloupe and Blueberries with Fresh Strawberry Sauce

This is a lovely, refreshing summer dessert. Serve with Double-Chocolate Cookies (page 251) or New-Fangled Hermits (page 254).

2 cups	sliced fresh strawberries	500 mL
2 tbsp	granulated sugar	25 mL
2 tbsp	kirsch (optional)	25 mL
1 tbsp	fresh lemon juice	15 mL
1	cantaloupe	1
1 cup	blueberries	250 mL

1 In blender or food processor, purée strawberries. Add sugar, kirsch (if using) and lemon juice; process to mix.
2 Halve cantaloupe; scoop out seeds. Cut flesh into bite-size pieces. Spoon cantaloupe and blueberries into 4 stemmed glasses.
3 Drizzle sauce over fruit. *Makes 4 servings.*

Make ahead: Through step 2, cover and refrigerate for up to 6 hours. Remove from refrigerator 30 minutes before serving.

Brunch Menu

Mushroom Bruschetta (page 23)
Salmon and Spinach Strata (page 221) or
Asparagus and Mushroom Gratin (page 224)
Spinach Salad with Walnut Vinaigrette (page 38)
Cantaloupe and Blueberries with Fresh Strawberry Sauce (this page) or
Apple Berry Crisp (page 271)

Serving Tip
Garnish each serving with a strawberry fan. They are easy to make; just slice strawberry from tip almost but not completely through, then fan out slices.

Nutrition Tip
Cantaloupe is an excellent source of the antioxidants vitamin C and beta carotene. When cantaloupe is teamed with strawberries (also an excellent source of vitamin C), as it is here, one serving will provide more than 175 percent of your daily requirement of vitamin C and 43 percent of beta carotene (Vitamin A).

Per serving:

calories	114
protein	2 g
total fat	1 g
cholesterol	0 mg
carbohydrate	28 g
dietary fiber	4 g
sodium	16 mg

R.D.I. Vit A 43%, E 7%, C 173%, Folate 18%, Ca 3% (28 mg), Iron 5%, Zinc 4%.

Canada's Food Guide Serving:
3 🥕

Citrus Frozen Yogurt with Mango

I had this dynamic dessert at a dinner party hosted by Monda Rosenberg, Chatelaine
*magazine's food editor. It was so wonderful that I immediately asked her for the recipe.
The grated lemon and lime rind give the yogurt a fabulous fresh fruity flavor.
It would also be lovely with fresh berries or peaches — in fact, any fresh fruit in season.*

8 cups	**frozen vanilla yogurt**	2 L
2	**lemons**	2
2	**limes**	2
3	**large ripe mangoes, peeled and sliced**	3
	Fresh mint leaves	

1 Let yogurt stand at room temperature just until it can be stirred, 15 to 30 minutes.

2 Finely grate rind from lemons and limes. Squeeze 1 tbsp (15 mL) each of the lime and lemon juice; set aside.

3 Turn softened yogurt into large bowl. Stir in rinds and juices until mixed. Spoon back into yogurt container; cover and freeze until hard, about 1 hour.

4 Arrange scoops of frozen yogurt on dessert plates. Attractively surround with mangoes; garnish with fresh mint. *Makes 12 servings.*

Make ahead: Through step 3 for up to 1 month.

Per serving:

calories	**247**
protein	**6 g**
total fat	**7 g**
saturated fat	5 g
cholesterol	13 mg
carbohydrate	**42 g**
dietary fiber	**2 g**
sodium	**78 mg**

R.D.I. Vit A 28%, E 7%, C 37%,
Folate 5%, Ca 18% (194 mg), Iron 1%,
Zinc 7%.

Canada's Food Guide Serving:
½ ▌ ½ 🥕

Apple Berry Crisp

Caramba, one of my favorite restaurants in Whistler, B.C., has a fabulous berry crisp, packed with blackberries and raspberries. Here's my version to make anytime of year. Use any combination of frozen or fresh berries.

3/4 cup	granulated sugar	175 mL
1/4 cup	all-purpose flour	50 mL
	Grated rind of 1 lemon	
4 cups	sliced peeled apples (about 4)	1 L
1	pkg (300 g) frozen blueberries (2 cups/500 mL)	1
1	pkg (300 g) unsweetened frozen raspberries (2 cups/500 mL)	1
2 cups	fresh or frozen cranberries	500 mL
Topping:		
1-1/2 cups	quick-cooking rolled oats	375 mL
3/4 cup	packed brown sugar	175 mL
1/4 cup	whole wheat flour	50 mL
2 tsp	cinnamon	10 mL
1/4 cup	butter or soft margarine, melted	50 mL

1 In large bowl, stir together sugar, flour and lemon rind. Add apples, blueberries, raspberries and cranberries; stir gently to mix. Spoon into 13- x 9-inch (3 L) baking dish.

2 Topping: In small bowl, stir together oats, sugar, flour and cinnamon; drizzle with butter and toss to mix. Spoon over fruit. Bake in 375°F (190°C) oven for 40 to 50 minutes or until bubbling and topping is golden. Serve warm or at room temperature. *Makes 8 servings.*

Make ahead: Let stand for up to 6 hours; serve at room temperature or reheat.

Serving Tip

Serve with frozen vanilla yogurt or extra-thick plain yogurt mixed with grated lemon rind and sweetened to taste with sugar.

Fat-lowering Tip

Keep washed fresh fruit and canned fruit cups handy for instant, low-fat snacks.

Per serving:

calories	368
protein	4 g
total fat	8 g
saturated fat	4 g
cholesterol	16 mg
carbohydrate	75 g
dietary fiber	8 g
sodium	68 mg

R.D.I. Vit A 6%, E 8%, C 20%, Folate 5%, Ca 5% (52 mg), Iron 14%, Zinc 10%.

Canada's Food Guide Serving:

¾ 🌾 2 🥕

Strawberry Apple Cobbler

You can make this well-liked dessert any time of year with fresh or frozen strawberries.

1/2 cup	granulated sugar	125 mL
3 tbsp	all-purpose flour	50 mL
1 tsp	cinnamon	5 mL
	Grated rind of 1 medium lemon	
5 cups	fresh strawberries or 2 pkg (300 g each) frozen unsweetened (not thawed)	1.25 L
2 cups	coarsely chopped peeled apples	500 mL
2 tbsp	fresh lemon juice	25 mL
Topping:		
1 cup	all-purpose flour	250 mL
3 tbsp	granulated sugar	50 mL
1 tsp	baking powder	5 mL
1/4 tsp	each baking soda and salt	1 mL
3 tbsp	cold butter, cut in bits	50 mL
2/3 cup	buttermilk	150 mL

1 In bowl, mix sugar, flour, cinnamon and lemon rind; stir in strawberries, apples then lemon juice. Spread in 8-cup (2 L) shallow baking dish; bake in 400°F (200°C) oven for 10 minutes.

2 Topping: In bowl, mix flour, sugar, baking powder, baking soda and salt. Using fingers or two knives, cut in butter until crumbly.

3 With fork, stir in buttermilk until soft dough forms. Drop by spoonfuls onto fruit in 6 evenly spaced mounds. Bake for 30 to 40 minutes or until top is golden and undersides of biscuits are cooked. *Makes 6 servings.*

Make ahead: Through step 2; let stand for 2 hours. Or through step 3 for up to 4 hours; serve at room temperature or reheat.

Strawberry Rhubarb Cobbler

Increase sugar to 3/4 cup (175 mL); substitute 4 cups (1 L) coarsely chopped (3/4-inch/2 cm pieces) rhubarb for the apples; reduce strawberries to 3 cups (750 mL). If using frozen rhubarb, thaw first.

Nutrition Tip

Strawberries are an excellent source of vitamin C and high in fiber.

Per serving:

calories	302
protein	4 g
total fat	7 g
saturated fat	4 g
cholesterol	17 mg
carbohydrate	58 g
dietary fiber	4 g
sodium	277 mg

R.D.I. Vit A 6%, E 3%, C 90%, Folate 8%, Ca 7% (81 mg), Iron 12%, Zinc 5%.

Canada's Food Guide Serving:
1¼ 🌾 2 🥕

Apricot Raspberry Parfait

This delicious, creamy, low-fat dessert looks pretty garnished with fresh raspberries and mint leaves.

1	can (14 oz/398 mL) apricots (undrained)*	1
1/4 cup	granulated sugar	50 mL
1	pkg (7 g) unflavored gelatin	1
1 cup	1% or 2% plain yogurt	250 mL
2 tbsp	fresh lemon juice	25 mL
1/4 tsp	almond extract	1 mL
1	pkg (300 g) frozen unsweetened raspberries, thawed, or 2 cups (500 mL) fresh**	1

1   Drain apricots, pouring 1/4 cup (50 mL) of the juice into saucepan or microwaveable dish; stir in 3 tbsp (45 mL) of the sugar. Sprinkle gelatin over top; let stand for 5 minutes to soften. Cook over low heat or microwave at Medium (50% power) for 40 seconds or until gelatin is dissolved.

2   In food processor or blender, purée apricots. In bowl, stir apricot purée, yogurt, gelatin mixture, lemon juice and almond extract until smooth.

3   Press raspberries and juice through sieve over bowl; stir in remaining sugar. Reserve 1/4 cup (50 mL) of the raspberry purée for garnish. Stir remaining raspberry purée into apricot mixture. Spoon into four parfait or stemmed glasses. Cover and refrigerate for 1-1/2 hours or until set. Spoon reserved raspberry purée over top. *Makes 4 servings.*

Make ahead: Cover and refrigerate for up to 2 days.

* Substitution Tip

To use dried apricots instead of canned, cover and simmer 12 whole dried apricots (1/2 cup/125 mL) in 1/2 cup (125 mL) water for 20 minutes or until very tender. Purée with any liquid until smooth. Soften gelatin in 1/4 cup (50 mL) cold water.

** Substitution Tip

Raspberries add extra flavor and color. However, you can omit them and add another 1 cup (250 mL) yogurt.

Per serving:

calories	162
protein	6 g
total fat	1 g
saturated fat	trace
cholesterol	2 mg
carbohydrate	34 g
dietary fiber	1 g
sodium	53 mg

R.D.I. Vit A 19%, E 12%, C 37%, Folate 11%, Ca 12% (135 mg), Iron 5%, Zinc 10%.

Canada's Food Guide Serving:
1¾ 🥕   ¼ 🥛

273

Ginger Citrus Fruit Salad

Chopped preserved ginger adds zip to a fresh fruit salad. Jars of preserved ginger are usually available in supermarkets and specialty food stores, especially in the fall and winter for holiday baking. You can add other fresh or dried fruits, including grapes, berries, bananas or mango. For a more spectacular presentation, slice oranges into rounds and garnish with starfruit.

2	grapefruit	2
4	oranges	4
2	kiwifruit, peeled	2
1/2 cup	dried cranberries (optional)	125 mL
2 tbsp	finely chopped preserved or crystallized ginger	25 mL

1 Cut slice from top and bottom of each grapefruit and orange; cut off skin, removing outside membrane. Working over bowl to catch juices, cut away sections from inner membranes.

2 Cut kiwifruit in half lengthwise; cut crosswise into slices.

3 In serving bowl, combine grapefruit, oranges, kiwifruit, cranberries (if using) and ginger (if using preserved ginger, stir in 1 tbsp/15 mL syrup). Cover and let stand for 1 hour before serving. *Makes 4 servings.*

Make ahead: Cover and refrigerate for up to 8 hours; serve at room temperature.

Per serving:

calories	146
protein	2 g
total fat	0 g
cholesterol	0 mg
carbohydrate	36 g
dietary fiber	6 g
sodium	6 mg

R.D.I. Vit A 5%, E 10%, C 237%, Folate 24%, Ca 8% (92 mg), Iron 13%, Zinc 2%.

Canada's Food Guide Serving:
2½

Orange Mousse

Creamy and smooth, this sophisticated dessert is truly easy to make.
Garnish with fresh berries, orange sections or candied orange rind.

Lower-Fat Cooking

For a fat-restricted diet, substitute 1/2 cup (125 mL) plain yogurt for the whipping cream and increase sugar to 1/2 cup (125 mL). Calories will be reduced to 119 and fat to 1 gram per serving.

Lower-Sugar Cooking

For people with diabetes, substitute 1/3 cup (75 mL) Splenda for the sugar.

1	pkg (7 g) gelatin	1
2/3 cup	fresh orange juice	150 mL
1 cup	1% or 2% plain yogurt	250 mL
1/3 cup	granulated sugar	75 mL
2 tbsp	orange liqueur (optional)	25 mL
	Finely grated rind of 1 medium orange	
1/2 cup	whipping cream, lightly whipped	125 mL

1 In bowl or saucepan, sprinkle gelatin over orange juice; let stand for 5 minutes. Microwave at Medium-High (70% power) for 1 minute, or stir over medium-low heat for 1 minute, or until dissolved.

2 Stir in yogurt, sugar, liqueur (if using) and orange rind. Fold in whipped cream. Spoon into individual dishes or stemmed glasses. Refrigerate until set, about 1-1/2 hours. *Makes 6 servings.*

Make ahead: Cover and refrigerate for up to 1 day.

Per serving:

calories	**152**
protein	**4 g**
total fat	**7 g**
saturated fat	**5 g**
cholesterol	**27 mg**
carbohydrate	**18 g**
dietary fiber	**1 g**
sodium	**39 mg**

R.D.I. Vit A 9%, E 2%, C 27%, Folate 5%, Ca 9% (95 mg), Iron 1%, Zinc 4%.

Canada's Food Guide Serving: ¼

Deep-Dish Apple Apricot Phyllo Pie

Sweet apricots and tart lemon add a novel twist of flavor to this apple pie.
Using a minimum of butter between the phyllo layers makes this pie lower in fat than one
with a regular pastry crust.

9 cups	sliced peeled apples	2.25 L
3/4 cup	dried apricots, cut in strips	175 mL
	Grated rind of 1 lemon	
2 tbsp	fresh lemon juice	25 mL
1/2 cup	granulated sugar	125 mL
2 tbsp	all-purpose flour	25 mL
1-1/2 tsp	cinnamon	7 mL
Pinch	ground nutmeg	Pinch
1 cup	coarse fresh bread crumbs	250 mL
Phyllo Topping:		
1 tbsp	granulated sugar	15 mL
1/4 tsp	cinnamon	1 mL
4	sheets phyllo pastry	4
4 tsp	butter, melted	20 mL

1 In large bowl, combine apples, apricots, lemon rind and juice. Mix together sugar, flour, cinnamon and nutmeg; stir into apple mixture. Spoon into 13- x 9-inch (3 L) shallow baking dish. Sprinkle bread crumbs over top.

2 Phyllo Topping: Mix sugar with cinnamon. Lay one sheet of phyllo on work surface, keeping remainder covered to prevent drying out. Brush lightly with butter; sprinkle with one-quarter of the cinnamon mixture. Lay second sheet on top; brush with butter and sprinkle with another quarter of the cinnamon mixture. Repeat layers twice.

3 Trim 1-inch (2.5 cm) border from phyllo. Place phyllo on top of fruit; roll edges under and press into sides of pan. Using serrated knife, cut slits in top of pastry; score into 8 portions. Bake in 350°F (180°C) oven for 50 minutes or until golden brown and apples are tender. *Makes 8 servings.*

Make ahead: Can stand for up to 6 hours; reheat for 15 minutes to crisp pastry.

Per serving:

calories	231
protein	2 g
total fat	3 g
saturated fat	1 g
cholesterol	5 mg
carbohydrate	51 g
dietary fiber	5 g
sodium	109 mg

R.D.I. Vit A 10%, E 4%, C 12%, Folate 2%, Ca 2% (25 mg), Iron 11%, Zinc 3%.

Canada's Food Guide Serving:
½ 🌾 2 🥕

Easy, No-Roll Food Processor Pastry

This is as easy to make and similar in method as a graham cracker or cookie crust pastry. I prefer a pastry made with butter rather than with oil (even though butter is higher in saturated fat), because it is more tender and I prefer the flavor. I keep the butter to a minimum and make a single-crust pie.

Baked Pie Shell

To bake an unfilled pie shell, prick pastry with fork (to prevent shrinking or puffing up). Line with foil; cover foil with dried beans or pie weights. Bake in 375°F (190°C) oven for 20 minutes; remove foil and beans. Prick shell if puffed; bake for 10 minutes longer or until golden brown.

1-1/4 cups	all-purpose flour	300 mL
1/4 cup	cold (hard) butter	50 mL
2 tbsp	granulated sugar	25 mL
2 tbsp	cold water	25 mL
2 tsp	white vinegar	10 mL

1 In food processor, combine flour, butter and sugar; process using on/off turns until mixture resembles coarse crumbs. Add water and vinegar; process using on/off turns until mixture barely starts to hold together. (If you press a little of the mixture between fingers, it sticks together.)

2 Turn into 9-inch (23 cm) pie plate or flan pan; using hands or back of large spoon, spread evenly over bottom and up side of plate, pressing firmly so mixture holds together (similar to graham cracker crust). Refrigerate for 15 minutes.
Makes one 9-inch (23 cm) pie shell, or 8 servings.

Make ahead: Cover and refrigerate for up to 1 day.

Per 1/8 shell:

calories	134
protein	2 g
total fat	6 g
saturated fat	4 g
cholesterol	16 mg
carbohydrate	18 g
dietary fiber	1 g
sodium	59 mg

R.D.I. Vit A 5%, E 1%, Folate 2%, Ca 0% (5 mg), Iron 6%, Zinc 2%.

Canada's Food Guide Serving:

1

Peach Blueberry Pie

Juicy ripe peaches and blueberries, sparked with lemon, make a fabulous summer pie.

1/2 cup	granulated sugar	125 mL
1/4 cup	all-purpose flour	50 mL
1 tsp	cinnamon	5 mL
	Grated rind of 1 medium lemon	
5 cups	thickly sliced peeled peaches	1.25 L
1 cup	blueberries	250 mL
1 tbsp	fresh lemon juice	15 mL
1	unbaked 9-inch (23 cm) pie shell (see Easy, No-Roll Food Processor Pastry, opposite page)	1
Topping:		
1	large peach, peeled and thinly sliced	1
2 tsp	fresh lemon juice	10 mL

1 In bowl, stir together sugar, flour, cinnamon and lemon rind. Add peaches, blueberries and lemon juice; stir to mix. Spoon evenly into pie shell.

2 Bake in 400°F (200°C) oven for 50 minutes or until bubbling and peaches are fork-tender. (If top browns too quickly, cover loosely with foil.) Let stand for at least 30 minutes or for up to 8 hours.

3 Topping: Brush peach slices with lemon juice; arrange over pie. *Makes 8 servings.*

Peach Raspberry Pie: Substitute 1 cup (250 mL) raspberries for blueberries.

Plum Tart: Substitute 5 cups (1.25 L) sliced pitted ripe plums (any kind) for the peaches and blueberries; omit lemon juice; increase sugar to 1 cup (250 mL).

Nectarine and Plum Tart: Substitute 2-1/2 cups (625 mL) each sliced nectarines and plums (any kind of ripe plum) for peaches and blueberries. Just before serving, sprinkle with icing sugar.

Peach Cream Pie: Omit blueberries. Mix 1 cup (250 mL) light 5% sour cream and 1 egg, lightly beaten, with sugar mixture.

Cooking Tip

To peel peaches: Some peaches are so ripe, the skin peels off very easily. If not, immerse peaches in a bowl of boiling water for 1 minute before peeling. To prevent peaches from darkening, rub whole peeled peach with cut lemon or sprinkle lemon juice over sliced peaches.

Per serving:	
calories	263
protein	4 g
total fat	6 g
saturated fat	4 g
cholesterol	16 mg
carbohydrate	51 g
dietary fiber	3 g
sodium	61 mg

R.D.I. Vit A 11%, E 11%, C 17%, Folate 4%, Ca 2% (17 mg), Iron 9%, Zinc 4%.

Canada's Food Guide Serving:
1 🌾 1½ 🥕

Lemon Chocolate Tart

This amazing pie is genuinely magical. During baking, some of the bottom chocolate crust rises to the top, leaving a lemon layer in the middle.

2 cups	chocolate wafer crumbs	500 mL
2 tbsp	butter, melted	25 mL
2 tbsp	corn syrup	25 mL
Lemon Filling:		
3	eggs	3
2	egg whites	2
3/4 cup	granulated sugar	175 mL
	Grated rind of 2 medium lemons	
1/2 cup	fresh lemon juice	125 mL
2 tsp	icing sugar	10 mL

1 In food processor, pulse chocolate wafer crumbs until fine. Mix butter with corn syrup. With machine running, drizzle butter mixture into crumbs, processing until mixed. Spray 9-inch (23 cm) pie plate or flan pan with nonstick cooking spray. Using hands or back of large spoon, spread chocolate mixture over bottom and up sides, pressing firmly so mixture holds together. Bake in 375°F (190°C) oven for 10 minutes.

2 Lemon Filling: In bowl, whisk together eggs, egg whites and sugar until well mixed. Whisk in lemon rind and juice. Pour into baked chocolate crust. Bake in 375°F (190°C) oven for 18 to 20 minutes or until top is barely set. Let cool.

3 Just before serving, sift icing sugar over top. *Makes 8 servings.*

Make ahead: Through step 1, let stand for up to 1 day. Through step 2, cover and refrigerate for up to 6 hours.

Per serving:

calories	278
protein	5 g
total fat	9 g
saturated fat	4 g
cholesterol	96 mg
carbohydrate	45 g
dietary fiber	1 g
sodium	109 mg

R.D.I. Vit A 8%, D 7%, E 8%, C 12%, Folate 5%, Ca 3% (30 mg), Iron 8%, Zinc 5%.

Canada's Food Guide Serving:
½

Strawberries with Lemon Cream in Phyllo Pastry Cups

Superb with strawberries, this dessert can show off other fruit, too.
I often use seasonal treats such as blueberries and mango, and even a combination of
berries. I garnish each cup with a fresh mint leaf or sometimes
pour a little Strawberry Sauce (page 269) over each.

4	sheets phyllo pastry	4
4 tsp	butter, melted	20 mL
3/4 cup	light tub cream cheese	175 mL
1/3 cup	1% or 2% plain yogurt	75 mL
3 tbsp	granulated sugar	50 mL
	Finely grated rind of 1 lemon	
3 cups	sliced strawberries	750 mL
1 tbsp	icing sugar	15 mL

1 Lay one sheet of phyllo on work surface, keeping remainder covered with a damp tea towel to prevent drying out. Brush with 1 tsp (5 mL) of the butter. Using scissors, cut crosswise into three 5-inch (12 cm) wide strips; fold each strip into thirds to form square. Round off corners; gently mold into muffin cups. Repeat with remaining phyllo to make 12 cups. Bake in 400°F (200°C) oven for 5 minutes or until golden.

2 In bowl, mix together cream cheese, yogurt, sugar and lemon rind until smooth.

3 Divide filling among pastry cups; spoon strawberries over filling. Sift icing sugar over top. *Makes 6 servings, 2 each.*

Make ahead: Through step 1, store in airtight container at room temperature for up to 2 weeks. Through step 2, cover and refrigerate for up to 2 days. Fill shells just before serving.

Per tart:	
calories	96
protein	3 g
total fat	4 g
saturated fat	2 g
cholesterol	11 mg
carbohydrate	12 g
dietary fiber	1 g
sodium	113 mg

R.D.I. Vit A 3%, E 2%, C 37%, Folate 5%, Ca 2% (21 mg), Iron 3%, Zinc 2%.

Canada's Food Guide Serving:
¼ 🌾 ½ 🥕

French Lemon Tart

It's hard to believe that something that tastes this good is so easy to make.
This is a lightened-up version of the traditional French tart au citron *with its thin,*
intense-flavored filling. I usually make the crust in a flan pan or quiche pan.

Cooking Tip

If your pie plate is shallow, omit the orange juice. This amount of filling fits best into a flan pan or deeper dish pie plate.

3	eggs	3
2	egg whites	2
3/4 cup	granulated sugar	175 mL
	Grated rind of 2 medium lemons	
1/2 cup	fresh lemon juice	125 mL
1/4 cup	fresh orange juice	50 mL
1	baked 9-inch (23 cm) pie shell (see Easy, No-Roll Food Processor Pastry, page 278)	1
2 tsp	icing sugar	10 mL

1 In bowl, using electric mixer, beat eggs, egg whites and sugar for 4 minutes or until thick and creamy. Beat in lemon rind. Beating constantly, slowly drizzle in lemon juice and orange juice. Pour into baked pie shell. Place on baking sheet.

2 Bake in 350°F (180°C) oven for 25 to 30 minutes or until filling is slightly puffed, browned on top and barely set (may still wobble slightly in center). Let cool completely.

3 Just before serving, sift icing sugar over top. *Makes 8 servings.*

Make ahead: Through step 2, cover and refrigerate for up to 8 hours.

Per serving:

calories	249
protein	5 g
total fat	8 g
saturated fat	4 g
cholesterol	96 mg
carbohydrate	40 g
dietary fiber	1 g
sodium	97 mg

R.D.I. Vit A 9%, D 7%, E 4%, C 15%, Folate 6%, Ca 2% (18 mg), Iron 8%, Zinc 4%.

Canada's Food Guide Serving:
1 ✹   ½ 〉

Lemon Cheesecake with Raspberry Glaze

This cheesecake is so rich and creamy tasting that no one will believe how low it is in fat. Yogurt and cottage cheese replace some of the cream cheese called for in traditional recipes. Light cream cheese instead of regular reduces the fat further.

Cooking Tip

To prepare without a food processor or blender, press cottage cheese through sieve; beat with cream cheese until smooth. In large bowl, beat eggs and whites until foamy; beat in sugar. Add lemon rind and juice; sprinkle with flour. Add vanilla and yogurt mixture; beat until smooth.

2 cups	1% or 2% plain yogurt or 1 cup (250 mL) extra-thick yogurt	500 mL
2	medium lemons	2
1 cup	granulated sugar	250 mL
2 cups	1% or 2% cottage cheese	500 mL
8 oz	light cream cheese, cubed and softened	250 g
2	eggs	2
3	egg whites	3
1/4 cup	all-purpose flour	50 mL
1 tsp	vanilla	5 mL
Crust:		
1 cup	graham cracker crumbs	250 mL
1 tbsp	butter, melted	15 mL
2 tbsp	light corn syrup	25 mL
Raspberry Glaze:		
1	pkg (300 g) individually frozen raspberries, thawed*	1
4 tsp	cornstarch	20 mL
2 tbsp	icing sugar	25 mL
4 tsp	fresh lemon juice	20 mL

Per serving:

calories	268
protein	12 g
total fat	8 g
saturated fat	4 g
cholesterol	60 mg
carbohydrate	38 g
dietary fiber	1 g
sodium	373 mg

R.D.I. Vit A 4%, D 3%, E 3%, C 13%, Folate 9%, Ca 12% (127 mg), Iron 6%, Zinc 8%.

Canada's Food Guide Serving:
½ 🌾 ¼ 🥕 ¼ 🥛

1 In cheesecloth-lined sieve set over bowl, drain plain yogurt (not extra-thick) in refrigerator for at least 3 hours or until reduced to 1 cup (250 mL). Discard liquid.

2 Spray bottom of 10-inch (3 L) springform pan with nonstick cooking spray or line with parchment paper. Center pan on foil; press foil to side of pan to keep water out when baking.

*If unavailable, substitute 1 pkg (425 g) frozen raspberries in light syrup; thaw and press through sieve. Use 1-1/3 cups (325 mL) of the juice.

3 Crust: In food processor, mix crumbs with butter. Add corn syrup; process until mixture starts to hold together. Press evenly into bottom of pan. Bake in 350°F (180°C) oven for 10 minutes.

4 Grate rind from lemons and squeeze juice to make 1/2 cup (125 mL). In food processor, mix sugar, lemon juice and rind. Add cottage cheese; process until smooth, scraping down side of bowl. Add yogurt and cream cheese; process until smooth. Add eggs, egg whites, flour and vanilla; process until smooth. Pour over prepared crust.

5 Set springform pan in larger pan; pour in enough hot water to come halfway up side of springform pan. Bake in 325°F (160°C) oven for 1-1/4 hours or until set around edge yet still jiggly in center. Turn oven off; quickly run knife around cake. Let stand in oven for 1 hour.

6 Remove from larger pan and remove foil; let cool completely on rack. Cover and refrigerate for at least 2 hours or for up to 2 days.

7 Raspberry Glaze: In sieve set over bowl, drain raspberries, pressing berries to remove seeds and extract about 1-1/3 cups (325 mL) juice. In saucepan, whisk juice with cornstarch until smooth. Bring to boil over medium-high heat, stirring constantly; cook, stirring, until thickened and clear, about 1 minute. Stir in sugar and lemon juice; let cool. Pour evenly over cheesecake; refrigerate for at least 1 hour or until set. Remove side of pan. *Makes 12 servings.*

Make ahead: Through step 6, cover and refrigerate for up to 2 days. Through step 7, cover and refrigerate for up to 4 hours.

Lower-Fat Tip

Reduce the fat from dairy products (milk, yogurt, cottage cheese, sour cream) by choosing products with 1% or less fat.

Cooking Tip

Before adding raspberry glaze, line pan sides with 2 inch (5 cm) high waxed- or parchment-paper collar to prevent glaze from touching sides of pan. If it touches, discoloration may result.

Cranberry Yogurt Flan

Tart cranberries add flavor, juiciness and color to this easy cheesecakelike dessert, which is one of my favorites. It works just as tastily with blueberries or raspberries instead of the cranberries.

Cranberry Yogurt Squares
Prepare and bake as directed, but use a 9-inch (2.5 L) square cake pan; cut into squares.

Raspberry Yogurt Flan
Substitute 3 cups (750 mL) fresh raspberries or 1 package (300 g) individually frozen (not thawed) for the cranberries.

Blueberry Yogurt Flan
Substitute 3 cups (750 mL) fresh or frozen blueberries (not thawed) for the cranberries.

1-1/2 cups	all-purpose flour	375 mL
1/2 cup	granulated sugar	125 mL
1-1/2 tsp	baking powder	7 mL
1/3 cup	butter or soft margarine	75 mL
2	egg whites	2
1 tsp	vanilla	5 mL
2 cups	cranberries (fresh or frozen)	500 mL
Topping:		
2 tbsp	all-purpose flour	25 mL
2 cups	1% or 2% plain yogurt	500 mL
1	egg, lightly beaten	1
2/3 cup	granulated sugar	150 mL
2 tsp	grated lemon or orange rind	10 mL
1 tsp	vanilla	5 mL
2 tsp	icing sugar	10 mL

1 In food processor or bowl, combine flour, sugar, baking powder, butter, egg whites and vanilla, mixing well. Press into bottom of lightly greased 10-inch (3 L) springform pan; sprinkle evenly with cranberries.

2 Topping: In bowl, sprinkle flour over yogurt. Add egg, sugar, lemon rind and vanilla; mix until smooth. Pour over cranberries.

3 Bake in 350°F (180°C) oven for 60 to 70 minutes or until crust is golden. Serve warm or cold. Sift icing sugar over top just before serving. *Makes 12 servings.*

Make ahead: Cover and refrigerate for up to 1 day.

Per serving:

calories	227
protein	5 g
total fat	6 g
saturated fat	4 g
cholesterol	33 mg
carbohydrate	38 g
dietary fiber	1 g
sodium	129 mg

R.D.I. Vit A 6%, D 1%, E 2%, C 3%, Folate 4%, Ca 9% (95 mg), Iron 6%, Zinc 6%.

Canada's Food Guide Serving:
¾ ▓ ¼ 🌱 ¼ 🥛

Black Forest Frozen Yogurt Cake or Pie

All family members will love this frozen dessert. I particularly like the combination of frozen cherry and chocolate yogurt, but other flavors will taste fine, too.

2 tbsp	butter, melted	25 mL
2 tbsp	corn syrup	25 mL
1 tbsp	water	15 mL
1-1/2 cups	chocolate wafer cookie crumbs	375 mL
3 cups	chocolate frozen yogurt or ice cream	750 mL
2 cups	cherry frozen yogurt*	500 mL
1	can (14 oz/398 mL) pitted dark cherries	1

Cherry Sauce:

4 tsp	cornstarch	20 mL
2 tbsp	fresh lemon juice	25 mL
2 tbsp	kirsch or black currant liqueur (cassis) or nectar	25 mL

1 In bowl, mix together butter, corn syrup and water; mix in crumbs. Firmly press into bottom and up sides of 9-inch (23 cm) pie plate or springform pan. Bake in 350°F (180°C) oven for 12 minutes; let cool. Freeze for 10 minutes or until firm.

2 Transfer chocolate and cherry frozen yogurt to refrigerator to soften slightly. Coarsely chop half of the cherries, reserving juice for sauce.

3 Working quickly, press frozen cherry yogurt into prepared crust. Sprinkle with chopped cherries. Press chocolate frozen yogurt on top, smoothing with spatula. Cover and freeze for 30 to 45 minutes or until firm.

4 Cherry Sauce: In saucepan, whisk reserved cherry juice with cornstarch; cook over medium-high heat, stirring constantly, until clear and thickened, about 2 minutes. Remove from heat. (Alternatively, in microwaveable dish, microwave on High for 2-1/2 minutes, stirring twice.) Stir in remaining cherries, lemon juice and liqueur; let cool. Pour over individual pieces of frozen cake when serving. *Makes 8 servings.*

Make ahead: Through step 3, cover and freeze for up to 1 week. Through step 4, cover and refrigerate sauce for up to 1 day.

Lower-Fat Tip

Light ice cream, frozen yogurts, sherbet and non-dairy frozen treats are good alternatives to regular and gourmet ice cream. Compare 1/2 cup (125 mL) of gourmet ice cream at about 17 grams of fat to a gourmet frozen yogurt at 2 grams of fat.

Cooking Tip

To make chocolate crumbs; process cookies in food processor.

* Substitution Tip

If cherry frozen yogurt isn't available, you can substitute strawberry, raspberry or vanilla.

Per serving:

calories	342
protein	7 g
total fat	9 g
saturated fat	4 g
cholesterol	20 mg
carbohydrate	60 g
dietary fiber	1 g
sodium	134 mg

R.D.I. Vit A 7%, E 6%, C 5%, Folate 8%, Ca 16% (179 mg), Iron 7%, Zinc 9%.

Canada's Food Guide Serving:

¼ 🥕 ½ 🥛

Orange Mousse Meringue Pie

Rich tasting and luscious, this pie is light because of its meringue crust and whipped evaporated milk filling. Be sure the evaporated milk is well chilled in order for it to whip.

3	egg whites	3
1/4 tsp	cream of tartar	1 mL
2/3 cup	granulated sugar	150 mL
1 tbsp	cornstarch	15 mL
Orange Mousse Filling:		
1	pkg (7 g) unflavored gelatin	1
	Grated rind of 2 medium oranges	
1-1/2 cups	fresh orange juice	375 mL
2	egg yolks	2
1/2 cup	granulated sugar	125 mL
3/4 cup	chilled 2% evaporated milk	175 mL

1 In bowl, beat egg whites with cream of tartar until soft peaks form. Gradually beat in sugar, 1 tbsp (15 mL) at a time, until stiff glossy peaks form. Blend in cornstarch.

2 Line baking sheet with parchment paper or foil; spread meringue into 9-inch (23 cm) circle, forming 1-inch (2.5 cm) high rounded rim. Bake in 300°F (150°C) oven for 1 hour or until lightly golden and crisp. Turn oven off; let meringue stand in oven for 12 hours. Gently peel off paper; place on serving plate.

3 Orange Mousse Filling: Sprinkle gelatin over 1/2 cup (125 mL) of the orange juice; set aside. In nonaluminum saucepan, whisk egg yolks lightly; add remaining orange juice, orange rind and sugar. Cook over medium heat, stirring constantly, for 5 to 10 minutes or until mixture thickens slightly and coats back of metal spoon. Remove from heat. Stir in gelatin mixture until dissolved. Cover and refrigerate for about 15 minutes or until thickened slightly.

4 In separate bowl, beat chilled evaporated milk until thickened and foamy, about 1 minute; fold into gelatin mixture until combined. Spoon into meringue pie shell; refrigerate for about 30 minutes or until set or for up to 8 hours. *Makes 8 servings.*

Make ahead: Through step 2, store in cardboard box or tin at room temperature for up to 1 week.

Dietary Help for Irritable Bowels

Irritable Bowel Syndrome (IBS) affects some 20% of otherwise healthy Canadians. Sufferers typically experience abdominal pain that is relieved with a bowel movement; alternating bouts of constipation with explosive diarrhea; and gas and bloating. Although there is no known cause or cure for IBS, diet can help control the symptoms. Since people respond differently to the changes suggested here, think of this advice as a starting point and be prepared to fine-tune it to suit yourself.

HEALTHY EATING TIPS: Irritable Bowels

- Keep a daily food journal. Look for links between foods eaten and onset of symptoms and eliminate suspect foods one at a time.
- Improve your eating habits overall. Eat 4 to 5 lower-fat meals and snacks, spaced regularly throughout the day.
- Fiber is a regulator, good for both diarrhea and constipation. Gradually increase your fiber intake by eating more whole grain foods, vegetables, fruit and legumes. Expect to suffer more from gas and bloating at first but this reaction shouldn't continue beyond a couple of months.
- If constipation is severe, add 1 tbsp (15 mL) of natural wheat bran to your diet each day, gradually increasing this to 3 to 4 tbsp (45 to 60 mL) daily over the next few months. Since bran works by absorbing moisture, drink 1 to 2 glasses of water along with the bran-containing food.
- If you suffer from diarrhea, choose foods high in soluble fiber such as oat bran, oatmeal, barley, legumes if tolerated, apples, applesauce, citrus fruits, psyllium-containing breakfast cereal; avoid foods containing the sweeteners sorbitol or mannitol; cut down on or eliminate caffeine-containing beverages, alcohol and spices.
- If excessive gas and bloating persist, try the suggestions given on page 128. Also consider eliminating lactose, the natural sugar in milk, by using lactose-reduced milk (sold alongside other milks) and avoiding processed cheese. Aged cheese and yogurt are low in lactose and shouldn't bother you.

Notes on Ingredients

Balsamic vinegar: This dark, rich-flavored, slightly sweet, mellow vinegar from Italy is available in supermarkets. If necessary, you can substitute 1 tbsp (15 mL) red wine vinegar plus a pinch of sugar for 1 tbsp (15 mL) balsamic vinegar.

Black bean sauce: A sauce, which is made from fermented black beans, is used in Chinese seafood, meat, poultry and vegetable dishes. It is available bottled in Asian grocery stores and the specialty section of supermarkets. I prefer the whole bean sauce to the purée.

Cheese: The fat content of cheese is listed on the label as a percentage of butter fat (b.f.) or milk fat (m.f.). This number indicates the percent of fat by weight and should not be confused with percent of calories from fat. Cheese labeled "light" is not necessarily a low-fat food. The term means simply that the cheese has at least 25% less fat than the regular kind. I often use the light Provolone-style cheese(12%) and the cheeses that are naturally lower in fat such as danbo at 9 to 13%, feta at 15 to 22% and creamy goat cheese (chèvre) 15 to 20%. Quark is a smooth, creamy, unripened soft cheese at 1 to 7%.

Chili paste or hot chili sauce: This red sauce, used in Asian cooking, is made from hot chili peppers, garlic and salt. A little goes a long way. It keeps well in the refrigerator for months. You can substitute hot pepper sauce.

Chinese noodles: Vacuum-packed, fresh Chinese wheat noodles (sometimes called chow mein noodles) are available in the vegetable section of many supermarkets. Some brands keep for at least 2 weeks in the refrigerator and are a great convenience food since they cook in boiling water in 2 to 3 minutes. If unavailable use Italian egg noodles. Rice noodles, usually dried, come in a variety of shapes, including rice vermicelli which are very thin. Soak rice noodles in warm water for 15 minutes then drain and use in soups or stir-frys. Cellophane (bean thread) noodles are made from ground mung beans. Soak 5 minutes in warm water before using.

Coconut milk: Coconut milk is a blend of freshly grated coconut and boiling water. It is used in soups, curries and sauces and is a staple in Thai cooking. Canned, light coconut milk has 12 to 20 grams of fat per cup; the regular kind is 75% higher in fat. Stir canned coconut milk well before using. Powdered coconut milk has an excellent flavor and is easy to use. However, it has about 4 grams fat per 1 tbsp (15 mL) powder. You can make your own light version by mixing less powder than called for with the water. For example, if you mix 5 tbsp (75 mL) powder with 1 cup (250 mL) water,

you will have 20 grams fat. Don't confuse coconut milk with sweetened coconut cream, which is used mainly for desserts and drinks, or with coconut water, the liquid inside a coconut.

Curry paste: Bottled or packaged Thai and Indian curry pastes are available in some supermarkets and specialty stores. They are a blend of spices, seasonings, vinegar and, sometimes, chili peppers. Use the paste in place of curry powder for a fresh flavor. Experiment with the pastes available; they vary widely in hotness and flavor. Pastes bought in a jar keep for months in the refrigerator.

Fish sauce: A staple in Thai cooking, fish sauce lends a salty fish flavor to dishes. You can sometimes substitute soy sauce but fish sauce has more flavor. All bottled fish sauce is high in sodium, although the amount varies widely from one brand to another. If you are concerned about sodium, look for brands with nutrition information on the label and choose the one lower in sodium. I use one that is lower than most yet has 760 mg sodium per 1 tbsp (15 mL). Fish sauce keeps in the cupboard for at least a year.

Five-spice powder: This fragrant pungent seasoning is a mixture of star anise, Szechuan peppercorns, fennel, cloves and cinnamon. It is found in the spice section of many supermarkets and in Chinese grocery stores. It keeps indefinitely in a sealed jar and is used in marinades and sauces.

Gingerroot: Fresh gingerroot adds wonderful flavor to vegetables, salads, sauces, marinades and stir-frys. Buy smooth, shiny, firm, not shriveled or moldy, gingerroot. Peel the ginger with a vegetable peeler or paring knife. Store in the refrigerator. It can also be frozen. Dried powdered ginger is a poor substitute.

Herbs: Use fresh herbs if possible. When buying dried herbs, choose the leaf not the powdered form. When substituting fresh for dried herbs, a rough guide is to use about 1 tbsp (15 mL) chopped fresh for 1 tsp (5 mL) dried leaf form. For basil or dill, I use 2 to 4 tbsp (25 to 50 mL) chopped fresh for 1 tsp (5 mL) dried. To store fresh herbs, wrap the roots or cut ends in a damp paper towel, refrigerate in a ziplock bag. Wash herbs just before using.

Hoisin sauce: Widely used in Chinese cooking, Hoisin sauce is made from soybeans, vinegar, sugar and spices and is available in Asian markets and most supermarkets. Use this dark, sweet sauce in stir-frys, marinades or pasta sauces. Or spread over salmon, chicken or pork chops before grilling. It keeps in the refrigerator for months.

Italian seasoning: Premixed Italian seasoning is a convenience. To make your own, mix 1/2 tsp (2 mL) dried oregano, 3/4 tsp (4 mL) dried basil, a large pinch each of thyme, rosemary and marjoram.

Oyster sauce: Made from oysters and soy sauce but without a fishy taste, this thick, brown sauce is used in Chinese dishes. It is available bottled in Chinese grocery stores and some supermarkets. It will keep indefinitely in the refrigerator.

Rice: There are many kinds of rice. Brown rice is the most nutritious because it is whole grain and contains the bran. White rice, the most common, has had the bran removed during processing. Instant or pre-cooked rice is white rice that has been cooked then dehydrated. Parboiled or converted rice has been processed to force the nutrients from the bran into the center (the endosperm) of the rice. It is more nutritious than white rice. Basmati rice from India and Pakistan and jasmine rice from Thailand are long-grain rices with a fragrant nut-like aroma and flavor. Arborio rice is a short- to medium-grain rice imported from Italy used in risotto. (See page 116 for cooking instructions.)

Saffron: This most expensive of all spices is the rust-colored stigmas of a small crocus. Because of its strong aromatic flavor it is used in small amounts and should not be combined with other strong spices or herbs. For the most flavor, steep the threads in a small amount of hot water before adding to a dish. Buy saffron threads from Spain in small amounts rather than the powder, which tends to lose its flavor. Instead of saffron you can use turmeric to produce the bright yellow color; however, the flavor will be different.

Salt: When a recipe calls for "salt to taste," the amount of sodium in the salt is not included in the amount of sodium per serving given in the recipe's nutrition information box. If you add 1/2 tsp (2 mL) salt, you will add about 1200 mg sodium to the total recipe. Divide the amount by the number of servings to give you the added sodium per serving.

Sesame oil: This dark, nutty-flavored oil made from roasted sesame seeds is used for seasoning not as a cooking oil. It is usually added at the end of cooking and is delicious in stir-frys. Look for bottled sesame oil from Japan as North American brands are less flavorful. I don't use "light" sesame oil, which is light in color and flavor not in fat or calories.

Sodium: See Salt.

Soy sauce: This staple in Asian cooking is made from soy beans, salt and water. Reduced sodium soy sauce can be used in all recipes, but in some you may want to adjust the seasonings. One brand of "lite" or sodium-reduced soy sauce has 100 mg of sodium per 1/2 tsp (2 mL) soy sauce, which is 40% less sodium than the regular.

Vegetable oil: Most recipes call for "vegetable oil" rather than a specific oil such as canola or safflower because either works well in the recipe and we need a variety of fats in our diet. (For information on the types of fats in oils and their effect on health see the Appendix on page 292.) For a general all-purpose oil I use canola oil, which is very bland in flavor and lowest in saturated fat. For salad dressings and pasta sauces and for a stronger flavor, I use extra virgin olive oil. I don't buy bottles labeled "vegetable oil" unless the label also specifies the type of vegetable oil. I don't use "light" oils because they are light in color and flavor not in fat and calories.

Wasabi: Often called Japanese horseradish, wasabi is made from the root of an Asian plant. It is the hot green paste used in sushi and is available in either paste or powder form in Japanese markets or Asian food stores. To use the powder, mix with a small amount of water.

Yogurt cheese or drained yogurt: Yogurt cheese has a thick creamy texture and is a substitute for higher-fat dairy products such as sour cream or cream cheese in spreads and dips. When mixed with sugar, it is a delicious substitute for a whipped cream topping. To drain yogurt, place plain, low-fat yogurt made without gelatin in a cheesecloth-lined sieve set over a bowl (or use a yogurt drainer or coffee-filter sieve) and refrigerate for 6 hours or until about half the volume remains. For a thicker spread, drain for up to 48 hours. You can substitute extra-thick yogurt, available in some supermarkets, or some varieties of Greek-style yogurts.

Zest: The outermost layer of citrus fruits, mainly oranges or lemons, zest is removed with a zester (see photo page 276), paring knife or vegetable peeler. (Be sure to remove only the yellow or orange layer not the bitter white pith.) Zest contains aromatic oils which add intense flavor to sweet or savory dishes.

Appendix: Types of Fat

Some types of fat are better for you than others. The characteristic of each type and its effect on your health are largely determined by the fat's fatty acid makeup.

Fatty acids are chains of carbon and hydrogen atoms that form the basic building blocks of fat. The length of the carbon chain and the bonds between the carbon and hydrogen molecules determine the physical and chemical properties of each type of fat and its effect on your health.

Saturated fat is saturated because the fatty acids that make it up are fully loaded with hydrogen. Unsaturated fat, on the other hand, contains fatty acids that can still take on more hydrogen. Adding hydrogen to unsaturated fat is what hydrogenation is all about. An unsaturated liquid oil is made into a solid and saturated-like fat by adding hydrogen. The process changes the physical and chemical properties of the original fat as well as its health effects.

Polyunsaturated Fat (PUF or PUFA)
Two major kinds:
Omega-3 fat: eicosapentenoic (EPA) and docosahexanoic (DHA)
- linked to heart health
- shows anti-inflammatory effect in arthritis

Found mainly in
- fatty fish such as mackerel, herring, salmon, swordfish, trout, cod, bluefish

Omega-6 fat: linoleic acid
- use in small amounts as a source of an essential fatty acid
- linked to heart health but also to increased cancer risk when consumed in large amounts.

Found mainly in
- oils: safflower, sunflower, corn
- margarine made from these oils
- nuts, seeds

Monounsaturated Fat (MUF or MUFA)
- use in small amounts
- linked to heart health

Found mainly in
- oils: olive, canola, peanut
- margarine made with these oils
- nuts and seeds

Saturated Fat (SF or SFA)
- limit as much as possible
- linked to increased risk of heart disease

Found mainly in
- meat, poultry
- milk, cheese, yogurt, except skim milk products
- butter, lard
- palm, palm kernel, coconut oil

Trans fat (TF or TFA)
- avoid as much as possible
- increases risk of heart disease

Found in
- partially hydrogenated vegetable oils such as shortening
- hard, brick margarines

About the Nutrient Analysis

Nutrient analysis of the recipes was performed by Info Access (1988) Inc., Don Mills, Ontario, using the nutritional accounting system component of the CBORD Menu Management System. The nutrient database was the 1997 Canadian Nutrient File supplemented when necessary with documented data from reliable sources.

The analysis was based on:

- imperial measure and weights (except for foods typically packaged and used in metric quantity),
- smaller ingredient quantity when there was a range and
- the first ingredient listed when there was a choice.

Recipes were analyzed using canola vegetable oil, 1% milk, canned chicken broth and fish sauce containing 765 mg sodium per tablespoon (15 mL). Calculations of meat and poultry recipes assumed that only the lean portion was eaten.

Optional ingredients and ingredients in unspecified amounts (including salt to taste) were not included in the analysis. (Note 1/4 tsp /1mL salt contributes approximately 600 mg sodium.)

Nutrient values were rounded to the nearest whole number with non-zero values of 0.49 and less appearing as "trace." Selected vitamins and minerals* are presented as percentages of Recommended Daily Intakes (RDI) established for labeling purposes (*Guide to Food Labelling and Advertising, March 1996,* Agriculture and Agri-Food Canada). The RDIs are a reference standard developed for use in the nutrition labeling of foods in Canada. They reflect the highest recommended intake of each nutrient for each age/sex group, omitting supplemental needs for pregnancy and lactation.

Canada's Food Guide Servings

Canada's Food Guide to Healthy Eating contains daily serving recommendations for foods from four groups (grain products, vegetables and fruit, milk products, and meat and alternatives) and displays serving sizes for selected items. The number of Canada's Food Guide servings contributed by each recipe portion was calculated using custom software developed by Info Access. For items with variable Canada's Food Guide serving size, calculations were based on 50 grams of meat, poultry or fish, 1 egg and 1/2 cup (125 mL) canned or cooked dried legumes. Serving sizes for ingredients not specifically mentioned in Canada's Food Guide were approximated with reference to serving size and nutrient contribution of other foods in the same food group. Canada's Food Guide servings were rounded to quarter servings.

---

*Minerals and vitamins reported are those that are low in the diets of some Canadians (calcium, iron, zinc and folate) and others of widespread interest (vitamins A, D, E and C). B vitamins other than folate are not reported because they are prevalent in a variety of foods that Canadians regularly consume.

Daily Nutrient Values

The nutrient analysis that accompanies each recipe in this book tells you how much of each nutrient a serving or portion of that recipe contains. To find out how much of each nutrient you need on a daily basis, refer to the charts on this page. The values given here are general guidelines for healthy adults and do not reflect special additions or restrictions some people may require — for example, sodium restriction or extra iron to treat iron-deficiency anemia. Unless otherwise noted, these recommendations reflect Canada's Nutrition Recommendations, 1990.

mg = milligrams   mcg = micrograms   RE = Retinol Equivalents   I.U. = International Units

Age	Sex	Energy[1] (calories)	Protein (grams)	Carbohydrate[2] (grams)	Fiber[3] (grams)	Fat[4] 25% (grams)	Fat 30% (grams)	Cholesterol (mg)	Sodium[5] (mg)
19-24	Males	3000	61	413	25-35	83	100	300 or less	2000 or less
	Females	2100	50	289	25-35	58	70	300 or less	2000 or less
25-49	Males	2700	64	371	25-35	75	90	300 or less	2000 or less
	Females	1900	51	261	25-35	53	63	300 or less	2000 or less
50-74	Males	2300	63	316	25-35	64	77	300 or less	2000 or less
	Females	1800	54	248	25-35	50	60	300 or less	2000 or less
75 +	Males	2000	59	275	25-35	56	67	300 or less	2000 or less
	Females	1700	55	234	25-35	47	57	300 or less	2000 or less

VITAMINS

Age	Sex	A[6] (includes Beta Carotene) RE (I.U.)	D[7] mcg (I.U.)	E mg (I.U.)	C[8] (mg)	Folic Acid[9] mcg (mg)	Calcium[10] (mg)	Iron (mg)	Zinc (mg)
19-24	Males	1000 (5700)	5 (200)	10 (16)	40	220 (.22)	1000	9	12
	Females	800 (4600)	5 (200)	7 (12)	30	180 (.18)	1000	13	9
25-49	Males	1000 (5700)	5 (200)	9 (15)	40	230 (.23)	1000	9	12
	Females	800 (4600)	5 (200)	6 (10)	30	185 (.19)	1000	13	9
				(up to age 70)					
50-74	Males	1000 (5700)	10 (400)	7 (12)	40	230 (.23)	1200	9	12
	Females	800 (4600)	10 (400)	6 (10)	30	195 (.20)	1200	8	9
				(age 71 +)					
75 +	Males	1000 (5700)	15 (600)	6 (10)	40	215 (.22)	1200	9	12
	Females	800 (4600)	15 (600)	5 (8)	30	200 (.20)	1200	8	9

[1] Calories are based on the energy needs of a moderately active, average person.

[2] Carbohydrate values have been calculated based on the nutrition recommendation that approximately 55% of the days' calories should come from carbohydrate. This includes both starch and sugar.

[3] Fiber values represent a daily fiber intake generally recognized as necessary for good health.

[4] Fat values are based on fat providing 25% or 30% of the day's calories. The former value is commonly used for cholesterol-lowering diets. The latter represents a goal for general, healthy eating.

[5] The sodium value represents practical healthy eating advice set at the mid-range of advice that ranges from 1800-2300 mg a day.

[6] Vitamin A includes beta carotene; preformed vitamin A is found only in foods of animal origin, whereas beta carotene comes primarily from plant sources.

[7] Vitamin D values are taken from the 1997 recommendations of the National Academy of Sciences.

[8] Vitamin C intakes should increase by 50% for smokers.

[9] Folic acid values reflect what you need to get to meet basic nutrition requirements, not extra amounts recommended to prevent neural tube defects.

[10] Calcium values are taken from the 1997 recommendations of the National Academy of Sciences.

Canadian Diabetes Association Food Choice Value

The Canadian Diabetes Association Food Choice Values contained in the following table are part of the Good Health Eating Guide system of meal planning (1998). This system is based on Canada's Food Guide to Healthy Eating. A dietitian can tailor the meal plan to meet individual needs.

People using the Good Health Eating Guide system can see how to fit recipes into their personalized meal plan. Some recipes may exceed the recommended number of servings on the meal plan at a particular meal. These can be incorporated by reducing the portion size.

Nutrient values displayed with the recipes in this book have been rounded to the nearest whole number. Canadian Diabetes Association Food Choice Values have been assigned on the basis of nutrient values rounded to one decimal point.

For more information on diabetes, the Good Health Eating Guide or the Canadian Diabetes Association, please contact: The Canadian Diabetes Association National Office, Suite 800, 15 Toronto Street, Toronto, Ontario M5C 2E3. 1-800-Banting (226-8464) or on the World Wide Web at www.diabetes.ca.

The following Canadian Diabetes Association Food Choice Values refer to the main recipe indicated, not to recipe variations that may appear on those pages.

FOOD CHOICE VALUE PER SERVING

Page		STARCH	FRUITS & VEGETABLES	MILK	SUGARS	PROTEIN	FATS & OILS	EXTRA
	Appetizers							
8	Grilled Quesadillas: Avocado 1/8 of recipe	1 1/2	1/2			1/2	1 1/2	
9	Shrimp Quesadillas 1 wedge (1/24 of recipe)	1/2				1/2		
10	Mini Phyllo Tart Shells 1 tart (1/36 of recipe)							1
11	Mango Salsa in Mini Phyllo Tarts 1 tart (1/30 of recipe)							1
12	Spicy Hummus 2 tbsp (1/16 of recipe)		1/2					
13	Caramelized Onion and Basil Dip 2 tbsp (1/20 of recipe)		1/2					
14	Creamy Crab Dip 2 tbsp (1/20 of recipe)					1/2		
15	Black Bean Dip with Veggie Topping 2 tbsp (1/16 of recipe)		1/2					
20	Creamy Coriander Mint Dip 2 tbsp (1/13.3 of recipe)			1/2 1%				
21	Smoked Trout Spread: Yogurt 2 tbsp (1/13.3 of recipe)					1/2		
22	Herbed Yogurt-Cheese 2 tbsp (1/8 of recipe)			1/2 1%				
23	Mushroom Bruschetta 1 piece (1/12 of recipe)	1/2				1/2	1/2	1
24	Marinated Mussels 1/45 of recipe							1
28	Crab Cakes 1/6 of recipe	1/2				3		1
29	Spiced Shrimp 3 pieces (1/13.3 of recipe)					1		
30	Hoisin Smoked-Turkey Spirals 2 pieces (1/20 of recipe)	1/2				1/2		
31	Sesame Wasabi Spirals with light mayonnaise 2 pieces 1/20 of recipe	1/2					1/2	
32	Roasted Red Pepper and Arugula Spirals 2 pieces (1/20 of recipe)	1/2					1/2	

Page		STARCH	FRUITS & VEGETABLES	MILK	SUGARS	PROTEIN	FATS & OILS	EXTRA
32	Smoked Salmon and Cream Cheese Spirals							
	Yogurt Cheese 2 pieces (1/20 of recipe)	1/2				1/2		
	Herbed Light Cream Cheese 2 pieces (1/20 of recipe)	1/2				1/2	1/2	
33	Teriyaki Chicken Bites 1/24 of recipe					1/2		
35	Citrus Mint Iced Tea 1/6 of recipe		1/2		1			

Salads

Page		STARCH	FRUITS & VEGETABLES	MILK	SUGARS	PROTEIN	FATS & OILS	EXTRA
38	Spinach Salad with Walnut Vinaigrette 1/8 of recipe						1	1
39	Carrot Slaw with Radicchio 1/4 of recipe		1				1	
40	Garlic Green Beans with Flavored Oil 1/8 of recipe		1/2				1/2	
41	Fresh Beet and Onion Salad 1/4 of recipe		1				1/2	
42	Watercress, Orange and Chick-Pea Salad 1/4 of recipe	1/2	1			1/2		
43	Indonesian Coleslaw 1/8 of recipe		1/2		1/2		1/2	
44	Thai Vegetarian Salad 1/4 of recipe		1			1	1/2	
45	Black Bean and Corn Salad 1/8 of recipe	1				1/2		1
46	Marinated Shrimp and Mango Salad 1/6 of recipe		2 1/2		1	4 1/2		
48	Arugula Salad with Grilled Chèvre 1/8 of recipe		1/2			1/2	1 1/2	
50	Curried Lentil, Wild Rice and Orzo Salad 1/8 of recipe	1 1/2	1/2			1/2	1 1/2	1
51	Chicken Penne Salad with Thai Dressing 1/6 of recipe	2	1/2			3 1/2		
53	Tomato and Corn Pasta Salad 1/8 of recipe	3 1/2				1	1	1
54	Pesto Pasta Salad with Chicken and Sun-Dried Tomatoes 1/6 of recipe	4				3		
55	Couscous, Orange and Carrot Salad 1/6 of recipe	2	2				1	
56	Yogurt Parsley Dressing 1 tbsp (1/26.7 of recipe)						1/2	
57	Herb and Ginger Vinaigrette 1 tbsp (1/8 of recipe)				1/2		1/2	

Soups

Page		STARCH	FRUITS & VEGETABLES	MILK	SUGARS	PROTEIN	FATS & OILS	EXTRA
60	Tortellini Vegetable Soup 1/4 of recipe	1 1/2	1/2			1 1/2	1/2	
61	Portuguese Chick-Pea and Spinach Soup 1/6 of recipe	1	1/2			1		
62	Soup au Pistou 1/6 of recipe	1	1			1 1/2	1/2	
63	Winter Vegetable Soup 1/4 of recipe	1	1			1/2	1	
66	Sweet Potato and Ginger Soup 1/8 of recipe	1 1/2					1	
67	Lightly Curried Carrot and Ginger Soup 1/6 of recipe		1	1/2 2%			1/2	
68	Asian Carrot and Mushroom Noodle Soup 1/5 of recipe	1/2	1/2			1 1/2		
70	Spicy Thai Chicken Noodle Soup 1/6 of recipe	1				2		1
71	Chinese Shrimp and Scallop Soup 1/4 of recipe	1				1 1/2		
72	Thai Coconut, Ginger and Chicken Soup 1/4 of recipe	1/2				1	1/2	

Page		STARCH	FRUITS & VEGETABLES	MILK	SUGARS	PROTEIN	FATS & OILS	EXTRA
73	Porcini Mushroom Bisque 1/6 of recipe		1/2	1/2 2%			1/2	1
75	Lentil, Barley and Sweet Potato Soup 1/8 of recipe	1	1			1/2		
76	Mulligatawny Soup 1/6 of recipe		1 1/2			2 1/2		
77	Quick Black Bean, Corn and Tomato Soup 1/6 of recipe	1	1 1/2			1/2		
78	Onion and Potato Soup 1/8 of recipe	1/2	1/2			1/2	1/2	
79	Gazpacho 1/8 of recipe		1			1/2		

Pasta

Page		STARCH	FRUITS & VEGETABLES	MILK	SUGARS	PROTEIN	FATS & OILS	EXTRA
82	Pasta with Chick-Peas and Spinach 1/3 of recipe	3 1/2				1 1/2		1
83	Easy Creamy Turkey Fettuccine 1/3 of recipe	3 1/2	1	1 1/2 2%		4		
84	Summer Corn and Tomato Pasta 1/10 of recipe	2				1/2	1	
85	Fettuccini with Pesto 1/4 of recipe	4 1/2				1	1 1/2	
87	Linguine with Shrimp and Fresh Basil 1/4 of recipe	4	1 1/2			3 1/2		
88	Pad Thai 1/4 of recipe	3	1		1/2	2 1/2	1	
90	Penne with Tomato, Tuna and Lemon 1/3 of recipe	3 1/2	1			2 1/2		
91	Thai Noodle and Vegetable Stir-Fry 1/4 of recipe	1 1/2	1/2			1/2	1	
92	Singapore-Style Noodles 1/4 of recipe	2	2			1 1/2	1	
93	Chinese Noodle and Shrimp Party Platter 1/10 of recipe	1 1/2	1			2 1/2		
96	Wild Mushroom and Spinach Lasagna 1/6 of recipe	2 1/2	1/2	1 1/2 1%		2 1/2	1/2	1
98	Grilled Italian Sausage and Red Peppers with Penne 1/4 of recipe	4	1 1/2			3	2	
99	Vegetable Tortellini Casserole with Cheese Topping 1/6 of recipe	3	2			2 1/2	1 1/2	
100	Penne with Sweet Red Peppers, Black Olives and Arugula 1/4 of recipe	3				1	2	1
102	Skillet Pork Curry with Apples and Chinese Noodles 1/6 of recipe	2	1 1/2	1/2 1%	1/2	4 1/2		
103	Lemon, Dill and Parsley Orzo 1/4 of recipe	2					1	
105	Beef, Tomato and Mushroom Rigatoni 1/6 of recipe	2 1/2	1 1/2			3		1
106	Spicy Chicken with Broccoli and Chinese Noodles 1/6 of recipe	1 1/2	1 1/2			4 1/2		
107	Two-Cheese Pasta and Tomatoes 1/6 of recipe	2 1/2	1/2			2	1/2	

Vegetarian Main Dishes

Page		STARCH	FRUITS & VEGETABLES	MILK	SUGARS	PROTEIN	FATS & OILS	EXTRA
111	Mediterranean Vegetable Stew 1/4 of recipe	2	1/2			1/2	1	
113	Vegetarian Paella 1/6 of recipe	4 1/2	2			1	1	1
115	Artichoke, Goat Cheese, Fresh Tomato and Onion Pizza 1/6 of recipe	2	1/2			1	1/2	
116	Leek and Rice Pilaf 1/4 of recipe	2 1/2					1	1
117	Potato Vegetable Curry 1/4 of recipe	1	1			1/2	1/2	
118	Sweet Potato, Squash and Bulgur Casserole 1/4 of recipe	1 1/2	2				1	
120	Mushroom Lentil Burgers 1/4 of recipe	1 1/2	1/2			1		

Page		STARCH ▢	FRUITS & VEGETABLES ◪	MILK ◈	SUGARS ✳	PROTEIN ⊘	FATS & OILS ▲	EXTRA ✚
121	Chick-Pea Burgers 1/4 of recipe	1 1/2	1/2			1/2	1/2	
123	Sunflower Veggie Tofu Burgers 1/4 of recipe	2	1/2			2	1	
124	Grilled Portobello Mushroom Burgers 1 burger (1/4 of recipe)	2	1/2			1 1/2	1 1/2	1
125	Coconut Rice 1/4 of recipe	2 1/2					1/2	1
126	Mexican Brown Rice with Tomatoes and Corn 1/4 of recipe	4	1 1/2				1	
127	Couscous with Tomato and Basil 1/4 of recipe	2	1/2				1/2	
129	Tuscan White Kidney Beans with Sage 1/4 of recipe	1				1		
130	Quinoa Pilaf 1/3 of recipe	1 1/2	1/2			1/2	1	
131	Tofu Vegetable Shish Kebabs 1/4 of recipe		1			1 1/2		
132	Lentil and Vegetable Curry 1/6 of recipe	1 1/2	1			1		
133	Barley and Black Bean Casserole 1/10 of recipe	2					1/2	

Vegetable Side Dishes

Page		STARCH ▢	FRUITS & VEGETABLES ◪	MILK ◈	SUGARS ✳	PROTEIN ⊘	FATS & OILS ▲	EXTRA ✚
136	Spanish-Style Asparagus 1/4 of recipe		1/2				1/2	
136	Roasted Asparagus with Parmesan 1/4 of recipe					1/2	1/2	1
137	Asparagus with Shaved Parmesan 1/4 of recipe		1/2			1/2		
137	Make-Ahead Cumin-Spiced Broccoli 1/4 of recipe		1/2			1/2	1/2	
138	Spiced Cabbage and Spinach 1/4 of recipe		1/2				1	
139	Spinach with Tomatoes and Cumin 1/3 of recipe		1/2			1/2		
140	Beet Greens with Lemon and Almonds 1/3 of recipe					1/2	1/2	1
141	Tomato Gratin 1/4 of recipe	1/2	1/2			1/2	1	
142	Tomatoes Provençal 1/6 of recipe		1/2				1/2	1
143	New Potatoes with Mint Pesto 1/6 of recipe	1					1/2	1
144	Sesame-Spiced Oven-Fried Potatoes 1/4 of recipe	2 1/2					1	
146	Herb-Roasted Potatoes and Onions 1/4 of recipe	1 1/2					1 1/2	
147	Skillet Sweet Potatoes 1/3 of recipe	2					1/2	
147	Carrots Provençal 1/4 of recipe		1				1/2	
148	Two-Potato Scallop 1/4 of recipe	3				1/2	1/2	
149	Broccoli Carrot Stir-Fry 1/4 of recipe		1 1/2				1	
150	Carrot and Squash Purée with Citrus 1/4 of recipe		1 1/2					
151	Braised Fennel with Parmesan 1/6 of recipe					1/2		1
154	Grilled Marinated Portobello Mushrooms 1/4 of recipe		1/2				1/2	
155	Roasted Eggplant Slices with Roasted Garlic Purée 1/4 of recipe		1/2				1	1
155	Roasted Garlic Purée 1/4 of recipe (1 tbsp)		1/2					
157	Roasted Winter Vegetables 1/8 of recipe	1/2	1 1/2				1	

Page		STARCH	FRUITS & VEGETABLES	MILK	SUGARS	PROTEIN	FATS & OILS	EXTRA
202	Grilled Teriyaki Tuna 1/4 of recipe					4		1
203	Fish Fillets, Tomato and Mushroom Packets 1/2 of recipe		1/2			4 1/2		
204	Baked Whole Salmon with Lime Ginger Mayonnaise 3 oz serving					3		
205	Lime Ginger Mayonnaise 1 tbsp (1/16 of recipe)						1/2	
206	Phyllo-Wrapped Salmon Fillets and Coconut Rice 1/4 of recipe	3 1/2	1/2			4	1	
207	Salmon in Black Bean Sauce 1/4 of recipe				1/2	4		
209	Tomotoes, Mussels and Rice 1/3 of recipe	2 1/2	1/2			1 1/2	1/2	
210	Cioppino 1/6 of recipe		1			3		
213	Shrimp and Scallops in Coconut Milk 1/6 of recipe		1/2			4		
215	Shrimp and Scallop Skewers 1/4 of recipe		1		1	4 1/2		
216	Shrimp Provençal Casserole 1/6 of recipe	2	1			4		
217	Pan-Seared Sea Bass with Red Onion and Lemon 1/4 of recipe					3		1

Brunch

Page		STARCH	FRUITS & VEGETABLES	MILK	SUGARS	PROTEIN	FATS & OILS	EXTRA
221	Salmon and Spinach Strata 1/8 of recipe	1/2	1/2	1/2 1%		2 1/2		
222	Potato and Onion Tortilla Espanola 1/2 of recipe	1 1/2	1/2			3	1	
224	Asparagus and Mushroom Gratin 1/8 of recipe	1/2	1/2			1	1/2	
225	Fresh Fruit, Granola and Yogurt Trifle 1/8 of recipe	1/2	1 1/2	1 1%	1 1/2		1/2	
228	Roasted Red Pepper Smoked Mackerel Focaccia Sandwich 1/6 of recipe	2 1/2	1/2			1 1/2	1	
230	Avocado Cheese Focaccia Sandwich 1/6 of recipe (1 sandwich)	2 1/2	1/2			1 1/2	2 1/2	
231	Seafood Salad 1/6 of recipe			1/2 1%		3		
233	Roasted Red Pepper, Onion and Hummus Pita Wrap 1/6 of recipe	3				1	1	
234	Tuna and Veggie Pita Wrap 1/6 of recipe	1 1/2	1/2			1 1/2		
236	Spinach and Mushroom Calzones 1/8 of recipe	2				1	1 1/2	
237	Scrambled Eggs and Smoked Salmon on Focaccia 1/8 of recipe	2	1/2			2	1	

Baking

Page		STARCH	FRUITS & VEGETABLES	MILK	SUGARS	PROTEIN	FATS & OILS	EXTRA
240	Pumpkin Orange Streusel Muffins 1/12 of recipe	1			1		1 1/2	
241	Blueberry Oat Bran Muffins 1/12 of recipe	1			1	1/2	1	
242	Lemon Zucchini Muffins 1/12 of recipe	1			1		1	
243	Strawberry-Glazed Banana Pineapple Muffins 1/12 of recipe	1	1/2		1		1	
244	Cranberry Orange Bran Muffins 1/12 of recipe	1			1		1	
245	Fig and Cottage Cheese Quick Bread 1/16 of recipe	1	1/2				1/2	
246	Focaccia 1/10 of recipe	1 1/2					1/2	
248	Festive Fruit Soda Bread 1/20 of recipe	1 1/2	1/2		1/2		1/2	

Page		STARCH	FRUITS & VEGETABLES	MILK	SUGARS	PROTEIN	FATS & OILS	EXTRA
249	Apple Raisin Spice Loaf 1/18 of recipe	1	1/2		1/2		1/2	
251	Double-Chocolate Cookies 1 cookie (1/60 of recipe)				1		1/2	
252	Oatmeal and Rice Crisp Squares 1/24 of recipe	1/2	1/2		1		1/2	
253	Cranberry Pecan Squares 1/18 of recipe	1/2	1/2		1/2		1	
254	New-Fangled Hermits 1/30 of recipe	1/2	1/2		1		1/2	
255	Chocolate Banana Cupcakes 1/12 of recipe	1			2 1/2		1	
256	Lemon Blueberry Coffee Cake 1/16 of recipe	1 1/2			1 1/2		1/2	
257	Chocolate Chip Coffee Cake 1/12 of recipe	1 1/2			2		2	

Desserts

Page		STARCH	FRUITS & VEGETABLES	MILK	SUGARS	PROTEIN	FATS & OILS	EXTRA
260	Lemon Cake without sauce 1/16 of recipe	1 1/2			3		1 1/2	
261	Lemon Cream 2 tbsp (1/10 of recipe)			1/2 1%	1/2			
261	Raspberry Sauce 1/4 cup (1/8 of recipe)		1/2		1/2			
263	Apple Cranberry Streusel Cake 1/12 of recipe	1	1/2		2		1	
264	Easy Chocolate Cake with Chocolate Buttermilk Icing 1/16 of recipe	1			3 1/2	1/2	1	
266	Chocolate Buttermilk Icing 4 tsp (1/12 of recipe)				1			
269	Cantaloupe and Blueberries with Fresh Strawberry Sauce 1/4 of recipe		2		1/2			
270	Citrus Frozen Yogurt with Mango 1/12 of recipe		1	1 1%	2 1/2		1 1/2	
271	Apple Berry Crisp 1/8 of recipe	1	1		4		1 1/2	1
272	Strawberry Apple Cobbler 1/6 of recipe	1 1/2	1		2		1 1/2	
273	Apricot Raspberry Parfait 1/4 of recipe		1 1/2	1/2 1%	1			
274	Ginger Citrus Fruit Salad 1/4 of recipe		2 1/2		1/2			
276	Orange Mousse 1/6 of recipe		1/2	1/2 1%	1		1 1/2	
	Orange Mousse (lower fat variation) 1/6 of recipe		1/2	1/2 1%	1 1/2			
277	Deep-Dish Apple Apricot Phyllo Pie 1/8 of recipe	1/2	2 1/2		1 1/2		1/2	
278	Easy, No-Roll Food Processor Pastry 1/8 of recipe	1			1/2		1	
279	Peach Blueberry Pie 1/8 of recipe	1	1 1/2		1 1/2		1	
280	Lemon Chocolate Tart 1/8 of recipe	1			3	1/2	1 1/2	
281	Strawberries with Lemon Cream in Phyllo Pastry Cups 1/12 of recipe	1/2			1/2		1	
282	French Lemon Tart 1/8 of recipe	1			2 1/2	1/2	1	
284	Lemon Cheesecake with Raspberry Glaze 1/12 of recipe	1/2	1/2	1/2 1%	2	1	1	
286	Cranberry Yogurt Flan 1/12 of recipe	1		1/2 1%	2		1	
287	Black Forest Frozen Yogurt Cake 1/8 of recipe	1		1 1%	4		1 1/2	
288	Orange Mousse Meringue Pie 1/8 of recipe			1/2 2%	3	1/2		

Index of Nutrition Information

Index of Recipes